AIR FRYER
Cookbook

600 Effortless Air Fryer Recipes for Beginners and Advanced Users

Jenson William

CONTENTS

SNACKS & SIDE DISHES 39

PORK, BEEF & LAMB 64

POULTRY 91

FISH & SEAFOOD 120

VEGETABLES & VEGETARIAN 137

SWEETS & DESSERTS 162

MEASUREMENT CONVERSIONS 172

AIR FRYER COOKING CHART 173

INDEX 174

INTRODUCTION

Hello…and welcome to my book about the fantastic air fryers!

Did you know that you can get healthy, lose weight, save dollars and still enjoy delicious, indulgent, utterly yummy foods? Does it sound too good to be true? Or does it sounds like something you would hear in an infomercial? No, it's not. It's 100% true. You just need to join the art of air frying! You'll love this book if you're new to air fryer cooking and also if you're an experienced air fryer user. It contains fantastic recipes for great meals that everyone will enjoy.

The air fryer is a brilliant kitchen appliance - it lets you cook delicious food without using lots of fat and oil. You'll be able to create yummy dishes that are healthy too!

You'll find the recipes in this book can be used with any brand and model of an air fryer. And go ahead and modify any of the recipes for the air fryer you have, such as the temperature and time. Or adjust the number of ingredients if you want to make more or less than the recipe calls for.

No matter what type of recipe you're looking for… I've got one for you. Breakfast, snacks, appetizers, meat, seafood, and desserts. There are also vegan and vegetarian options that are sure to delight.

When it comes to breakfast and dessert, I've got some healthy choices for you with decadent and delicious recipes, using ingredients that are sure to make your mouth water in anticipation.

Be warned – the recipes in this book aren't for those who are watching their weight and stick to their diet all day, every day. These are recipes that are to be savored and enjoyed. But even if you're watching what you eat, it all comes down to balancing your diet. Use this cookbook to create delightful meals when you're having a cheat day and want to treat yourself to something tasty.

Let's jump into what an air fryer is and how it works, and then you can start cooking!

WHAT IS AN AIR FRYER?

An air fryer is a kitchen appliance that fits nicely on your kitchen countertop. Foods are cooked and fried when hot air circulates through the fryer. You'll be able to enjoy fried foods without all the extra fat a deep fryer usually uses. You get the same crunchy texture you want with traditional fried foods, but with a fraction of the calories. Some air fryers' models do more than just fry the food – they can bake, broil, roast, rotisserie, and steam as well. You can use your air fryer the same way as you would use your microwave, oven, and stove, and it's much more comfortable, faster, and healthier to use!

You can also use your air fryer for cooking batters and marinades; however, as a safety concern, the things you can't cook in your air fryer are soups or other foods with a lot of liquid, such as a broth.

Once you start cooking with your air fryer, you'll be amazed at all the benefits of this handy kitchen appliance.

BENEFITS OF THE AIR FRYER

Use less fat and oil

Perhaps the top reason for using an air fryer is so you can cook using less fat and oil. No more French fries or spring rolls' cooking in a deep fryer filled with all that fattening oil. Now you can cook them in your air fryer using no more than a tablespoon of oil. The circulating hot oil cooks the fries, keeping the inside tender and the outside nice and crisp.

Your air fryer not only cuts down the amount of fat and oil you use, but it also reduces your daily calorie intake. When you use the air fryer, you'll enjoy the foods you love while still eating a healthy diet. French fries when you're watching your weight? Absolutely! Eating healthy is all about consuming nutritious foods and still being able to enjoy those treats you love.

Fits perfectly on your kitchen countertop

You'll be using your air fryer a lot, so it's a good thing it fits so perfectly on any countertop in your kitchen. Air fryers only take up a small amount of room – leaving your kitchen neat and tidy. You'll be able to cook all kinds of delicious meals without making a mess in your kitchen. And all the air fryer accessories can be stored within the air fryer, keeping your kitchen uncluttered.

Ease and versatility

Depending on what model air fryer you have, there are different features you can use. There are so many functions; you'll never use your microwave or oven again to cook a meal. And all of these functions are easy to use. This means you'll be able to cook with ease, without the hassle of using other kitchen appliances. All you need to do is get all the ingredients together for a recipe, pop them into the air fryer, and set the function, temperature, and timer. Then wait until your meal is cooked to perfection.

HOW TO USE YOUR AIR FRYER

Air fryers are designed to be super easy to use. Here's a little guide to get you started.

Choose a recipe

Pick up a recipe that you want to cook in your air fryer. Remember that most foods you cook in your microwave or oven, or on the stovetop, can be prepared in the air fryer – except for those meals with a lot of fat or liquids. There are plenty of suitable recipes in this cookbook.

Prepare the air fryer

Read through the recipe from start to end, so you know what accessories you need for cooking. Some recipes call for using the basket, rack, or rotisserie that comes with the air fryer (*some air fryer brands won't include them, but I recommend you get them as soon as you can). Other recipes use cake or muffin pans that you can insert into the fryer. Just be sure these accessories fit into the fryer and are safe to use.

Prepare the ingredients

Gather the ingredients for the recipe and prep them according to the instructions. When prepped, put the ingredients into the air fryer or in the basket, rack, or pans inside the air fryer. Use parchment baking paper or a light mist of oil spray to prevent food from sticking.

Never crowd food in the air fryer or over-fill. Food that is crowded in the air fryer won't cook evenly and can be raw or under-cooked. If you're preparing food for many people, you may have to cook more than one batch.

NOTE: Ingredients such as chicken breast are indicated for sale in most supermarkets as skinless peeled and boneless. If it comes otherwise, it will be specified as skin-on, bone-in, etc.

Setting the temperature and time

Check the recipe for the correct temperature and time setting. You can set manually, or you can use the digital setting for the temperature and time needed for the recipe. Most air fryers also have preset functions that make it easy to set according to each recipe.

Check food during cooking

Many air fryer recipes require you to check the food while it's cooking so that it cooks evenly and doesn't over-cook. All you need to do is remove the basket, shake, flip, or toss the food to distribute it. Or for some recipes, you'll need to turn the food around halfway through cooking so that it bakes and crisps thoroughly all the way through.

Cleaning the air fryer

Once the food is cooked, remove and unplug the air fryer. Let it cool completely before cleaning. Follow the instructions that come with the fryer for proper cleaning. Never scrub or use abrasive cleaners when cleaning the fryer or the fryer accessories.

AIR FRYER RECIPES

What air fryer should you use?

The recipes in my book can be used with any air fryer model. This includes oven-style fryers that have horizontal racks or fryers that have a basket and handle.

My recipes were developed for my air fryer – it **only** has a temperature and timer setting. But you'll able to make any of the recipes in my book even if your air fryer has preset functions or multiple functions for baking, broiling, and roasting. Choose a function that matches my recipe or use the manual setting if you're unsure.

Using the basket or rack

Some air fryers use a round basket where foods are cooked, while other models will have layered racks that fit into a square cooking space, much like a small oven. My recipes can be used for both baskets and racks.

Keep an eye on the timing

You'll find that air fryers cook at **different temperatures depending on what model you have.** This is why it's essential to check on foods during the cooking process, so you don't over or undercook them. If you cut back on quantities in some of my recipes, be sure to cut the cooking time down accordingly.

Using oil sprays

Most of my recipes in this book use oil spray – I use PAM. But you can use any brand you want. Or make your own by merely putting olive oil into a small spray bottle. Use a small amount of fat and spray over the basket and trays to prevent food from sticking. Some of my recipes require you to spray the food with oil directly.

AUTHOR'S NOTE

The book contains a table of contents, recipes, measurement conversions, air fryer cooking chart for essential items, and index for most common foods for your air fryer.

Inside the table of contents, the digits before each recipe title reflect the exact number of the **600 recipes** in this book, whilst the digits after the recipe title are the page numbers of the book.

The book has a great variety and selection of dishes, which means that some of the recipes contain unpopular ingredients. My idea's idea is to present not only standard and comfort foods, but also a certain twist, mainly with international dishes, in order to put in practice your air fryer to cook easy, tasty and appetizing recipes.

My goal is to offer to the dear reader and most new cooks a lot of **different and interesting recipes (600)** in an affordable and compact format.

Now that all safety requirements are met let's get to the FUN part!

QUICK & EASY

Classic French Fries

INGREDIENTS (2 Servings)

2 russet potatoes, peeled and cut into strips
1 tbsp olive oil

Salt and black pepper to taste
½ cup garlic aioli (or garlic mayo)

DIRECTIONS (Prep + Cook Time: 30 minutes)

Preheat the air fryer to 400 F. Spray the frying basket with cooking spray.

Place the potato strips in a bowl and toss with the olive oil, salt, and pepper. Arrange on the frying basket. AirFry for 20-22 minutes, turning once halfway through, until crispy. Serve with garlic aioli.

Curly Fries with Paprika

INGREDIENTS (2 Servings)

2 Yukon gold potatoes, spiralized
1 tbsp olive oil

1 tsp all-purpose seasoning blend
1 tsp paprika

DIRECTIONS (Prep + Cook Time: 30 minutes)

Coat the potatoes with olive oil. Place them in the frying basket and AirFry for 20-22 minutes at 390 F, tossing them at the 10-minute mark. Sprinkle with the blend and paprika and serve immediately.

Simple Baked Potatoes

INGREDIENTS (4 Servings)

4 Yukon gold potatoes, clean and dried
2 tbsp olive oil

2 tbsp butter
Salt and black pepper to taste

DIRECTIONS (Prep + Cook Time: 45 minutes)

Preheat the air fryer to 400 F. Brush the potatoes with olive oil and season with salt and black pepper. Arrange them on the frying basket and AirFry for 30 minutes at 400 F until fork-tender, flipping once.

Let cool slightly, then cut slit down the center of each baked potato. Use a fork to fluff the insides of the potatoes. Top with butter, sprinkle with salt and black pepper. Serve immediately and enjoy!

Avocado Egg Rolls

INGREDIENTS (4 Servings)

2 ripe avocados, roughly chopped
8 egg roll wrappers

1 tomato, peeled and chopped
Salt and black pepper to taste

DIRECTIONS (Prep + Cook Time: 15 minutes)

Place the avocados, tomato, salt, and black pepper in a bowl. Mash with a fork until somewhat smooth. Divide the mixture between the egg wrappers. Fold the edges in and over the filling, roll up tightly, and seal the wrappers with a bit of water. Arrange them on the greased frying basket. Spray the rolls with cooking spray and Bake for 10 minutes at 350 F, turning halfway through until crispy and golden.

Balsamic Brussels Sprouts

INGREDIENTS (2 Servings)

½ lb Brussels sprouts, trimmed and halved
1 tbsp butter, melted

Salt and black pepper to taste
1 tbsp balsamic vinegar

DIRECTIONS (Prep + Cook Time: 20 minutes)

Preheat the air fryer to 380 F. In a bowl, mix Brussels sprouts with butter, salt, and black pepper. Place the sprouts in the greased frying basket and AirFry for 5-7 minutes. Shake and cook until the sprouts are caramelized but tender on the inside, 5-7 more minutes. Drizzle with balsamic vinegar to serve.

Zucchini-Parmesan Chips

INGREDIENTS (4 Servings)

2 medium zucchinis, sliced
1 cup breadcrumbs
2 eggs, beaten
1 cup Parmesan cheese, grated
Salt and black pepper to taste
1 tsp smoked paprika

DIRECTIONS (Prep + Cook Time: 20 minutes)

Preheat the air fryer to 390 F. In a bowl, mix breadcrumbs, salt, pepper, Parmesan, and paprika. Dip zucchini slices in the eggs and then in the cheese mix; press to coat well. Spray the coated slices with cooking spray and place them in the frying basket. AirFry for 12-14 minutes, flipping once. Serve hot.

Onion Rings

INGREDIENTS (2 Servings)

1 onion, sliced into 1-inch rings
1 egg, beaten
¼ cup milk
Salt and garlic powder to taste
½ cup all-purpose flour
¼ cup panko breadcrumbs

DIRECTIONS (Prep + Cook Time: 20 minutes)

Preheat the air fryer to 350 F. Dust the onion rings with some flour and set aside. In a bowl, mix the remaining flour, garlic powder, and salt. Stir in the egg and milk. Dip onion rings into the flour mixture, then coat them in the crumbs. Lay the rings into the frying basket and spray with cooking spray. AirFry for 8-11 minutes until golden and crispy, shaking once. Serve with honey-mustard dipping sauce.

Breaded Mushrooms

INGREDIENTS (4 Servings)

1 lb white button mushrooms, cleaned
1 cup breadcrumbs
2 eggs, beaten
Salt and black pepper to taste
1 cup Parmesan cheese, grated

DIRECTIONS (Prep + Cook Time: 20 minutes)

Preheat the air fryer to 360 F. Pour breadcrumbs into a bowl and add in the Parmesan cheese, salt, and pepper; mix well. Dip each mushroom into the eggs, then coat in the cheese mixture. Spray with cooking spray and Bake in the fryer for 10-12 minutes, shaking once halfway through. Serve warm.

Herb & Cheese Stuffed Mushrooms

INGREDIENTS (4 Servings)

1 lb brown mushrooms, stems removed
1 cup Grana Padano cheese, grated
½ tsp dried thyme
½ tsp dried rosemary
Salt and black pepper to taste
1 tbsp olive oil

DIRECTIONS (Prep + Cook Time: 20 minutes)

Preheat the air fryer to 360 F. In a bowl, mix Grana Padano cheese, herbs, salt, and black pepper. Spoon the mixture into the mushrooms and press down so that it sticks. Drizzle with olive oil and place in the air fryer. Bake for 8-10 minutes or until the cheese has melted. Serve warm.

Hot Air Fried Green Tomatoes

INGREDIENTS (4 Servings)

8 green tomato slices
2 egg whites
½ cup flour
1 cup breadcrumbs

1 tsp cayenne pepper
½ tsp mustard powder
Salt and black pepper to taste

DIRECTIONS (Prep + Cook Time: 15 minutes)

Preheat the air fryer to 390 F. In a bowl, beat the egg whites with a pinch of salt. In a separate bowl, mix the flour, mustard powder, cayenne pepper, salt, and black pepper. Add the breadcrumbs to a third bowl.

Dredge the tomato slices in the flour mixture, then in the egg whites, and finally in the crumbs. Spray with oil and arrange in the greased frying basket. AirFry for 8 minutes, turning once. Serve warm.

Classic Zucchini Fries

INGREDIENTS (2 Servings)

1 zucchini, cut lengthways into strips
½ cup panko breadcrumbs
½ cup all-purpose flour

1 egg
Salt and garlic powder to taste
½ cup garlic mayonnaise

DIRECTIONS (Prep + Cook Time: 20 minutes)

Preheat the air fryer to 400 F. Sift the flour into a bowl with a pinch of salt. Whisk the egg in another bowl with some salt. Pour the breadcrumbs in a third one and mix with garlic powder. Coat the zucchini strips in the flour, then in the beaten egg, and finally in the crumbs. Lightly spray the strips with cooking spray and AirFry until crispy, 10-12 minutes, flipping once halfway through. Serve with garlic mayo.

Corn on the Cob

INGREDIENTS (2 Servings)

2 ears fresh corn, cut into halves
2 tbsp fresh parsley, chopped

2 tbsp butter, softened
Garlic salt to taste

DIRECTIONS (Prep + Cook Time: 20 minutes)

Preheat the air fryer to 390 F. Spritz the corn with cooking spray and Bake for 12-14 minutes, turning a few times until slightly charred. Brush the corn with the butter. Sprinkle with garlic salt and parsley.

Perfect Air Fryer Eggs

INGREDIENTS (6 Servings)

6 large eggs

Salt and black pepper to taste

DIRECTIONS (Prep + Cook Time: 20 minutes)

Preheat the air fryer to 270 F. Lay the eggs in the basket (or in a muffin tray) and cook for 10 minutes for runny or 15 minutes for hard. Using tongs, place the eggs in a bowl with cold water to cool for 5 minutes. When cooled, remove the shells, cut them in half, and sprinkle with salt and pepper. Serve.

Air Fried Mac & Cheese

INGREDIENTS (2 Servings)

8 oz elbow macaroni, cooked
1 cup cheddar cheese, grated
1 cup warm milk

1 tbsp Parmesan cheese, grated
Salt and black pepper to taste

DIRECTIONS (Prep + Cook Time: 20 minutes)

Preheat the air fryer to 350 F. Add the macaroni to a baking dish and stir in cheddar, milk, salt, and pepper. Place the dish in the fryer and Bake for 16 minutes. Serve sprinkled with Parmesan cheese.

Morning Frittata

INGREDIENTS (4 Servings)

8 eggs
½ cup heavy cream
Salt and black pepper to taste
1 cup spinach, finely chopped

½ red onion, chopped
½ cup tomatoes, diced
1 cup mozzarella cheese, shredded
2 tsp fresh parsley for garnishing

DIRECTIONS (Prep + Cook Time: 30 minutes)

Preheat the air fryer to 330 F. Grease a baking dish that fits in your air fryer with cooking spray.

In a bowl, whisk the eggs and heavy cream until pale. Add in spinach, red onion, tomatoes, mozzarella, salt, and pepper. Mix to combine. Pour the mixture into the baking dish and Bake in the air fryer for 20-23 minutes, or until the eggs are set in the center. Sprinkle with parsley and cut into wedges to serve.

Mediterranean Bruschetta

INGREDIENTS (4 Servings)

8 french baguette slices
2 tbsp olive oil
2 garlic cloves, haled

1 cup mozzarella cheese, grated
1 tsp fresh basil, chopped
1 cup mixed cherry tomatoes, quartered

DIRECTIONS (Prep + Cook Time: 15 minutes)

Brush the bread with olive oil and rub with garlic. Scatter mozzarella cheese on top. Arrange the slices in the frying basket and Bake for 8-10 minutes at 360 F. Top with cherry tomatoes and basil to serve.

Mozzarella Cheese Sticks

INGREDIENTS (4 Servings)

12 oz mozzarella cheese sticks
½ cup flour
1 cup breadcrumbs

2 eggs
¼ cup Parmesan cheese, grated
1 cup marinara sauce (optional)

DIRECTIONS (Prep + Cook Time: 15 minutes)

Preheat the air fryer to 380 F. Pour the breadcrumbs into a bowl. Beat the eggs in another bowl. In a third bowl, mix Parmesan cheese and flour. Dip each cheese stick in the flour, then in the eggs, and finally in breadcrumbs. Place them in the greased frying basket and AirFry until golden brown, about 6-8 minutes, shaking the basket once or twice. Serve with marinara sauce.

"Bikini" Ham & Cheese Sandwich

INGREDIENTS (1 Serving)

2 tbsp butter
2 slices bread

2 slices cheddar cheese
1 slice ham

DIRECTIONS (Prep + Cook Time: 15 minutes)

Preheat the air fryer to 370 F. Spread 1 tsp of butter on the outside of each of the bread slices. Place the cheese on the inside of one bread slice. Top with ham and the other cheese slice. Close with the second bread slice. AirFry for 8 minutes, flipping once halfway through. Cut diagonally and serve.

Homemade Arancini (Rice Balls)

INGREDIENTS (4 Servings)

2 cups cooked rice
½ cup flour
1 green onion, chopped
2 garlic cloves, minced
2 eggs, lightly beaten

½ cup Parmesan cheese, grated
Salt and black pepper to taste
1 cup breadcrumbs
1 tsp dried mixed herbs
1 cup arrabbiata sauce

DIRECTIONS (Prep + Cook Time: 25 minutes + chilling time)

Place the flour, beaten eggs, and breadcrumbs into 3 separate bowls. Combine the cooked rice, onion, garlic, Parmesan cheese, herbs, salt, and pepper in a bowl. Shape into 10 balls. Roll them in the flour, shake off any excess, then dip in the eggs, and finally coat in the breadcrumbs. Let chill for 20 minutes.

Preheat the air fryer to 390 F. Spray the arancini with cooking spray and AirFry them for 12-14 minutes, turning once halfway through cooking, until golden and crispy. Serve with arrabbiata sauce.

Cheddar Hash Browns

INGREDIENTS (4 Servings)

4 russet potatoes, peeled and grated
1 brown onion, chopped
2 garlic cloves, minced
½ cup cheddar cheese, grated

1 egg, lightly beaten
Salt and black pepper to taste
1 tbsp fresh thyme, chopped

DIRECTIONS (Prep + Cook Time: 30 minutes)

In a bowl, mix the potatoes, onion, garlic, cheddar cheese, egg, salt, black pepper, and thyme. Spread the mixture in the greased frying basket and AirFry in the preheated air fryer for 20-22 minutes at 400 F. Shake once halfway through cooking, until golden and crispy. Serve hot with ketchup (optional).

Bacon-Wrapped Chicken Breasts

INGREDIENTS (4 Servings)

2 chicken breasts
8 oz cream cheese
1 tbsp butter

6 turkey bacon slices
Salt to taste
1 tbsp fresh parsley, chopped

DIRECTIONS (Prep + Cook Time: 25 minutes)

Preheat the air fryer to 390 F. Stretch out the bacon and lay the slices in 2 sets; 3 bacon strips together on each side. Place the chicken on each bacon set. Use a knife to smear the cream cheese on both.

Spread the butter on top and sprinkle with salt. Wrap the turkey bacon around the chicken and secure the ends into the wrap. Place the wrapped chicken in the greased frying basket and AirFry for 16-18 minutes, turning halfway through. Top with fresh parsley and serve with steamed greens (optional).

Air-Fried Chicken Popcorn

INGREDIENTS (4 Servings)

2 chicken breasts, cut into small cubes
2 cups panko breadcrumbs

Salt and black pepper to taste
1 tsp garlic powder

DIRECTIONS (Prep + Cook Time: 30 minutes)

Preheat the air fryer to 360 F. Rub the chicken cubes with salt, garlic powder, and black pepper. Coat in the panko breadcrumbs and place them in the greased frying basket. Spray with cooking spray and AirFry for 16-18 minutes, flipping once until nice and crispy. Serve with tzatziki sauce if desired.

Sweet Garlicky Chicken Wings

INGREDIENTS (4 Servings)

16 chicken wings
¼ cup butter
1 tsp honey

½ tbsp salt
4 garlic cloves, minced
¾ cup potato starch

DIRECTIONS (Prep + Cook Time: 20 minutes)

Preheat the air fryer to 370 F. Coat the chicken with potato starch and place in the greased frying basket. Bake for 5 minutes. Whisk the rest of the ingredients in a bowl. Remove the wings from the fryer, pour the sauce over them, and Bake for another 10 minutes, until crispy. Serve immediately.

Spicy Buffalo Chicken Wings

INGREDIENTS (4 Servings)

2 lb chicken wings
½ cup cayenne pepper sauce
2 tbsp coconut oil
2 tbsp Worcestershire sauce
Salt to taste

½ cup sour cream
¼ cup mayonnaise
1 tbsp scallions, chopped
1 tbsp fresh parsley, chopped
1 garlic clove, minced

DIRECTIONS (Prep + Cook Time: 25 minutes + marinating time)

In a mixing bowl, combine cayenne pepper sauce, coconut oil, Worcestershire sauce, and salt. Add in the chicken wings and toss to coat. Cover with a lid and marinate for 1 hour in the fridge.

Preheat the air fryer to 400 F. Place the chicken in a greased frying basket and AirFry for 15-18 minutes or until the marinade becomes sticky and the wings are cooked through.

Meanwhile, in a small bowl, mix together sour cream, mayonnaise, garlic, parsley, and salt. Top the wings with scallions and serve with the prepared sauce on the side. Enjoy!

Effortless Chicken Drumsticks

INGREDIENTS (4 Servings)

1 lb chicken drumsticks
1 tsp garlic powder
1 tsp cayenne pepper

½ cup flour
¼ cup milk
Salt and black pepper to taste

DIRECTIONS (Prep + Cook Time: 25 minutes)

Preheat the air fryer to 390 F. Spray the frying basket with cooking spray. In a small bowl, mix garlic powder, cayenne pepper, salt, and black pepper. Rub the chicken drumsticks with the mixture.

In a separate bowl, pour the flour. Dunk the chicken in the milk, then roll in the flour to coat. Place the drumsticks in the frying basket and spray with cooking spray. AirFry for 14-16 minutes, flipping once.

Hot Chicken Wingettes

INGREDIENTS (4 Servings)

1 lb chicken wingettes
Salt and black pepper to taste

⅓ cup hot sauce
½ tbsp white wine vinegar

DIRECTIONS (Prep + Cook Time: 25 minutes)

Preheat the air fryer to 360 F. Season the wingettes with black pepper and salt and spray them with oil. AirFry them for 15-18 minutes, until golden, tossing every 5 minutes. In a bowl, mix vinegar with hot sauce. When the wingettes are ready, transfer them to a plate and pour the sauce over. Serve warm.

Turkey Scotch Eggs

INGREDIENTS (4 Servings)

4 hard-boiled eggs, peeled
1 cup panko breadcrumbs
1 egg, beaten in a bowl

1 lb ground turkey
½ tsp dried rosemary
Salt and black pepper to taste

DIRECTIONS (Prep + Cook Time: 20 minutes)

Preheat the air fryer to 400 F. In a bowl, mix panko breadcrumbs with rosemary. In another bowl, pour the ground turkey and mix it with salt and pepper. Shape into 4 balls.

Wrap the balls around the boiled eggs to form a large ball with the egg in the center. Dip in the beaten egg and coat with breadcrumbs. Place in the greased frying basket and Bake for 12-14 minutes, shaking once. Serve and enjoy!

Air Fried Pork Popcorn Bites

INGREDIENTS (4 Servings)

4 boneless pork chops, cut into 1-inch cubes
Salt and black pepper to taste
1 cup flour
¼ tsp garlic powder

¼ tsp onion powder
1 tsp paprika
2 eggs
1 cup ranch sauce

DIRECTIONS (Prep + Cook Time: 20 minutes)

Preheat the Air fryer to 390 F. Spray the basket with cooking spray. In a bowl, combine the flour, garlic and onion powders, paprika, salt, and black pepper and mix well. In another bowl, whisk the eggs with a bit of salt. Dip the pork in the flour first, then in the eggs, and back again in the flour; coat well.

Spray with cooking spray and place in the frying basket. AirFry for 15 minutes, shaking once halfway through. Remove to a serving plate and serve with ranch sauce.

Sesame Pork Skewers

INGREDIENTS (4 Servings)

1 lb pork tenderloin, cut into 1-inch chunks
1 red pepper, cut into 1-inch chunks
2 tbsp sesame oil
1 garlic clove, minced

2 tbsp soy sauce
Salt and black pepper to taste
1 tbsp honey
1 tsp sesame seeds

DIRECTIONS (Prep + Cook Time: 20 minutes + marinating time)

In a bowl, mix the honey, sesame oil, soy sauce, salt, and black pepper. Coat the pork in the mixture. Cover with a lid and let sit for 30 minutes. Preheat the air fryer to 400 F. Thread the pork onto skewers, alternating the cubes of meat with chunks of red pepper. Place them in the greased frying basket.

Spritz them with cooking spray and AirFry the skewers for 8-10 minutes. Flip them over and cook further for 5-7 minutes until golden brown. Top with sesame seeds and serve.

Teriyaki Pork Ribs

INGREDIENTS (4 Servings)

1 lb pork ribs
2 tbsp olive oil
Salt and black pepper to taste
1 tsp sugar
1 tsp ginger paste
1 tsp five-spice powder

1 tbsp teriyaki sauce
1 tbsp light soy sauce
1 garlic clove, minced
½ tsp honey
2 tbsp water
1 tbsp tomato sauce

DIRECTIONS (Prep + Cook Time: 20 minutes + marinating time)

In a bowl, mix teriyaki sauce, sugar, five-spice powder, ginger paste, salt, and black pepper. Add in the pork ribs and stir to coat. Cover with foil and marinate for 2 hours in the fridge. Preheat the air fryer to 350 F. Add the ribs to the greased frying basket and Bake for 18-20 minutes, flipping once until crispy.

Heat the olive oil in a skillet over medium heat and stir in the soy sauce, garlic, honey, water, and tomato sauce. Cook the sauce for 1-2 minutes until it thickens slightly. Pour it over the ribs and serve.

Gorgonzola Cheese Burgers

INGREDIENTS (4 Servings)

1 lb ground beef
½ cup Gorgonzola cheese, crumbled
1 tbsp olive oil
1 tsp Worcestershire sauce
½ tsp hot sauce
½ garlic clove, minced

4 bread buns
4 yellow cheese slices
2 tbsp mayonnaise
1 tsp ketchup
1 dill pickle, sliced
Salt and black pepper to taste

DIRECTIONS (Prep + Cook Time: 35 minutes)

Preheat the air fryer to 360 F. In a mixing bowl, place the ground beef, Worcestershire sauce, hot sauce, gorgonzola cheese, garlic, salt, and pepper. Mix well. Shape the mixture into 4 burgers.

Grease the frying basket with a thin layer of olive oil. Add the burgers and AirFry for 20 minutes, flipping once halfway through. On bread buns, spread the mayonnaise and add the dill pickles. Place the burgers over the top and lay the yellow cheese. Top with ketchup and serve.

Beef Steak Fingers

INGREDIENTS (4 Servings)

1 lb beef steak, cut into strips
1 tbsp olive oil
½ cup flour
½ cup panko breadcrumbs
¼ tsp cayenne pepper
2 eggs, beaten

½ cup milk
Salt and black pepper to taste
1 lb tomatoes, chopped
1 tbsp tomato paste
1 tsp honey
1 tbsp white wine vinegar

DIRECTIONS (Prep + Cook Time: 30 minutes)

Place the tomatoes, tomato paste, honey, and vinegar in a deep skillet over medium heat. Cook for 6-8 minutes, stirring occasionally until the sauce thickens; set aside to cool. Grease the basket with oil.

Preheat the air fryer to 390 F. In a bowl, combine flour, salt, black pepper, and cayenne pepper. In a second bowl, whisk the eggs with the milk. Dredge the steak strips in the flour mixture, then coat with the egg mixture, and finally in the breadcrumbs until completely coated. AirFry the dredged steak strips for 8 minutes. Turn them over and spray with a little bit of olive oil. Continue to cook for another 5-7 minutes until golden and crispy. Spoon into paper cones and serve with the tomato sauce.

Easy Salmon Fillets

INGREDIENTS (2 Servings)

2 salmon fillets
1 tbsp olive oil

Salt to taste
1 lemon, cut into wedges

DIRECTIONS (Prep + Cook Time: 15 minutes)

Preheat the air fryer to 380 F. Brush the salmon with olive oil and season with salt. Place the fillets in the greased frying basket and Bake for 8 minutes until tender, turning once. Serve with lemon wedges.

Classic Fish & Chips

INGREDIENTS (4 Servings)

2 tbsp olive oil
4 potatoes, cut into thin slices
Salt and black pepper to taste
4 white fish fillets

1 cup flour
2 eggs, beaten
1 cup breadcrumbs
Salt and black pepper to taste

DIRECTIONS (Prep + Cook Time: 30 minutes)

Preheat the air fryer to 400 F. Drizzle the potatoes with olive oil and season with salt and black pepper; toss to coat. Place them in the greased frying basket and AirFry for 10 minutes.

Season the fillets with salt and black pepper. Coat them with flour, then dip in the eggs, and finally into the crumbs. Shake the potatoes and add in the fish; cook until the fish is crispy, 8-10 minutes. Serve.

Chipotle-Lime Prawn Bowls

INGREDIENTS (4 Servings)

1 lb prawns, deveined, peeled
2 tsp olive oil
2 tsp lime juice
1 tsp honey
1 garlic clove, minced

1 tsp chipotle powder
2 cups cooked brown rice
1 (15-oz) can black beans, warmed
1 large avocado, chopped
1 cup sliced cherry tomatoes

DIRECTIONS (Prep + Cook Time: 25 minutes + marinating time)

Toss the lime juice, olive oil, honey, garlic, and chipotle powder in a bowl. Mix well to make a marinade. Add the prawns and toss to coat. Transfer them to the fridge for at least 30 minutes.

Preheat the air fryer to 390 F. Remove the prawns to the fryer and AirFry them for 10-15 minutes, tossing once, until golden and cooked through. Divide the rice, beans, avocado, and tomatoes between 4 bowls and top with the prawns. Serve.

Simple Calamari Rings

INGREDIENTS (4 Servings)

1 lb calamari rings
½ cup cornstarch
2 large eggs, beaten

2 garlic cloves, minced
1 cup breadcrumbs
1 lemon, sliced

DIRECTIONS (Prep + Cook Time: 30 minutes)

In a bowl, coat the calamari with cornstarch. In another bowl, mix the eggs with garlic. Dip the calamari in the egg and roll them up in the crumbs. Transfer to the fridge for 10 minutes. Remove calamari from the fridge and arrange them on the greased frying basket. AirFry for 12 minutes at 390 F, shaking onc halfway through cooking. Serve with lemon slices.

Gambas al Ajillo (Garlic Shrimp)

INGREDIENTS (4 Servings)

1 lb shrimp, peeled and deveined
½ tsp Cajun seasoning
10 lettuce leaves

1 tbsp olive oil
¼ tsp garlic powder
2 tbsp lemon juice, chopped

DIRECTIONS (Prep + Cook Time: 25 minutes)

Mix the garlic powder, half of the lemon juice, olive oil, and Cajun seasoning in a bowl to make a marinade. Toss the shrimp to coat thoroughly. Cover with a plastic wrap and refrigerate for 30 minutes.

Preheat the air fryer to 400 F. Place the shrimp in the greased frying basket and AirFry for 5 minutes. Shake the basket and cook for 7-8 more minutes, until cooked through. Arrange the lettuce leaves on a plate and top with the shrimp. Drizzle with the remaining lemon juice and serve.

Crispy Fish Finger Sticks

INGREDIENTS (4 Servings)

2 fresh white fish fillets, cut into 4 fingers each
1 egg
½ cup buttermilk

1 cup panko breadcrumbs
Salt and black pepper to taste
1 cup aioli (or garlic mayo)

DIRECTIONS (Prep + Cook Time: 20 minutes)

Preheat the air fryer to 380 F. In a bowl, beat the egg and buttermilk. On a plate, combine breadcrumbs, salt, and pepper. Dip each finger into the egg mixture, roll it up in the crumbs, and spritz it with cooking spray. Arrange on the greased frying basket and AirFry for 10 minutes, turning once. Serve with aioli.

Raspberry & Vanilla Pancakes

INGREDIENTS (4 Servings)

1 ½ cups all-purpose flour
1 cup milk
3 eggs, beaten
1 tsp baking powder

2 tbsp brown sugar
1 tsp vanilla extract
½ cup frozen raspberries, thawed
2 tbsp maple syrup

DIRECTIONS (Prep + Cook Time: 15 minutes)

Preheat the air fryer to 370 F. In a bowl, mix the flour, baking powder, milk, eggs, vanilla, and brown sugar. Gently stir in the raspberries to avoid coloring the batter. Working in batches, drop the batter into a greased baking pan using a spoon. Bake for 6-8 minutes, flipping once. Repeat the process with the remaining batter. Serve the pancakes with maple syrup.

Cinnamon French Toast Sticks

INGREDIENTS (2 Servings)

4 white bread slices, cut them into strips
2 eggs
1 ½ tbsp butter
¼ tsp cinnamon powder + some for dusting

¼ nutmeg powder
¼ clove powder
2 tbsp brown sugar
1 tbsp icing sugar

DIRECTIONS (Prep + Cook Time: 15 minutes)

Preheat the air fryer to 350 F. In a bowl, add the eggs, brown sugar, clove powder, nutmeg powder, and cinnamon powder. Beat the mixture using a whisk until well combined. Dip the strips into the egg mixture. Arrange them on the greased frying basket and spritz with cooking spray. Bake for 2 minutes. Flip the toasts and cook for 3 more minutes. Dust the toasts with cinnamon and icing sugar to serve.

Air Fried Cinnamon Apples

INGREDIENTS (2 Servings)

2 apples, cored, bottom intact
2 tbsp butter, cold
3 tbsp sugar

3 tbsp crushed walnuts
2 tbsp raisins
1 tsp cinnamon

DIRECTIONS (Prep + Cook Time: 25 minutes)

Preheat the air fryer to 350 F. In a bowl, add butter, sugar, walnuts, raisins, and cinnamon. Mix well until you obtain a crumble. Stuff the apples with the filling mixture. Bake in the air fryer for 20 minutes.

BRUNCH

Easy Breakfast Potatoes

INGREDIENTS (6 Servings)

4 large potatoes, cubed
2 bell peppers, cut into 1-inch chunks
½ onion, diced
2 tsp olive oil

1 garlic clove, minced
½ tsp dried thyme
½ tsp cayenne pepper
Salt to taste

DIRECTIONS (Prep + Cook Time: 35 minutes)

Preheat the air fryer to 390 F. Place the potato cubes in a bowl and sprinkle with garlic, cayenne pepper, and salt. Drizzle with some olive oil and toss to coat. Arrange the potatoes in an even layer in the greased frying basket. AirFry for 10 minutes, shaking once halfway through cooking.

In the meantime, add the remaining olive oil, garlic, thyme, and salt in a mixing bowl. Add in the bell peppers and onion and mix well. Pour the veggies over the potatoes and continue cooking for 10 more minutes. At the 5-minute mark, shake the basket and cook for 5 minutes. Serve warm.

Morning Potato Skins

INGREDIENTS (4 Servings)

4 eggs
2 large russet potatoes, scrubbed
1 tbsp olive oil
2 tbsp cooked bacon, chopped

1 cup cheddar cheese, shredded
1 tbsp chopped chives
¼ tsp red pepper flakes
Salt and black pepper to taste

DIRECTIONS (Prep + Cook Time: 35 minutes)

Preheat the air fryer to 360 F. Using a fork, poke holes all over the potatoes, then cook them in the microwave on high for 5 minutes. Flip them and cook in the microwave for another 3-5 minutes. Test with a fork to make sure they are tender. Halve the potatoes lengthwise and scoop out most of the 'meat,' leaving enough potato, so 'boat' sides don't collapse.

Coat the skin side of the potatoes with olive oil, salt, and black pepper for taste. Arrange the potatoes, skin down, in the lightly greased frying basket. Crack an egg and put it in the scooped potato, one egg for each half. Divide the bacon and cheddar cheese between the potatoes and sprinkle with salt and pepper. For a runny yolk, AirFry for 5-6 minutes, and for a solid yolk, AirFry for 7-10 minutes. Sprinkle with red pepper flakes and chives to serve.

Chili Potato Latkes (Hash Browns)

INGREDIENTS (4 Servings)

1 lb potatoes, peeled and shredded
Salt and black pepper to taste
1 tsp garlic powder
1 tsp chili flakes

1 tsp onion powder
1 egg, beaten
1 tbsp olive oil

DIRECTIONS (Prep + Cook Time: 25 minutes + cooling time)

Heat olive oil in a skillet over medium heat and sauté potatoes for 10 minutes; transfer to a bowl to cool. When cooled, add in the egg, black pepper, salt, chili flakes, onion powder, and garlic powder; mix well. On a flat plate, spread the mixture and pat it firmly with your fingers. Refrigerate for 20 minutes.

Preheat the air fryer to 350 F. Shape the cooled mixture into patties. Arrange them on the greased frying basket and AirFry for 12 minutes, flipping once halfway through. Serve warm.

Kaiserschmarrn (German Torn Pancake)

INGREDIENTS (4 Servings)

3 eggs, whites and yolks separated
1 tbsp sugar
2 tbsp butter, melted
1 cup flour

2 tbsp sugar, powdered
½ cup milk
2 tbsp raisins, soaked in rum
1 cup plum sauce

DIRECTIONS (Prep + Cook Time: 30 minutes)

Preheat the air fryer to 350 F. In a bowl, mix flour, milk, and egg yolks until fully incorporated; stir in the drained raisins. Beat the egg whites with sugar until stiff. Gently fold the whites into the yolk mixture. Grease a baking pan with butter and pour in the batter. Place the pan inside the frying basket.

Bake for 6-8 minutes until the pancake is fluffy and golden brown. Break the pancake into pieces using two forks and dust with powdered sugar. Serve with plum sauce and enjoy!

Three Meat Cheesy Omelet

INGREDIENTS (2 Servings)

1 beef sausage, chopped
4 slices prosciutto, chopped
3 oz salami, chopped
1 cup mozzarella cheese, grated

4 eggs
1 green onion, chopped
1 tbsp ketchup
1 tsp fresh parsley, chopped

DIRECTIONS (Prep + Cook Time: 20 minutes)

Preheat the air fryer to 350 F. Whisk the eggs with ketchup in a bowl. Stir in the green onion, mozzarella, salami, and prosciutto. AirFry the sausage in a greased baking pan inside the fryer for 2 minutes. Slide out and pour the egg mixture over. Bake for 8-10 more minutes until golden. Serve topped with parsley.

Masala Omelet The Indian Way

INGREDIENTS (1 Serving)

1 garlic clove, crushed
1 green onion
½ chili powder
½ tsp garam masala

2 eggs
1 tbsp olive oil
1 tbsp fresh cilantro, chopped
Salt and black pepper to taste

DIRECTIONS (Prep + Cook Time: 15 minutes)

Preheat the air fryer to 360 F. In a bowl, whisk the eggs with salt and black pepper. Add in the green onion, garlic, chili powder, and garam masala; stir well. Transfer to a greased baking pan. Bake in the fryer for 8 minutes until the top is golden and the eggs are set. Scatter with fresh cilantro and serve.

Japanese-Style Omelet

INGREDIENTS (1 Serving)

½ cup cubed tofu
3 whole eggs
Salt and black pepper to taste
¼ tsp ground coriander

¼ tsp cumin
1 tsp soy sauce
1 tbsp green onions, chopped
¼ onion, chopped

DIRECTIONS (Prep + Cook Time: 20 minutes)

In a bowl, mix eggs, onion, soy sauce, ground coriander, cumin, black pepper, and salt. Add in the tofu and pour the mixture into a greased baking pan. Place in the preheated air fryer and Bake for 8 minutes at 360 F. Remove, and let cool for 2 minutes. Sprinkle with green onions and serve.

Baked Kale Omelet

INGREDIENTS (2 Servings)

5 eggs
3 tbsp cottage cheese, crumbled
1 cup kale, chopped

½ tbsp fresh basil, chopped
½ tbsp fresh parsley, chopped
Salt and black pepper to taste

DIRECTIONS (Prep + Cook Time: 15 minutes)

Beat the eggs, salt, and black pepper in a bowl. Stir in the rest of the ingredients. Pour the mixture into a greased baking pan and fit in the air fryer. Bake for 10 minutes at 330 F until slightly golden and set.

Ham & Cheddar Omelet

INGREDIENTS (2 Servings)

4 eggs
3 tbsp cheddar cheese, grated

1 tsp soy sauce
½ cup ham, chopped

DIRECTIONS (Prep + Cook Time: 20 minutes)

Preheat the air fryer to 350 F. In a bowl, whisk the eggs with soy sauce. Fold in the chopped ham and mix well to combine. Spoon the egg mixture into a greased baking pan and pour into the frying basket. Bake for 6-8 minutes until golden on top. Sprinkle with the cheddar cheese and serve warm.

Omelet Bread Cups

INGREDIENTS (4 Servings)

4 crusty rolls
5 eggs, beaten
½ tsp thyme, dried

3 strips cooked bacon, chopped
2 tbsp heavy cream
4 Gouda cheese thin slices

DIRECTIONS (Prep + Cook Time: 25 minutes)

Preheat the air fryer to 330 F. Cut the tops off the rolls and remove the inside with your fingers. Line the rolls with a slice of cheese and press down, so the cheese conforms to the inside of the roll.

In a bowl, mix the eggs, heavy cream, bacon, and thyme. Stuff the rolls with the egg mixture. Lay them in the greased frying basket and Bake for 6-8 minutes or until the eggs become puffy, and the roll shows a golden brown texture. Remove and let them cool for a few minutes before serving.

Greek-Style Frittata

INGREDIENTS (4 Servings)

5 eggs
1 cup baby spinach
½ cup grape tomatoes, halved
½ cup feta cheese, crumbled

10 Kalamata olives, sliced
Salt and black pepper to taste
2 tbsp fresh parsley, chopped

DIRECTIONS (Prep + Cook Time: 30 minutes)

Preheat the air fryer to 360 F. Beat the eggs, salt, and black pepper in a bowl, until well combined. Add in the spinach and stir until well mixed. Pour half the mixture into a greased baking pan.

On top of the mixture, add half of the tomatoes, olives, and feta cheese. Cover the pan with foil, making sure to close it tightly around the edges, then place it inside the air fryer and Bake for 12 minutes.

Remove the foil and cook for an additional 5-7 minutes, until the eggs are fully cooked. Place the finished frittata on a serving plate and repeat the above instructions for the remaining ingredients. Decorate with fresh parsley and cut into wedges. Serve hot or at room temperature.

Spanish Chorizo Frittata

INGREDIENTS (2 Servings)

4 eggs
1 large potato, boiled and cubed
¼ cup Manchego cheese, grated
1 tbsp parsley, chopped

1 Spanish chorizo, chopped
½ small red onion, chopped
¼ tsp paprika
Salt and black pepper to taste

DIRECTIONS (Prep + Cook Time: 20 minutes)

Preheat the air fryer to 330 F. In a bowl, beat the eggs with paprika, salt, and pepper. Stir in all of the remaining ingredients, except for the parsley. Spread the egg batter on the greased baking pan and insert it into the air fryer. Bake for 8-10 minutes until the top is golden. Garnish with parsley to serve.

Vienna Sausage & Cherry Tomato Frittata

INGREDIENTS (2 Servings)

2 Vienna sausages, sliced
Salt and black pepper to taste
1 tbsp fresh parsley, chopped
½ cup milk

4 eggs
½ tsp red pepper flakes, crushed
4 cherry tomatoes, halved
2 tbsp Parmesan cheese, shredded

DIRECTIONS (Prep + Cook Time: 15 minutes)

Preheat the air fryer to 360 F. In a bowl, whisk the eggs and milk. Stir in the Parmesan cheese, red pepper flakes, salt, parsley, and black pepper. Add the mixture to a lightly greased baking pan and top with sausage slices and cherry tomatoes. Bake in the fryer for 8 minutes until the eggs are set. Serve hot.

Air Fried Shirred Eggs

INGREDIENTS (2 Servings)

2 tsp butter, melted
4 eggs
2 tbsp heavy cream
4 smoked ham slices

3 tbsp Parmesan cheese, grated
¼ tsp paprika
Salt and black pepper to taste
2 tsp fresh chives, chopped

DIRECTIONS (Prep + Cook Time: 20 minutes)

Preheat the air fryer to 320 F. Lightly grease 4 ramekins with butter. Line the bottom of each ramekin with a piece of smoked ham. Crack the eggs on top of the ham and season with salt and pepper. Drizzle with heavy cream and sprinkle with Parmesan cheese. AirFry for 10-12 minutes until the eggs are completely set. Garnish with paprika and fresh chives to serve.

Prosciutto, Mozzarella & Eggs in a Cup

INGREDIENTS (2 Servings)

4 prosciutto slices
2 eggs
4 tomato slices
¼ tsp balsamic vinegar

2 tbsp mozzarella cheese, grated
¼ tsp maple syrup
2 tbsp mayonnaise
Salt and black pepper to taste

DIRECTIONS (Prep + Cook Time: 20 minutes)

Preheat the air fryer to 350 F. Grease 2 cups with cooking spray. Line the bottom and sides of each cup with prosciutto, patching up any holes using little pieces if necessary. Place the tomato slices on top and divide the mozzarella cheese between the cups. Crack the eggs over the mozzarella cheese and drizzle with maple syrup and balsamic vinegar. Season with salt and pepper. Bake in the fryer until the egg whites are just set, about 10-12 minutes. Top with mayonnaise and serve.

Buttered Eggs in Hole

INGREDIENTS (2 Servings)

2 bread slices
2 eggs

Salt and black pepper to taste
1 tbsp butter, softened

DIRECTIONS (Prep + Cook Time: 15 minutes)

Preheat the air fryer to 360 F. Place a heatproof pan in the frying basket and brush with butter. Make a hole in the middle of the bread slices with a bread knife and place in the heatproof pan in 2 batches. Crack an egg into the center of each hole; adjust the seasoning. Bake in the air fryer for 4 minutes. Turn the bread with a spatula and cook for another 4 minutes. Serve warm.

Breakfast Shrimp & Egg Muffins

INGREDIENTS (4 Servings)

4 eggs, beaten
2 tbsp olive oil
½ small red bell pepper, finely diced
1 garlic clove, minced

4 oz shrimp, cooked, chopped
4 tsp ricotta cheese, crumbled
1 tsp dry dill
Salt and black pepper to taste

DIRECTIONS (Prep + Cook Time: 35 minutes)

Preheat the air fryer to 360 F. Warm the olive oil in a skillet over medium heat. Sauté the bell pepper and garlic until the pepper is soft, then add the shrimp. Season with dill, salt, and pepper and cook for about 5 minutes. Remove from the heat and mix in the eggs. Grease 4 ramekins with cooking spray.

Divide the mixture between the ramekins. Place them in the air fryer and Bake for 6 minutes. Remove and stir the mixture. Sprinkle with ricotta and return to the fryer. Bake for 5 more minutes until the eggs are set, and the top is lightly browned. Let sit for 2 minutes, invert on a plate while warm, and serve.

Cheese & Ham Breakfast Egg Cups

INGREDIENTS (6 Servings)

4 eggs, beaten
1 tbsp olive oil
½ cup Colby cheese, shredded

2 ¼ cups frozen hash browns, thawed
1 cup smoked ham, chopped
½ tsp Cajun seasoning

DIRECTIONS (Prep + Cook Time: 20 minutes)

Preheat the air fryer to 360 F. Gather 12 silicone muffin cups and coat with olive oil. Whisk the eggs, hash browns, smoked ham, Colby cheese, and Cajun seasoning in a large bowl and add a heaping spoonful into each muffin cup. Put the muffin cups in the frying basket and AirFry 8-10 minutes until golden brown and the center is set. Transfer to a wire rack to cool completely. Serve.

Turkey & Mushroom Sandwich

INGREDIENTS (1 Serving)

⅓ cup leftover turkey, shredded
⅓ cup sliced mushrooms, sauteed
½ tbsp butter, softened
2 tomato slices

½ tsp red pepper flakes
Salt and black pepper to taste
1 hamburger bun, halved

DIRECTIONS (Prep + Cook Time: 10 minutes)

Preheat the air fryer to 350 F. Brush the bun bottom with butter and top with shredded turkey. Arrange the mushroom slices on top of the turkey. Cover with tomato slices and sprinkle with salt, black pepper, and red flakes. Top with the bun top and AirFry for 5-8 minutes until crispy. Serve and enjoy!

Air Fried Sourdough Sandwiches

INGREDIENTS (2 Servings)

4 slices sourdough bread
2 tbsp mayonnaise
2 slices ham

2 lettuce leaves
1 tomato, sliced
2 slices mozzarella cheese

DIRECTIONS (Prep + Cook Time: 20 minutes)

Preheat the air fryer to 350 F. On a clean working board, lay the bread slices and spread them with mayonnaise. Top 2 of the slices with ham, lettuce leaves, tomato slices, and mozzarella. Cover with the remaining bread slices to form two sandwiches. AirFry for 12 minutes, flipping once. Serve hot.

Loaded Egg Pepper Rings

INGREDIENTS (4 Servings)

4 eggs
1 bell pepper, cut into four ¾-inch rings

5 cherry tomatoes, halved
Salt and black pepper to taste

DIRECTIONS (Prep + Cook Time: 15 minutes)

Preheat the air fryer to 360 F. Add the bell pepper rings to a greased baking pan and crack an egg into each one. Season with salt and black pepper. Top with the halved cherry tomatoes. Put the pan into the air fryer and AirFry for 6-9 minutes, or until the eggs are have set. Serve and enjoy!

Sausage & Egg Casserole

INGREDIENTS (6 Servings)

2 tbsp olive oil
1 lb Italian sausages
6 eggs
1 red pepper, diced
1 green pepper, diced

1 yellow pepper, diced
1 sweet onion, diced
1 cup cheddar cheese, shredded
Salt and black pepper to taste
2 tbsp fresh parsley, chopped

DIRECTIONS (Prep + Cook Time: 20 minutes)

Warm the olive oil in a skillet over medium heat. Add the sausages and brown them slightly, turning occasionally, about 5 minutes. Once done, drain any excess fat derived from cooking and set aside.

Arrange the sausages on the bottom of a greased casserole dish that fits in your air fryer. Top with onion, red pepper, green pepper, and yellow pepper. Sprinkle with cheddar cheese on top.

In a bowl, beat the eggs with salt and pepper. Pour the mixture over the cheese. Place the casserole dish in the frying basket and Bake at 360 F for 15 minutes. Serve warm garnished with fresh parsley.

Grilled Tofu Sandwich with Cabbage

INGREDIENTS (1 Serving)

2 slices of bread
1 tofu slice, 1-inch thick
¼ cup red cabbage, shredded

2 tsp olive oil
¼ tsp vinegar
Salt to taste

DIRECTIONS (Prep + Cook Time: 20 minutes)

Preheat the air fryer to 350 F. Add the bread slices to the frying basket and AirFry for 3 minutes; set aside. Brush the tofu with some olive oil and place in the air fryer. AirFry for 5 minutes on each side.

Mix the cabbage, remaining olive oil, and vinegar. Season with salt. Place the tofu on top of one bread slice, place the cabbage over, and top with the other bread slice. Serve with cream cheese-mustard dip.

French Toast with Vanilla Filling

INGREDIENTS (3 Servings)

6 white bread slices
2 eggs
¼ cup milk
3 tbsp caramel sauce

⅓ cup cream cheese, softened
1 tsp vanilla extract
⅓ cup sugar mixed with 1 tsp ground cinnamon

DIRECTIONS (Prep + Cook Time: 15 minutes)

In a bowl, mix the cream cheese, caramel sauce, and vanilla. Spread three of the bread slices with the cheese mixture around the center. Place the remaining three slices on top to form three sandwiches.

Whisk the eggs and milk in a bowl. Dip the sandwiches into the egg mixture. Arrange them in the greased frying basket and AirFry for 10 minutes at 340 F, turning once. Dust with the cinnamon mixture.

Brioche Toast with Nutella

INGREDIENTS (2 Servings)

4 slices of brioche
3 eggs
4 tbsp butter
6 oz Nutella spread

½ cup heavy cream
1 tsp vanilla extract
1 tbsp icing sugar
½ cup fresh strawberries, sliced

DIRECTIONS (Prep + Cook Time: 15 minutes)

Preheat the air fryer to 350 F.

Beat the eggs along with heavy cream and vanilla in a small bowl. Dip the brioche slices in the egg mixture and AirFry in the greased frying basket for 7-8 minutes in total, shaking once or twice. Spread two pieces of the toast with a thin layer of Nutella and cover with the remaining toast pieces. Dust with icing sugar and top with strawberries. Serve and enjoy!

Bacon & Egg Sandwich

INGREDIENTS (1 Serving)

1 egg, fried
1 slice English bacon
Salt and black pepper to taste

2 bread slices
½ tbsp butter, softened

DIRECTIONS (Prep + Cook Time: 10 minutes)

Preheat the air fryer to 400 F. Spread butter on one side of the bread slices. Add the fried egg on top and season with salt and black pepper. Top with the bacon and cover with the other slice of the bread. Place in the frying basket and AirFry for 4-6 minutes. Serve warm.

Mediterranean Avocado Toast

INGREDIENTS (2 Serving)

2 slices thick whole grain bread
4 thin tomato slices
1 ripe avocado, pitted, peeled, and sliced

1 tbsp olive oil
1 tbsp pinch of salt
½ tsp chili flakes

DIRECTIONS (Prep + Cook Time: 7 minutes)

Preheat the air fryer to 370 F. Arrange the bread slices in the frying basket and toast them for 3 minutes. Add the avocado to a bowl and mash it up with a fork until smooth. Season with salt.

When the toasted bread is ready, remove it to a plate. Spread the avocado and cover with thin tomato slices. Drizzle with olive oil, sprinkle the toasts with chili flakes and serve.

Very Berry Breakfast Puffs

INGREDIENTS (4 Servings)

1 puff pastry sheet
1 tbsp strawberries, mashed
1 tbsp raspberries, mashed

¼ tsp vanilla extract
1 cup cream cheese
1 tbsp honey

DIRECTIONS (Prep + Cook Time: 30 minutes)

Preheat the air fryer to 375 F. Roll the puff pastry out on a lightly floured surface into a 1-inch thick rectangle. Cut into 4 squares. Spread the cream cheese evenly on top of them. In a bowl, combine the berries, honey, and vanilla. Spoon the mixture onto the pastry squares. Fold in the sides over the filling. Pinch the ends to form a puff. Place the puffs in the greased frying basket. Bake in the air fryer for 15 minutes until the pastry is puffed and golden all over. Let it cool for 10 mins before serving.

Romanian Polenta Fries

INGREDIENTS (4 Servings)

2 cups milk
1 cup instant polenta

Salt and black pepper to taste
2 tbsp fresh thyme, chopped

DIRECTIONS (Prep + Cook Time: 30 minutes + cooling time)

Line a baking dish with parchment paper. Pour 2 cups of milk and 2 cups of water into a saucepan and let simmer. Keep whisking as you pour in the polenta. Continue to whisk until the polenta thickens and bubbles; season to taste. Add polenta into the lined dish and spread out. Refrigerate for 45 minutes.

Preheat the air fryer to 380 F. Slice the polenta into batons. Arrange the chips in the greased frying basket and sprinkle with thyme. AirFry for 14-16 minutes, turning once, until the fries are crispy.

Soppressata Pizza

INGREDIENTS (2 Servings)

1 pizza crust
½ tsp dried oregano
½ cup passata

½ cup mozzarella cheese, shredded
4 oz soppressata, chopped
4 basil leaves

DIRECTIONS (Prep + Cook Time: 15 minutes)

Preheat the air fryer to 370 F. Spread the passata over the pizza crust, sprinkle with oregano, mozzarella, and finish with soppressata. Bake in the fryer for 10 minutes. Top with basil leaves and serve.

Air Fried Italian Calzone

INGREDIENTS (4 Servings)

1 pizza dough
4 oz cheddar cheese, grated
1 oz mozzarella cheese, grated
1 oz bacon, diced
2 cups cooked turkey, shredded

1 egg, beaten
4 tbsp tomato paste
½ tsp dried basil
½ tsp dried oregano
Salt and black pepper to taste

DIRECTIONS (Prep + Cook Time: 20 minutes)

Preheat the air fryer to 350 F. Divide the pizza dough into 4 equal pieces, so you have the dough for 4 pizza crusts. Combine the tomato paste, basil, and oregano in a small bowl. Brush the mixture onto the crusts; make sure not to go all the way to avoid brushing near the edges of each crust.

Scatter half of the turkey on top and season with salt and black pepper. Top with bacon, mozzarella and cheddar cheeses. Brush the edges with the beaten egg. Fold the crusts and seal with a fork. Bake for 10-12 minutes until puffed and golden, turning it over halfway through cooking. Serve warm.

Breakfast Banana Bread

INGREDIENTS (2 Servings)

1 cup flour
¼ tsp baking soda
1 tsp baking powder
⅓ cup sugar
2 bananas, mashed
¼ cup vegetable oil

1 egg, beaten
1 tsp vanilla extract
¾ cup walnuts, chopped
¼ tsp salt
2 tbsp peanut butter, softened
2 tbsp sour cream

DIRECTIONS (Prep + Cook Time: 35 minutes)

Preheat the air fryer to 350 F. Sift the flour into a large bowl and add salt, baking powder, and baking soda; stir to combine. In another bowl, combine bananas, vegetable oil, egg, peanut butter, vanilla, sugar, and sour cream; stir well. Mix both mixtures and fold in the walnuts. Pour the batter into a greased baking dish and place in the fryer. Bake for 20-25 minutes until nice and golden. Serve chilled.

Prosciutto & Mozzarella Bruschetta

INGREDIENTS (2 Servings)

½ cup tomatoes, finely chopped
3 oz mozzarella cheese, grated
3 prosciutto slices, chopped

1 tbsp olive oil
1 tsp dried basil
6 small French bread slices

DIRECTIONS (Prep + Cook Time: 7 minutes)

Preheat the air fryer to 350 F. Add in the bread slices and fry for 3 minutes to toast them. Remove and top the slices with tomatoes, prosciutto, and mozzarella cheese. Sprinkle basil all over and drizzle with olive oil. Return to the fryer and AirFry for 1 more minute, just to heat through. Serve warm.

Quick Feta Triangles

INGREDIENTS (3 Servings)

1 cup feta cheese
1 onion, chopped
½ tsp parsley dried

1 egg yolk
2 tbsp olive oil
3 sheets filo pastry

DIRECTIONS (Prep + Cook Time: 30 minutes)

Cut each of the filo sheets into 3 equal-sized strips. Brush the strips with some olive oil.

In a bowl, mix onion, feta cheese, egg yolk, and parsley. Divide the mixture between the strips and fold each diagonally to make triangles. Arrange them in the a greased frying basket and brush the tops with the remaining olive oil. Place in the fryer and Bake for 8 minutes at 360 F. Serve warm.

Toasted Herb & Garlic Bagel

INGREDIENTS (1 Serving)

1 tbsp butter, softened
¼ tsp dried basil
¼ tsp dried parsley
¼ tsp garlic powder

1 tbsp Parmesan cheese, grated
Salt and black pepper to taste
1 bagel, halved

DIRECTIONS (Prep + Cook Time: 10 minutes)

Preheat the air fryer to 370 degrees. Place the bagel halves in the frying basket and AirFry for 3 minutes. Mix butter, Parmesan cheese, garlic, basil, and parsley in a bowl. Season with salt and pepper. Spread the mixture onto the toasted bagel and return to the fryer to AirFry for 3 more minutes.

Pumpkin & Sultanas' Bread

INGREDIENTS (6 Servings)

1 cup pumpkin, peeled and shredded
1 cup flour
1 tsp ground nutmeg
½ tsp salt
¼ tsp baking powder
2 eggs
½ cup sugar

¼ cup milk
2 tbsp butter, melted
½ tsp vanilla extract
2 tbsp sultanas, soaked
1 tbsp honey
1 tbsp canola oil

DIRECTIONS (Prep + Cook Time: 30 minutes + cooling time)

Preheat the air fryer to 350 F. In a bowl, beat the eggs and add pumpkin, sugar, milk, canola oil, sultanas, and vanilla. In a separate bowl, sift the flour and mix in nutmeg, salt, butter, and baking powder.

Combine the 2 mixtures and stir until a thick cake mixture forms. Spoon the batter into a greased baking dish and place it in the air fryer. Bake for 25 minutes until a toothpick inserted in the center comes out clean and dry. Remove to a wire rack to cool completely. Drizzle with honey and serve.

Grilled Apple & Brie Sandwich

INGREDIENTS (1 Serving)

2 bread slices
½ apple, thinly sliced

2 tsp butter
2 oz brie cheese, thinly sliced

DIRECTIONS (Prep + Cook Time: 10 minutes)

Spread butter on the outside of the bread slices and top with apple slices. Place the brie slices on top of the apple and cover with the other slice of bread. Bake in the air fryer for 5 minutes at 350 F. When ready, remove and cut diagonally to serve.

Blueberry & Maple Toast

INGREDIENTS (2 Servings)

2 eggs, beaten
4 bread slices
1 tbsp maple syrup
1 ½ cups corn flakes

⅓ cup milk
¼ tsp ground nutmeg
1 cup fresh blueberries

DIRECTIONS (Prep + Cook Time: 15 minutes)

Preheat the air fryer to 390 F. In a bowl, mix the eggs, nutmeg, and milk. Dip the bread slices in the egg mixture, then thoroughly coat them in corn flakes. AirFry them in the greased frying basket for 8 minutes, turning once halfway through cooking. Drizzle with maple syrup and top blueberries. Serve.

Spicy Egg & Bacon Tortilla Wraps

INGREDIENTS (3 Servings)

3 flour tortillas
2 eggs, scrambled
3 slices bacon, cut into strips

3 tbsp salsa
3 tbsp cream cheese
1 cup Pepper Jack cheese, grated

DIRECTIONS (Prep + Cook Time: 15 minutes)

Preheat the air fryer to 390 F. Spread cream cheese on the tortillas. Add the eggs and bacon and top with salsa. Scatter with grated Pepper Jack cheese and roll up tightly. Place in the frying basket and AirFry for 10 minutes or until golden. Cut in half and serve warm.

Paprika Rarebit

INGREDIENTS (2 Servings)

4 toasted bread slices
1 tsp smoked paprika
2 eggs, beaten

1 tsp Dijon mustard
4 ½ oz cheddar cheese, grated
Salt and black pepper to taste

DIRECTIONS (Prep + Cook Time: 15 minutes)

Preheat the fryer to 360 F. In a bowl, combine the eggs, mustard, cheddar, and paprika. Season with salt and pepper. Spread the mixture on the bread slices and AirFry them for 10 minutes or until golden.

Mango Bread

INGREDIENTS (6 Servings)

½ cup butter, melted
1 egg, lightly beaten
½ cup brown sugar
1 tsp vanilla extract
3 ripe mangoes, mashed

1 ½ cups flour
1 tsp baking powder
½ tsp grated nutmeg
½ tsp ground cinnamon

DIRECTIONS (Prep + Cook Time: 30 minutes)

Line a loaf tin with baking paper. In a bowl, whisk melted butter, egg, sugar, vanilla, and mangoes. Sift in flour, baking powder, nutmeg, and ground cinnamon and stir without overmixing. Pour the batter into the tin and place it in the frying basket. Bake for 18-20 minutes at 330 F. Let cool before slicing. Serve.

Crustless Mediterranean Feta Quiche

INGREDIENTS (2 Servings)

4 eggs
½ cup tomatoes, chopped
1 cup feta cheese, crumbled
½ tbsp fresh basil, chopped
½ tbsp fresh oregano, chopped

¼ cup Kalamata olives, sliced
¼ cup onions, chopped
½ cup milk
Salt and black pepper to taste

DIRECTIONS (Prep + Cook Time: 40 minutes)

Preheat the air fryer to 340 F. Beat the eggs with the milk, salt, and pepper in a bowl. Stir in all the remaining ingredients. Pour the egg mixture into a greased baking pan that fits in your air fryer and Bake for 30 minutes or until lightly golden. Serve warm with a green salad if desired.

Crustless Broccoli & Mushroom Pie

INGREDIENTS (4 Servings)

4 eggs, beaten
1 cup mushrooms, sliced
1 cup broccoli florets, steamed
½ cup cheddar cheese, shredded

½ cup mozzarella cheese, shredded
2 tbsp olive oil
¼ tsp ground allspice
Salt and black pepper to taste

DIRECTIONS (Prep + Cook Time: 25 minutes)

Preheat the air fryer to 360 F. Warm the olive oil in a pan over medium heat. Sauté the mushrooms for 3-4 minutes or until soft. Stir the broccoli for 1 minute; set aside.

Place the eggs, cheddar cheese, mozzarella cheese, allspice, salt, and pepper in a medium bowl and whisk well. Pour the mushrooms' mixture into the egg mixture and gently fold it in. Transfer the batter to a greased baking pan and into the fryer. AirFry for 5 minutes, then stir the mixture and cook until the eggs are done, about 3-5 more minutes. Cut into wedges and serve.

Flaxseed Porridge

INGREDIENTS (4 Servings)

1 cup steel-cut oats
1 tbsp flax seeds
1 tbsp peanut butter

1 tbsp butter
1 cup milk
2 tbsp honey

DIRECTIONS (Prep + Cook Time: 15 minutes)

Preheat the air fryer to 350 F. Combine all ingredients in an ovenproof bowl. Place the bowl in the air fryer and Bake for 10 minutes. Let cool for a few minutes before serving. Enjoy!

Zucchini Muffins

INGREDIENTS (4 Servings)

1 ½ cups flour
1 tsp cinnamon
3 eggs
2 tsp baking powder
½ tsp sugar
1 cup milk

2 tbsp butter, melted
1 tbsp yogurt
1 zucchini, shredded
A pinch of salt
2 tbsp cream cheese

DIRECTIONS (Prep + Cook Time: 25 minutes)

Preheat the air fryer to 350 F. In a bowl, whisk the eggs with sugar, salt, cinnamon, cream cheese, flour, and baking powder. In another bowl, combine the remaining ingredients, except for the zucchini.

Gently combine the dry and liquid mixtures. Stir in the zucchini. Grease 4 muffin tins with oil and pour the batter inside them. Place them in the air fryer and Bake for 18-20 minutes until golden. Serve.

Banana & Hazelnut Muffins

INGREDIENTS (6 Servings)

¼ cup butter, melted
¼ cup honey
1 egg, lightly beaten
2 ripe bananas, mashed
½ tsp vanilla extract

1 cup flour
½ tsp baking powder
½ tsp ground cinnamon
¼ cup hazelnuts, chopped
¼ cup dark chocolate chips

DIRECTIONS (Prep + Cook Time: 30 minutes)

Spray a muffin tin that fits in your air fryer with cooking spray. In a bowl, whisk butter, honey, egg, bananas, and vanilla until well combined. Sift in flour, baking powder, and cinnamon without overmixing.

Stir in the hazelnuts and chocolate chips. Pour the batter into the muffin holes and place in the air fryer. Bake for 20 minutes at 350 F, checking them around the 15-minute mark. Serve chilled.

Italian Sausage Patties

INGREDIENTS (4 Servings)

1 lb ground Italian sausage
¼ cup breadcrumbs
1 tsp red pepper flakes

Salt and black pepper to taste
¼ tsp garlic powder
1 egg, beaten

DIRECTIONS (Prep + Cook Time: 20 minutes)

Preheat the air fryer to 350 F. Thoroughly mix all the ingredients in a large bowl. Make balls out of the mixture using your hands. Flatten the balls to make the patties. Arrange them on the greased frying basket. Place them in the fryer and AirFry for 15 minutes, flipping once halfway through. Serve.

Kiwi Muffins with Pecans

INGREDIENTS (4 Servings)

1 cup flour
1 kiwi, mashed
¼ cup powdered sugar
1 tbsp milk

1 tbsp pecans, chopped
½ tsp baking powder
¼ cup oats
¼ cup butter, room temperature

DIRECTIONS (Prep + Cook Time: 25 minutes)

Preheat the air fryer to 350 F. Place the sugar, pecans, kiwi, and butter in a bowl and mix well. In another bowl, mix the flour, baking powder, and oats and stir well. Combine the two mixtures and stir in the milk. Pour the batter into a greased muffin tin that fits in the fryer and Bake for 15 minutes. Remove to a wire rack and leave to cool for a few minutes before removing the muffin from the tin. Enjoy!

Orange Creamy Cupcakes

Ingredients (4 Servings)

Lemon Frosting:
1 cup plain yogurt
2 tbsp sugar
1 orange, juiced
Cake:
1 tsp dark rum
2/3 cup flour
¼ tsp salt
½ cup sugar

1 tbsp orange zest
7 oz cream cheese

1 tsp vanilla extract
2 eggs
½ cup butter, softened

Directions (Prep + Cook Time: 25 minutes)

In a bowl, add yogurt and cream cheese and mix until smooth. Add in orange juice and zest and whisk well. Gradually add the sugar and stir until smooth. Make sure the frosting is not runny. Set aside.

Preheat the air fryer to 360 F.

For the cake, in a bowl, put the flour, rum, softened butter, eggs, vanilla extract, sugar, and salt. Beat with a whisk until smooth. Spoon the batter into 4 cupcake cases, ¾ way up. Place them in the air fryer and Bake for 12 minutes or until an inserted toothpick comes out clean. Once ready, remove and let cool. Design the cupcakes with the frosting and serve.

Coconut & Oat Cookies

INGREDIENTS (4 Servings)

¾ cup flour
4 tbsp sugar
½ cup oats
Filling:
1 tbsp white chocolate, melted
4 tbsp butter

1 egg
¼ cup coconut flakes

½ cup powdered sugar
1 tsp vanilla extract

DIRECTIONS (Prep + Cook Time: 30 minutes)

In a bowl, beat egg, sugar, oats, and coconut flakes with an electric hand mixer. Fold in the flour. Drop spoonfuls of the batter into a greased baking sheet and Bake in the air fryer at 350 F for 18 minutes. Let cool to firm up and to resemble cookies. Cook in batches if needed.

Meanwhile, prepare the filling by beating all filling ingredients together. Spread the filling on half of the cookies. Top with the other halves to make cookie sandwiches like oreo. Serve and enjoy!

Cherry & Almond Scones

INGREDIENTS (4 Servings)

2 cups flour + some more
⅓ cup sugar
2 tsp baking powder
½ cup sliced almonds

¾ cup dried cherries, chopped
¼ cup cold butter, cut into cubes
½ cup milk
1 egg

DIRECTIONS (Prep + Cook Time: 25 minutes)

Preheat the air fryer to 390 F. Line the frying basket with baking paper. Mix together flour, sugar, baking powder, sliced almonds, and dried cherries in a bowl. Rub the butter with hands into the dry ingredients to form a sandy, crumbly texture. Whisk together egg, and milk.

Pour into the dry ingredients and stir to combine. Sprinkle a working board with flour, lay the dough onto the board, and give it a few kneads. Shape into a rectangle and cut into 9 squares. Arrange the squares in the frying basket and AirFry for 12-14 minutes at 390 F. Work in batches if needed. Serve.

Blueberry Oat Bars

INGREDIENTS (12 bars)

2 cups rolled oats
¼ cup ground almonds
¼ cup sugar
1 tsp baking powder
½ tsp ground cinnamon

2 eggs, lightly beaten
½ cup canola oil
½ cup milk
1 tsp vanilla extract
2 cups blueberries

DIRECTIONS (Prep + Cook Time: 20 minutes)

Spray a baking pan that fits in your air fryer with oil. In a bowl, add oats, almonds, sugar, baking powder, and cinnamon; stir well. In another bowl, whisk eggs, canola oil, milk, and vanilla. Stir the wet ingredients into the oat mixture. Fold in the blueberries. Pour the mixture into the pan and place it inside the fryer. Bake for 10 minutes. Remove to a wire rack to cool and then cut into 12 bars.

Sweet Bread Pudding with Raisins

INGREDIENTS (4 Servings)

8 bread slices, cubed
½ cup buttermilk
¼ cup honey
1 cup milk
2 eggs
½ tsp vanilla extract

2 tbsp butter, softened
¼ cup sugar
4 tbsp raisins
2 tbsp chopped hazelnuts
Ground cinnamon for garnish

DIRECTIONS (Prep + Cook Time: 45 minutes)

Preheat the air fryer to 350 F. Beat the eggs along with buttermilk, honey, milk, vanilla, sugar, and butter in a bowl. Stir in raisins and hazelnuts, then add in the bread to soak, about 10 minutes. Transfer to a greased tin and Bake the pudding in the air fryer for 25 minutes. Dust with cinnamon. Serve

Simple Crispy Bacon

INGREDIENTS (4 Servings)

8 oz bacon, sliced

DIRECTIONS (Prep + Cook Time: 15 minutes)

Preheat the fryer to 390 F. Place the bacon slices in the frying basket. AirFry for 10 minutes, flipping once.

Crispy Croutons

INGREDIENTS (4 Servings)

2 cups bread cubes
2 tbsp butter, melted

1 tsp dried parsley
Garlic salt and black pepper to taste

DIRECTIONS (Prep + Cook Time: 20 minutes)

Mix the cubed bread with butter, parsley, garlic salt, and black pepper until well coated. Place them in the frying basket and AirFry for 6-8 minutes at 380 F, shaking once until golden brown.

Avocado Tempura

INGREDIENTS (4 Servings)

½ cup breadcrumbs
½ tsp salt

1 avocado, pitted, peeled, and sliced
½ cup soda water (club soda)

DIRECTIONS (Prep + Cook Time: 15 minutes)

Preheat the air fryer to 360 F. In a bowl, add the breadcrumbs and salt and mix well. Sprinkle the avocado with soda water and then coat in the breadcrumbs. Arrange the slices in the grease frying basket in one layer and AirFry for 8-10 minutes, shaking once or twice. Serve warm.

Baked Avocado with Eggs & Cilantro

INGREDIENTS (1 Serving)

1 ripe avocado, pitted and halved
2 eggs

Salt and black pepper, to taste
1 tsp fresh cilantro, chopped

DIRECTIONS (Prep + Cook Time: 20 minutes)

Preheat the air fryer to 400 F. Crack one egg into each avocado half and place in the air fryer. Bake for 8-12 minutes until the eggs are cooked through. Let cool slightly and season to taste. Top with freshly chopped cilantro and serve warm.

Roasted Asparagus with Serrano Ham

INGREDIENTS (4 Servings)

12 spears asparagus, trimmed
12 Serrano ham slices

¼ cup Parmesan cheese, grated
Salt and black pepper to taste

DIRECTIONS (Prep + Cook Time: 20 minutes)

Preheat the air fryer to 350 F. Season asparagus with salt and black pepper. Wrap each ham slice around each asparagus spear from one end to the other end to cover completely. Arrange them on the greased frying basket and AirFry for 10 minutes, shaking once or twice throughout cooking. When ready, scatter with Parmesan cheese and serve immediately.

Hearty Banana Pastry

INGREDIENTS (2 Servings)

3 bananas, sliced
3 tbsp honey

2 puff pastry sheets, cut into thin strips
1 cup fresh berries to serve

DIRECTIONS (Prep + Cook Time: 20 minutes)

Preheat the air fryer to 340 F. Place banana slices into a greased baking dish. Cover with pastry strips and drizzle with honey. Bake inside the air fryer for 12 minutes until golden. Serve with berries.

SNACKS & SIDE DISHES

Air-Fried Hot Wings

INGREDIENTS (4 Servings)

¼ tsp celery salt
¼ tsp bay leaf powder
Black pepper to taste
½ tsp cayenne pepper

¼ tsp allspice
1 tbsp thyme leaves
1 lb chicken wings

DIRECTIONS (Prep + Cook Time: 25 minutes)

Preheat the air fryer to 360 F. In a bowl, mix celery salt, bay leaf powder, black pepper, paprika, thyme, cayenne pepper, and allspice. Coat the wings in the mixture. Arrange the wings on the greased frying basket and AirFry for 10 minutes. Flip and cook for 6-8 more minutes until crispy on the outside.

Crispy Alfredo Chicken Wings

INGREDIENTS (4 Servings)

1 ½ lb chicken wings, pat-dried
Salt to taste

½ cup Alfredo sauce

DIRECTIONS (Prep + Cook Time: 25 minutes)

Preheat the air fryer to 370 F. Season the wings with salt. Arrange them in the greased frying basket, without overlapping, and AirFry for 12 minutes until no longer pink in the center. Flip them, increase the heat to 390 F, and cook for 5 more minutes. Work in batches if needed. Plate the wings and drizzle with Alfredo sauce to serve.

Crunchy Ranch Chicken Wings

INGREDIENTS (4 Servings)

2 lb chicken wings
2 tbsp olive oil

1 tbsp ranch seasoning mix
Salt to taste

DIRECTIONS (Prep + Cook Time: 25 minutes)

Preheat the air fryer to 390 F. Put the ranch seasoning, olive oil, and salt in a large, resealable bag and mix well. Add the wings, seal the bag, and toss until the wings are thoroughly coated.

Put the wings in the greased frying basket in one layer, spritz them with a nonstick cooking spray, and AirFry for 7 minutes. Turn them over and fry for 5-8 more minutes until the wings are light brown and crispy. Test for doneness with a meat thermometer. Serve with your favorite dipping sauce and enjoy!

Korean Chili Chicken Wings

INGREDIENTS (4 Servings)

8 chicken wings
Salt to taste
1 tsp sesame oil
Juice from half lemon

¼ cup sriracha chili sauce
1-inch piece ginger, grated
1 tsp garlic powder
1 tsp sesame seeds

DIRECTIONS (Prep + Cook Time: 20 minutes)

Preheat the air fryer to 370 F. Grease the air frying basket with cooking spray. In a bowl, mix salt, ginger, garlic, lemon juice, sesame oil, and chili sauce. Coat the wings in the mixture. Transfer the wings to the basket and AirFry for 15 minutes, flipping once. Sprinkle with sesame seeds and serve.

Teriyaki Chicken Wings

INGREDIENTS (4 Servings)

1 lb chicken wings
1 cup soy sauce
½ cup brown sugar
½ cup apple cider vinegar
2 tbsp fresh ginger, minced

1 garlic clove, minced
Black pepper to taste
2 tbsp cornstarch
2 tbsp cold water
1 tsp sesame seeds

DIRECTIONS (Prep + Cook Time: 20 minutes+ marinating time)

In a bowl, add the chicken wings and cover with half a cup of soy sauce. Refrigerate for 20 minutes. Drain and pat dry. Arrange them on the greased frying basket and AirFry for 14 minutes at 380 F, turning once halfway through cooking.

In a skillet over medium heat, stir the sugar, remaining soy sauce, vinegar, ginger, garlic, and black pepper, for 4 minutes. Dissolve 2 tbsp of cornstarch in cold water and stir in the sauce until it thickens, about 2 minutes. Pour the sauce over the wings and sprinkle with sesame seeds. Serve hot.

Chicken Wings with Gorgonzola Dip

INGREDIENTS (4 Servings)

8 chicken wings
1 tsp cayenne pepper
Salt to taste
2 tbsp olive oil
1 tsp red chili flakes

1 cup heavy cream
3 oz gorgonzola cheese, crumbled
½ lemon, juiced
½ tsp garlic powder

DIRECTIONS (Prep + Cook Time: 30 minutes)

Preheat the air fryer to 380 F. Coat the wings with cayenne pepper, salt, and olive oil. Place in the fryer and AirFry for 16 minutes until crispy and golden brown, flipping once. In a bowl, mix heavy cream, gorgonzola cheese, chili flakes, lemon juice, and garlic powder. Serve the wings with the cheese dip.

Piri Piri Chicken Wings

INGREDIENTS (4 Servings)

8 chicken wings
Salt and black pepper to taste
1 tsp smoked paprika
½ tsp ground ginger

½ tsp red chili powder
1 tsp ground cumin
1 cup mayonnaise mixed with 1 tbsp lemon juice

DIRECTIONS (Prep + Cook Time: 25 minutes)

Preheat the air fryer to 380 F. In a bowl, mix paprika, ginger, chili powder, cumin, salt, and pepper. Add the chicken wings and toss to coat. Place in the greased frying basket and AirFry for 16-18 minutes, flipping once halfway through. Let cool for a few minutes. Serve with lemon mayonnaise.

Air-Fried Chicken Thighs

INGREDIENTS (4 Servings)

1 ½ lb chicken thighs
2 eggs, lightly beaten
1 cup seasoned breadcrumbs

½ tsp oregano
Salt and black pepper to taste

DIRECTIONS (Prep + Cook Time: 20 minutes)

Preheat the air fryer to 390 F. Season the thighs with oregano, salt, and black pepper. In a bowl, add the beaten eggs. In a separate bowl, add the breadcrumbs. Dip the thighs in the egg wash.

Then roll them in the breadcrumbs and press firmly, so the breadcrumbs stick well. Spray the thighs with cooking spray and arrange them in the frying basket in a single layer, skin-side up. AirFry for 12 minutes, turn the thighs over, and cook for 6-8 more minutes until crispy. Serve and enjoy!

Mustard-Honey Chicken Thighs

Ingredients (4 Servings)

1 lb chicken thighs
Salt and garlic powder to taste
2 tbsp olive oil

1 tsp yellow mustard
1 tsp honey
¼ cup mayo mixed with 2 tbsp hot sauce

Directions (Prep + Cook Time: 30 minutes + marinating time)

Preheat the air fryer to 360 F. In a bowl, whisk the olive oil, honey, mustard, salt, and garlic powder. Add the thighs and stir to coat. Marinate for 10 minutes. Transfer the thighs to the greased frying basket, skin side down, and insert in the air fryer. AirFry for 18-20 minutes, flipping once until golden and crispy. Serve immediately with the hot mayo sauce. Enjoy!

Crispy Chicken Nuggets

INGREDIENTS (4 Servings)

1 lb chicken breasts, cut into large cubes
Salt and black pepper to taste
2 tbsp olive oil

5 tbsp plain breadcrumbs
2 tbsp panko breadcrumbs
2 tbsp grated Parmesan cheese

DIRECTIONS (Prep + Cook Time: 25 minutes)

Preheat the air fryer to 380 F. Season the chicken with black pepper and salt. In a bowl, mix the breadcrumbs and Parmesan cheese. Coat the chicken pieces with the olive oil. Then dip into the breadcrumb mixture, shake off the excess, and place in the greased frying basket. Lightly spray the nuggets with cooking spray and AirFry for 13-15 minutes, flipping once. Serve warm

Paprika Chicken Fingers

INGREDIENTS (4 Servings)

2 chicken breasts, cut into chunks
1 tsp paprika
2 tbsp milk
2 eggs

1 tsp garlic powder
Salt and black pepper to taste
1 cup flour
2 cups breadcrumbs

DIRECTIONS (Prep + Cook Time: 20 minutes + cooling time)

Preheat the air fryer to 370 F. In a bowl, mix paprika, garlic powder, salt, pepper, flour, and breadcrumbs. In another bowl, beat eggs with milk. Dip the chicken in the egg mixture, then roll in the crumbs. Place in the frying basket and spray with cooking spray. AirFry for 14-16 minutes, flipping once. Yummy!

Corn-Crusted Chicken Tenders

INGREDIENTS (4 Servings)

2 chicken breasts, cut into strips
Salt and black pepper to taste

2 eggs
1 cup ground cornmeal

DIRECTIONS (Prep + Cook Time: 25 minutes)

Preheat the air fryer to 390 F. In a bowl, mix cornmeal, salt, and black pepper. In another bowl, beat the eggs; season with salt and pepper. Dip the chicken in the eggs and then coat in the cornmeal. Spray the strips with cooking spray and place them in the frying basket in a single layer. AirFry for 6 minutes, slide the basket out, and flip the sticks. Cook for 6-8 more minutes until golden brown. Serve hot.

Chicken & Oat Croquettes

INGREDIENTS (4 Servings)

1 lb ground chicken
2 eggs
Salt and black pepper to taste

1 cup oats, crumbled
½ tsp garlic powder
1 tsp dried parsley

DIRECTIONS (Prep + Cook Time: 20 minutes)

Preheat the air fryer to 360 F. Mix the chicken with garlic, parsley, salt, and pepper. In a bowl, beat the eggs with a pinch of salt. In a third bowl, add the oats. Form croquettes out of the chicken mixture. Dip in the eggs and coat in the oats. AirFry them in the greased frying basket for 10 minutes, shaking once.

Crunchy Chicken Egg Rolls

INGREDIENTS (4 Servings)

2 tsp olive oil
2 garlic cloves, minced
¼ cup soy sauce
1 tsp grated fresh ginger
1 lb ground chicken

2 cups white cabbage, shredded
1 onion, chopped
1 egg, beaten
8 egg roll wrappers

DIRECTIONS (Prep + Cook Time: 30 minutes)

Heat olive oil in a pan over medium heat and add garlic, onion, ginger, and ground chicken. Sauté for 5 minutes until the chicken is no longer pink. Pour in the soy sauce and shredded cabbage and stir-fry for another 5-6 minutes until the cabbage is tender. Remove from the heat and let cool slightly.

Fill each egg wrapper with the mixture, arranging it just below the center of the wrappers. Fold in both sides and roll up tightly. Use the beaten egg to seal the edges. Brush the tops with the remaining beaten egg. Place the rolls in the greased frying basket, spray them with cooking spray, and AirFry for 12-14 minutes at 370 F until golden, turning once halfway through. Let cool slightly and serve.

Asian Veggie Spring Rolls

INGREDIENTS (4 Servings)

4 spring roll wrappers
½ cup cooked vermicelli noodles
1 garlic clove, minced
1 tbsp fresh ginger, minced
1 tbsp soy sauce

2 tsp sesame oil
½ red bell pepper, seeds removed, chopped
½ cup mushrooms, finely chopped
½ cup carrots, finely chopped
¼ cup scallions, finely chopped

DIRECTIONS (Prep + Cook Time: 30 minutes)

Warm sesame oil in a saucepan over medium heat and add garlic, ginger, soy sauce, bell pepper, mushrooms, carrots, and scallions and stir-fry for 5 minutes. Stir in vermicelli noodles and set aside.

Place the wrappers onto a working board. Spoon the veggie-noodle mixture at the center of the roll wrappers. Roll and tuck in the corners and edges to create neat and secure rolls. Spray with oil and place them in the frying basket. AirFry for 12-14 minutes at 340 F, turning once or twice until golden.

Herby Meatballs

INGREDIENTS (4 Servings)

1 lb ground beef
1 onion, finely chopped
2 garlic cloves, finely chopped
1 egg

1 cup breadcrumbs
½ cup Mediterranean herbs
Salt and black pepper to taste
1 tbsp olive oil

DIRECTIONS (Prep + Cook Time: 30 minutes)

In a bowl, add the ground beef, onion, garlic, egg, breadcrumbs, herbs, salt, and pepper and mix with your hands to combine. Shape into balls and brush them with olive oil. Arrange the meatballs in the frying basket and AirFry for 15-16 minutes at 380 F, turning once halfway through. Serve immediately.

Chili Cheese Balls

INGREDIENTS (4 Servings)

2 cups cottage cheese, crumbled
2 cups Parmesan cheese, grated
2 red potatoes, boiled and mashed
1 medium onion, finely chopped
1 ½ tsp red chili flakes

1 green chili, finely chopped
Salt to taste
2 tbsp fresh cilantro, chopped
1 cup flour
1 cup breadcrumbs

DIRECTIONS (Prep + Cook Time: 25 minutes)

In a bowl, combine the cottage and Parmesan cheeses, onion, chili flakes, green chili, salt, cilantro, flour, and mashed potatoes. Mold balls out of the mixture and roll them in breadcrumbs. Place them in the greased frying basket and AirFry for 14-16 minutes at 350 F, shaking once or twice. Serve warm.

Cheesy Sticks with Sweet Thai Sauce

INGREDIENTS (4 Servings)

12 sticks mozzarella cheese
2 cups breadcrumbs
3 eggs

1 cup sweet Thai sauce
4 tbsp skimmed milk

DIRECTIONS (Prep + Cook Time: 25 minutes + freezing time)

Pour the breadcrumbs into a bowl. Beat the eggs with milk in another bowl. One after the other, dip the sticks in the egg mixture, in the crumbs, then in the egg mixture again, and lastly in the crumbs again.

Freeze for 1 hour. Preheat the air fryer to 380 F. Arrange the sticks in the greased frying basket and AirFry for 10-12 minutes, flipping halfway through. Work in batches. Serve with sweet Thai sauce.

Potato Chips with Chives

INGREDIENTS (4 Servings)

1 lb potatoes, cut into thin slices
¼ cup olive oil
1 tbsp garlic paste

2 tbsp chives, chopped
A pinch of salt

DIRECTIONS (Prep + Cook Time: 40 minutes + marinating time)

Preheat the air fryer to 390 F. In a bowl, add olive oil, garlic paste, and salt and mix to obtain a marinade. Add the potatoes and let them sit for 30 minutes. Lay the potato slices into the frying basket and AirFry for 20 minutes. At the 10-minute mark, give the chips a turn and sprinkle with freshly chopped chives.

Quick Pickle Chips

INGREDIENTS (4 Servings)

36 sweet pickle chips, drained
1 tsp cayenne pepper

1 cup flour
¼ cup cornmeal

DIRECTIONS (Prep + Cook Time: 15 minutes)

Preheat the air fryer to 400 F. In a bowl, mix flour, cayenne pepper, and cornmeal. Dip the pickles in the flour mixture and spritz with cooking spray. AirFry for 10 minutes until golden brown, turning once.

Garlicky Potato Chips with Herbs

INGREDIENTS (2 Servings)

2 potatoes, thinly sliced
1 tbsp olive oil
1 garlic cloves, crushed

1 tsp each of fresh rosemary, thyme, oregano, chopped
Salt and black pepper to taste

DIRECTIONS (Prep + Cook Time: 40 minutes)

In a bowl, mix olive oil, garlic, herbs, salt, and pepper. Coat the potatoes thoroughly in the mixture. Arrange them in the frying basket and AirFry for 18-20 minutes at 360 F, shaking every 4-5 minutes.

Hot Carrot Crisps

INGREDIENTS (2 Servings)

2 large carrots, cut into strips
½ tsp oregano
½ tsp hot paprika

½ tsp garlic powder
1 tbsp olive oil
Salt to taste

DIRECTIONS (Prep + Cook Time: 25 minutes)

Put the carrots in a bowl and stir in the remaining ingredients; toss to coat. Arrange the carrots in the greased frying basket and AirFry for 13-15 minutes at 390 F, shaking once. Serve warm.

Root Vegetable Chips

INGREDIENTS (4 Servings)

1 carrot, sliced
1 parsnip, sliced
1 potato, sliced

1 daikon, sliced
2 tbsp olive oil
1 tbsp soy sauce

DIRECTIONS (Prep + Cook Time: 25 minutes)

Preheat the air fryer to 400 F. In a bowl, mix olive oil and soy sauce. Add in the veggies and toss to coat; marinate for 5 minutes. Transfer them to the fryer and AirFry for 15 minutes, tossing once.

Mexican-Style Air Fryer Nachos

INGREDIENTS (4 Servings)

8 corn tortillas, cut into wedges
1 tbsp olive oil
½ tsp ground cumin
½ tsp chili powder

½ tsp paprika
½ tsp cayenne pepper
½ tsp salt
½ tsp ground coriander

DIRECTIONS (Prep + Cook Time: 20 minutes)

Preheat the air fryer to 370 F. Brush the tortilla wedges with olive oil and arrange them in the frying basket in an even layer. Mix the spices thoroughly in a small bowl. Sprinkle the tortilla wedges with the spice mixture. AirFry for 2-3 minutes, shake the basket, and fry for another 2-3 minutes until crunchy and nicely browned. Serve the nachos immediately.

Air Fried Asparagus with Romesco Sauce

INGREDIENTS (4 Servings)

1 cup panko breadcrumbs
Salt and black pepper to taste
½ cup almond flour

1 lb asparagus spears, trimmed and washed
2 eggs
2 tomatoes, chopped

Romesco Sauce
2 roasted peppers, chopped
½ cup almond flour
½ tsp garlic powder
1 tbsp vinegar
2 slices toasted bread, torn into pieces

½ tsp paprika
1 tsp crushed red chili flakes
1 tbsp tomato purée
½ cup extra-virgin olive oil

DIRECTIONS (Prep + Cook Time: 25 minutes)

Preheat the air fryer to 390 F. On a plate, combine panko breadcrumbs, salt, and black pepper. On another shallow plate, whisk the eggs with salt and black pepper. On a third plate, pour the almond flour. Dip asparagus in the almond flour, followed by a dip in the eggs, and finally, coat with breadcrumbs.

Place in the greased frying basket and AirFry for 10 minutes, turning once halfway. Pulse all romesco sauce ingredients in a food processor until smooth. Serve asparagus with romesco sauce.

Parmesan Artichoke Hearts

INGREDIENTS (4 Servings)

1 can (14-oz) artichoke hearts, drained
2 eggs
¼ cup flour
¼ Parmesan cheese, grated

⅓ cup panko breadcrumbs
1 tsp garlic powder
Salt and black pepper to taste

DIRECTIONS (Prep + Cook Time: 25 minutes)

Preheat the air fryer to 390 F. Pat dry the artichokes with a paper towel and cut them into wedges. In a bowl, whisk the eggs with a pinch of salt. In another bowl, combine Parmesan cheese, breadcrumbs, and garlic powder. In a third bowl, pour the flour mixed with salt and black pepper.

Dip the artichokes in the flour, followed by a dip in the eggs, and finally coat with breadcrumbs. Place them in the frying basket and AirFry for 10 minutes, flipping once. Serve with mayo sauce if desired.

Air Fried Cheesy Brussels Sprouts

INGREDIENTS (4 Servings)

1 lb Brussels sprouts, halved
2 tbsp canola oil
1 cup breadcrumbs

1 tbsp paprika
2 tbsp Grana Padano cheese, grated
1 tbsp sage, chopped

DIRECTIONS (Prep + Cook Time: 30 minutes)

Preheat the air fryer to 400 F. Line the frying basket with parchment paper.

In a bowl, mix breadcrumbs and paprika with Grana Padano cheese. Drizzle the Brussels sprouts with canola oil and add them to the crumbs/cheese mixture; toss to coat. Place in the frying basket and AirFry for 15 minutes, shaking every 4-5 minutes. Serve sprinkled with chopped sage.

Crispy Kale Chips

INGREDIENTS (4 Servings)

4 cups kale leaves, stems removed, chopped
2 tbsp olive oil
1 tsp garlic powder

Salt and black pepper to taste
¼ tsp onion powder

DIRECTIONS (Prep + Cook Time: 20 minutes + cooling time)

In a bowl, mix kale and olive oil. Add in garlic and onion powders, salt, and black pepper; toss to coat. Arrange the kale in the frying basket and AirFry for 8 minutes at 350 F, shaking once. Serve cool.

Crispy Cauliflower in Buffalo Sauce

INGREDIENTS (4 Servings)

3 tbsp butter, melted
3 tbsp buffalo hot sauce
1 egg white

1 cup panko breadcrumbs
Salt and black pepper to taste
½ head cauliflower, cut into florets

DIRECTIONS (Prep + Cook Time: 35 minutes)

In a bowl, whisk butter, buffalo sauce, and egg white. In a separate bowl, mix breadcrumbs with salt and black pepper. Toss the florets in the buffalo mixture and roll them in the breadcrumbs to coat. Spritz with cooking spray and AirFry them for 14-16 minutes at 340 F, shaking twice. Serve hot.

Crunchy Cauliflower Bites

INGREDIENTS (4 Servings)

1 tbsp Italian seasoning
1 cup flour
1 cup milk

1 egg, beaten
1 head cauliflower, cut into florets

DIRECTIONS (Prep + Cook Time: 25 minutes)

Preheat the air fryer to 390 F. Grease the frying basket with cooking spray. In a bowl, mix flour, milk, egg, and Italian seasoning. Coat the cauliflower in the mixture and drain the excess liquid.

Place the florets in the frying basket, spray with cooking spray, and AirFry for 7 minutes. Shake and continue cooking for another 5 minutes. Allow to cool before serving.

Crispy Yellow Squash Chips

INGREDIENTS (4 Servings)

2 yellow squash, sliced into rounds
½ cup flour
Salt and black pepper to taste
2 eggs
1 tbsp soy sauce

¾ cup panko breadcrumbs
¼ tsp dried dill
¼ cup Parmesan cheese, grated
Greek yogurt dressing, for serving

DIRECTIONS (Prep + Cook Time: 25 minutes)

Preheat the air fryer to 380 F. Spray the frying basket with cooking spray.

In a bowl, mix the flour, dill, salt, and black pepper. In another bowl, beat the eggs with soy sauce. In a third, pour the breadcrumbs and Parmesan cheese, mix well.

Dip the squash rounds in the flour, then in the eggs, and then coat with breadcrumbs. Place in the frying basket and AirFry for 10 minutes, flipping once halfway through. Serve with Greek yogurt dressing.

Air Fryer Avocado Wedges

INGREDIENTS (4 Servings)

2 avocados, peeled, stoned, cut into wedges
1 cup panko breadcrumbs
2 egg, beaten
½ cup Greek yogurt

1 tbsp fresh cilantro, chopped
½ tsp sriracha sauce
Salt and garlic powder to taste

DIRECTIONS (Prep + Cook Time: 25 minutes)

Preheat the air fryer to 390 F. Add the yogurt, sriracha sauce, salt, garlic powder, and cilantro to a small bowl. Mix together until well incorporated. Place in the fridge to chill for 15 minutes.

In a bowl, whisk the eggs with a pinch of salt until frothy. In another bowl, mix the breadcrumbs with garlic powder and salt. Dip the avocado wedges into the eggs and then dredge in the breadcrumbs.

Arrange the wedges in the greased frying basket. Spritz with cooking spray, AirFry for 4 minutes, flip, and cook for 3-4 more minutes until crispy. Serve the avocado wedges with yogurt sauce.

Fried Pimiento-Stuffed Green Olives

INGREDIENTS (4 Servings)

½ (13-oz) jar pimiento-stuffed green olives
¼ cup flour
¼ cup Parmesan cheese, grated
Salt and black pepper to taste

½ cup panko breadcrumbs
1 egg, beaten
1 tsp cayenne pepper

DIRECTIONS (Prep + Cook Time: 30 minutes)

Preheat the air fryer to 390 F. In a bowl, combine flour, cayenne pepper, salt, and black pepper. In another bowl, add the beaten egg. Mix the breadcrumbs with Parmesan cheese in a third bowl.

Drain and pat dry the olives with a paper towel. Dredge the olives in flour, then in the egg, and finally in the breadcrumbs. Place in the frying basket, spray them with cooking spray, and AirFry for 8-10 minutes. Shake and cook for 3 more minutes. Let cool before serving.

Mini Spinach & Mushroom Empanadas

INGREDIENTS (4 Servings)

2 tbsp olive oil
10 oz spinach, chopped
1 onion, chopped
2 garlic cloves, minced
¼ cup mushrooms, chopped

1 cup ricotta cheese, crumbled
1 (13-oz) pizza crust
1 tbsp Italian seasoning
Salt and black pepper to taste
1 ½ cups marinara sauce

DIRECTIONS (Prep + Cook Time: 30 minutes)

Heat olive oil in a pan over medium heat and sauté garlic, onion, and mushrooms for 4 minutes or until tender. Stir in spinach for 2-3 minutes. Season with Italian seasoning, salt, and pepper. Pour in marinara sauce and cook until the sauce thickens, about 5 minutes. Turn off and mix in ricotta cheese.

On a floured work surface, roll the pizza crust out. Slice into 4 rectangles. Divide the mixture between the rectangles and close them by folding in half. Seal the edges and lightly flatten. Spritz with cooking spray and transfer to the frying basket. Bake for 14-16 minutes, turning once halfway through. Serve.

Kielbasa & Mushroom Pierogi

INGREDIENTS (4 Servings)

½ package puff pastry dough, at room temperature
½ lb Kielbasa smoked sausage, chopped
½ onion, chopped
½ lb mushrooms, chopped

½ tsp ground cumin
¼ tsp paprika
Salt and black pepper to taste
1 egg, beaten

DIRECTIONS (Prep + Cook Time: 25 minutes)

Preheat the air fryer to 360 F. In a bowl, mix Kielbasa sausage, onion, mushrooms, cumin, paprika, salt, and pepper. Place the pastry on a lightly floured surface. Using a glass, cut out 8 circles of the pastry.

Place 1 tbsp of the sausage mixture on each pastry circle, brush the edges with the beaten egg, and fold over. Seal the edges with a fork. Brush the empanadas with the remaining egg and spray with cooking spray. Place in the greased frying basket and Bake for 12-14 minutes until golden brown.

Low-Carb Radish Chips

INGREDIENTS (4 Servings)

10-15 radishes, thinly sliced

Salt to season

DIRECTIONS (Prep + Cook Time: 15 minutes)

Preheat the air fryer to 400 F. Grease the frying basket with cooking spray. Add in the sliced radishes and AirFry for 8 minutes, flipping once halfway through. Season with salt and consume immediately.

Green Bean Crisps

INGREDIENTS (4 Servings)

1 lb green beans, trimmed
2 tbsp olive oil
½ tsp garlic powder

½ tsp onion powder
½ tsp paprika
Salt and black pepper to taste

DIRECTIONS (Prep + Cook Time: 15 minutes)

Preheat the air fryer to 390 F. In a bowl, mix olive oil, garlic and onion powders, paprika, salt, and black pepper. Coat the green beans in the mixture and place them in the greased frying basket. AirFry for 10-12 minutes, shaking once halfway through cooking. Serve warm.

Smoked Fish Balls

INGREDIENTS (4 Servings)

1 cup smoked mackerel, flaked
2 cups cooked rice
2 eggs, lightly beaten
1 cup Grana Padano cheese, grated

¼ cup fresh thyme, chopped
Salt and black pepper to taste
1 cup panko breadcrumbs
Cooking spray

DIRECTIONS (Prep + Cook Time: 25 minutes)

In a bowl, add fish, rice, eggs, Grana Padano cheese, thyme, salt, and black pepper; stir to combine. Shape the mixture into 12 even-sized balls. Roll the balls in the crumbs, then spray with cooking spray. Place the balls in the frying basket and AirFry for 14-16 minutes at 400 F, shaking once, until crispy.

Salmon Mini Tarts

INGREDIENTS (4-6 Servings)

15 mini tart shells
4 eggs, lightly beaten
½ cup heavy cream

3 oz smoked salmon
6 oz cream cheese, divided into 15 pieces
2 tbsp fresh dill, chopped

DIRECTIONS (Prep + Cook Time: 20 minutes)

Mix together the eggs and heavy cream in a bowl. Arrange the tarts on a greased air fryer muffin tray. Pour the mixture into the tarts, about halfway up the side, and top with a piece of salmon and cheese. Bake in the fryer for 10 minutes at 340 F, regularly checking them to avoid overcooking. When ready, remove them from the tray and let cool. Sprinkle with freshly chopped dill and enjoy.

Easy Coconut Shrimp

INGREDIENTS (4 Servings)

1 lb jumbo shrimp, peeled and deveined
¾ cup coconut, shredded
1 tsp maple syrup

½ cup breadcrumbs
⅓ cup cornstarch
½ cup milk

DIRECTIONS (Prep + Cook Time: 30 minutes)

Pour the cornstarch and shrimp in a zipper bag and shake vigorously to coat. Mix maple syrup and milk in a bowl and set aside. In a separate bowl, mix the breadcrumbs and shredded coconut.

Remove the shrimp from the bag while shaking off excess starch. Dip each piece in the milk mixture and then in the crumbs mixture. Lay the shrimp in the frying basket and AirFry for 12-14 minutes at 350 F, flipping once halfway through. Serve with a coconut-based dip or sautéed green beans if desired.

Salmon Croquettes

INGREDIENTS (4 Servings)

1 (15 oz) tinned salmon, flaked
1 cup onions, grated
1 cup carrots, grated
3 large eggs
1 ½ tbsp fresh chives, chopped

4 tbsp mayonnaise
4 tbsp breadcrumbs
2 ½ tsp Italian seasoning
Salt and black pepper to taste
2 ½ tsp lemon juice

DIRECTIONS (Prep + Cook Time: 20 minutes + refrigerating time)

In a bowl, mix well the salmon, onions, carrots, eggs, chives, mayonnaise, crumbs, Italian seasoning, salt, black pepper, and lemon juice. Form croquettes out of the mixture and refrigerate for 45 minutes.

Preheat the air fryer to 400 F. Grease the basket with cooking spray. Arrange the croquettes in a single layer and spray with cooking spray. AirFry for 10-12 minutes until golden, flipping once.

Rich Cod Fingers

INGREDIENTS (4 Servings)

2 cups flour
Salt and black pepper to taste
1 tsp seafood seasoning
1 cup cornmeal

1 lb cod fillets, cut into fingers
2 tbsp milk
2 eggs, beaten
1 cup breadcrumbs

DIRECTIONS (Prep + Cook Time: 20 minutes)

Preheat the air fryer to 400 F. In a bowl, mix the eggs with milk, salt, and black pepper. In a separate bowl, mix the flour, cornmeal, and seafood seasoning. In a third bowl, pour the breadcrumbs.

Roll the cod fingers in the flour mixture, then dip in the egg mixture, and finally coat with the breadcrumbs. Place the fingers in the frying basket and AirFry for 12-14 minutes, shaking once or twice. Serve hot.

Parsley & Lemon Fried Shrimp

INGREDIENTS (4 Servings)

1 ½ lb shrimp, peeled and deveined
½ cup fresh parsley, chopped
Juice of 1 lemon
1 egg, beaten

½ cup flour
¾ cup seasoned breadcrumbs
2 tbsp chili garlic sauce

DIRECTIONS (Prep + Cook Time: 20 minutes + marinating time)

Add the shrimp, parsley, and lemon juice in a resealable bag and massage until well-coated. Place in the fridge to marinate for 20 minutes. Preheat the air fryer to 400 F.

Put beaten egg, flour, and breadcrumbs each in a bowl. Dredge shrimp in the flour, then in the egg, and finally in the crumbs. Add to the frying basket and spray with cooking spray. AirFry for 10-12 minutes, shaking once. Remove to a serving plate and drizzle with chili garlic sauce to serve.

Prawn & Cabbage Egg Rolls

INGREDIENTS (4 Servings)

2 tbsp olive oil
1-inch piece fresh ginger, grated
1 tbsp garlic paste
1 carrot, cut into strips
¼ cup chicken broth
2 tbsp soy sauce

1 tbsp sugar
1 cup Napa cabbage, shredded
1 tbsp sesame oil
8 cooked prawns, chopped
1 egg
8 egg roll wrappers

DIRECTIONS (Prep + Cook Time: 30 minutes + cooling time)

Warm olive oil in a skillet over medium heat. Sauté ginger, carrot, and garlic paste for 2 minutes. Pour in the broth, soy sauce, and sugar and bring to a boil. Add the cabbage, lower the heat, and let simmer until softened, about 4 minutes. Remove from the heat and stir in sesame oil; let cool for 15 minutes.

Strain the cabbage mixture and add in the chopped prawns. Whisk an egg in a small bowl. Divide the prawn mixture between the wrappers. Fold the bottom part over the filling and tuck under. Fold in both sides and tightly roll-up. Use the whisked egg to seal the wrappers. Place the rolls into the greased frying basket, spray them with oil and AirFry for 12 minutes at 370 F, turning once halfway through.

Mouth-Watering Beef Sticks

INGREDIENTS (4 Servings)

1 lb ground beef
1 tbsp thyme
½ tsp garlic powder

½ tsp chili powder
Salt to taste
1 tsp liquid smoke

DIRECTIONS (Prep + Cook Time: 30 minutes)

Place the ground beef, thyme, garlic powder, chili powder, salt, and liquid smoke in a bowl; mix well. Mold out 4 sticks with your hands and place them on a plate to stand for 10 minutes. After, place them in the frying basket and AirFry for 14-16 minutes at 350 F, flipping once halfway through. Serve warm.

Cheesy Bacon Fries

INGREDIENTS (4 Servings)

2 russet potatoes, boiled and chopped
5 slices bacon
2 tbsp olive oil
2 cups cheddar cheese, shredded

3 oz softened cream cheese
Salt and black pepper to taste
¼ cup scallions, chopped

DIRECTIONS (Prep + Cook Time: 35 minutes)

Preheat the air fryer to 400 F. Place the bacon in the frying basket and AirFry for 5 minutes, turning once; set aside to cool. To the air fryer, add the potatoes and drizzle them with olive oil. AirFry for 20-22 minutes, shaking once. Remove and season with salt and black pepper.

In a bowl, mix cheddar and cream cheeses. Pour over the potatoes and cook for 5 more minutes. Chop the fried bacon and scatter over the potatoes. Sprinkle with scallions and serve immediately.

Crispy Bacon with Butter Bean Dip

INGREDIENTS (2 Servings)

1 (14-oz) can butter beans
1 tbsp scallions, chopped
½ cup feta cheese, crumbled

Black pepper to taste
3 tbsp olive oil
2 oz bacon, sliced

DIRECTIONS (Prep + Cook Time: 15 minutes)

Preheat the air fryer to 390 F. Arrange the bacon slices in the frying basket and AirFry for 5 minutes. Flip and cook for 5 more minutes or until crispy. Remove to a paper towel-lined plate to drain.

Meanwhile, blend butter beans, olive oil, and black pepper in a blender. Add in the feta cheese and stir well. Serve the crispy bacon with the feta-bean dip and scatter fresh scallions on top.

Bacon-Wrapped Avocados

INGREDIENTS (4 Servings)

12 thick strips bacon
3 large avocados, sliced
⅓ tsp salt

⅓ tsp chili powder
⅓ tsp cumin

DIRECTIONS (Prep + Cook Time: 40 minutes)

Stretch the bacon strips to elongate and cut in half to make 24 pieces. Wrap each bacon piece around a slice of avocado. Tuck the end of bacon into the wrap, and season with salt, chili powder, and cumin.

Arrange the wrapped pieces in the frying basket and AirFry for 8-10 minutes at 350 F, flipping halfway through to cook evenly. Remove to a wire rack and repeat the process for the remaining avocados.

Bacon & Chicken Wrapped Jalapeños

INGREDIENTS (4 Servings)

8 jalapeño peppers, halved lengthwise and seeded
4 chicken breasts, halved and butterflied
6 oz cream cheese, softened
6 oz cheddar cheese, grated

16 slices bacon
1 cup breadcrumbs
Salt and black pepper to taste
2 eggs

DIRECTIONS (Prep + Cook Time: 40 minutes)

Season the chicken with black pepper and salt on both sides. In a bowl, add cream and cheddar cheeses, black pepper, and salt; mix well. Fill the jalapeños with the cheese mixture.

On a working board, flatten each piece of chicken and lay 2 bacon slices onto each one. Place a stuffed jalapeño on each laid out chicken and bacon set and wrap around the jalapeños.

Preheat the air fryer to 350 F. Add the eggs to a bowl and pour the breadcrumbs into another bowl. Dip the wrappers into the eggs first and then in the breadcrumbs. Arrange them on the greased frying basket and AirFry for 7-8 minutes, turn and cook further for 4-5 minutes. Serve warm.

Black Bean & Corn Flatbreads

Ingredients (4 Servings)

4 flatbreads, warm
2 oz cream cheese, softened
¼ cup cheddar cheese, shredded
½ (15-oz) can corn, drained and rinsed
½ (15-oz) can black beans, drained and rinsed

¼ cup chunky salsa
½ tsp ground cumin
½ tsp paprika
Salt and black pepper to taste
2 tbsp fresh cilantro, chopped

Directions (Prep + Cook Time: 20 minutes)

Preheat the air fryer to 320 F. Add the black beans, corn, chunky salsa, cream cheese, cheddar cheese, cumin, paprika, salt, and pepper in a bowl. Mix well.

Spread the mixture out on a baking dish and insert in the air fryer. AirFry for 9-11 minutes until heated through. Divide the mixture among the flatbreads. Top with cilantro and serve warm.

BBQ Chicken Naan Pizza

INGREDIENTS (1 Serving)

1 piece naan bread
¼ cup barbeque sauce
¼ cup mozzarella cheese, shredded
¼ cup Monterrey Jack cheese, shredded

2 tbsp red onions, thinly sliced
½ chicken sausage, sliced
½ tbsp fresh cilantro, chopped

DIRECTIONS (Prep + Cook Time: 20 minutes)

Spray naan's bread with cooking spray and place it on the greased frying basket. Brush with barbeque sauce, sprinkle with mozzarella and Monterrey Jack cheeses, and red onions. Top with the chicken sausage. Bake in the preheated fryer for 8-10 minutes at 400 F. Sprinkle with cilantro to serve.

Italian Pork Sausage Pizza

INGREDIENTS (2 Servings)

1 piece pizza crust dough
½ tsp dried oregano
¼ cup tomato sauce
¼ cup mozzarella cheese, shredded

1 shallot, thinly sliced
1 Italian pork sausage, sliced
4 fresh basil leaves
4 black olives

DIRECTIONS (Prep + Cook Time: 20 minutes)

Preheat the air fryer to 390 F. Spread tomato sauce over the pizza dough and sprinkle with oregano. Top with mozzarella cheese, shallot, and pork sausage slices.

Place the pizza dough on the greased frying basket. Bake for 10 minutes until the crust is golden and the cheese is melted. Scatter over basil leaves and olives to serve.

Chorizo Pita Pizzas

INGREDIENTS (4 Servings)

4 pita bread pieces
4 tbsp marinara sauce
12 chorizo rounds
8 button mushrooms, sliced

8 fresh basil leaves
2 cups cheddar cheese, grated
1 tsp chili flakes
Cooking oil

DIRECTIONS (Prep + Cook Time: 25 minutes)

Spray the pitas with oil and scatter marinara sauce over. Top with chorizo rounds, mushrooms, basil, cheddar cheese, and chili flakes. Bake in the fryer for 12-14 minutes at 360 F, checking regularly to ensure an even baking. Work in batches if needed. Serve warm with garlic mayo or yogurt dip.

Crispy Pepperoni Pizza

INGREDIENTS (2 Servings)

8 oz fresh pizza dough
⅓ cup tomato sauce
⅓ cup mozzarella cheese, shredded

8 pepperonis, sliced
1 tsp oregano, dried
Flour to dust

DIRECTIONS (Prep + Cook Time: 25 minutes)

On a floured surface, place pizza dough and dust with flour. Stretch with hands into greased frying basket. Spray the dish with cooking spray and place the pizza dough inside.

Spread the tomato sauce, leaving some space at the border. Scatter with mozzarella cheese and oregano and top with pepperoni slices. Bake for 14-16 minutes or until crispy at 340 F. Serve sliced.

Bacon-Wrapped Dates

INGREDIENTS (4 Servings)

2 tbsp maple syrup
16 dates, pits removed

⅓ cup blue cheese, softened
8 bacon slices, cut in half crosswise

DIRECTIONS (Prep + Cook Time: 25 minutes)

Preheat the air fryer to 370 F. Grease the frying basket with cooking oil. Using a sharp knife, make a deep cut into each date to create a pocket. Stuff the dates with blue cheese and pinch to lock up.

Lay the bacon slices on the chopping board. Put a date on one side of each slice and roll up. Secure with toothpicks. Brush the wrapped dates with maple syrup and AirFry for 10-12 minutes, turning halfway through cooking until the bacon is crispy. Let cool for 5 minutes and serve.

Delicious Chicken Tortillas

INGREDIENTS (4 Servings)

1 cup cooked chicken, shredded
1 cup mozzarella cheese, shredded
¼ cup salsa

¼ cup Greek yogurt
Salt and black pepper to taste
8 flour tortillas

DIRECTIONS (Prep + Cook Time: 20 minutes)

In a bowl, mix the chicken, mozzarella, salsa, Greek yogurt, salt, and black pepper. Lay 2 tbsp of the mixture at the center of the tortillas. Roll tightly around the mixture. Spray the taquitos with cooking spray and arrange them in the frying basket. AirFry for 12-14 minutes at 380 F, turning once. Serve.

Chicken Burgers with Horseradish Sauce

INGREDIENTS (4 Servings)

1 lb ground chicken
½ cup seasoned breadcrumbs
¼ cup Parmesan cheese, grated
1 egg, beaten
1 tbsp minced garlic

1 tbsp olive oil
1 tsp horseradish sauce
4 tbsp Greek yogurt
4 buns, halved
4 tomato slices

DIRECTIONS (Prep + Cook Time: 25 minutes)

Preheat the air fryer to 380 F. In a bowl, combine ground chicken, breadcrumbs, Parmesan, egg, and garlic. Mix well. Form balls and flatten to make patties. Brush them with olive oil and place in the greased frying basket. AirFry for 16-18 minutes, flipping once until nice and golden.

Mix the yogurt with horseradish sauce. Assemble the burgers by spreading the yogurt mixture on the bun bottoms, then add the patties and fresh tomato slices. Cover with the bun tops and serve.

Classic Beef Meatballs

INGREDIENTS (4 Servings)

1 lb ground beef
1 tsp grated ginger
1 tbsp hot sauce
½ tbsp white wine vinegar

½ tsp lemon juice
½ cup tomato ketchup
¼ tsp dry mustard
Salt and black pepper to taste

DIRECTIONS (Prep + Cook Time: 25 minutes)

In a bowl, mix well ground beef, ginger, hot sauce, vinegar, lemon juice, ketchup, mustard, black pepper, and salt. With greased hands, shape the mixture into 2-inch sized balls. Add the balls to the fryer without overcrowding. AirFry at 370 F for 13-15 minutes, shaking once. Serve with tomato dip if desired.

Paprika Beef Fajitas

INGREDIENTS (4 Servings)

1 lb beef sirloin steak, cut into strips
2 garlic cloves, minced
1 tsp paprika
½ red bell pepper, sliced
½ orange bell pepper, sliced
2 shallots, sliced

2 tbsp Cajun seasoning
2 tbsp olive oil
8 tortilla wraps
½ cup cheddar cheese, shredded
Salt and black pepper to taste

DIRECTIONS (Prep + Cook Time: 35 minutes)

Preheat the air fryer to 360 F. In a bowl, combine the beef, shallots, bell peppers, and garlic. Season with Cajun seasoning, paprika, salt, and black pepper; toss to combine. Transfer the mixture to a greased frying basket and place it inside the frying basket. Bake for 10 minutes, shaking once or twice throughout cooking. Serve on the tortilla wraps, topped with cheddar cheese.

South Asian Pork Momos

INGREDIENTS (4 Servings)

1 lb ground pork
2 tbsp olive oil
1 carrot, shredded
1 onion, chopped

1 tsp soy sauce
16 wonton wrappers
Salt and black pepper to taste

DIRECTIONS (Prep + Cook Time: 25 minutes)

Preheat the air fryer to 320 F. Warm olive oil in a pan over medium heat and stir-fry ground pork, onion, carrot, soy sauce, salt, and black pepper for 8-10 minutes or until the meat is browned.

Divide the filling between the wrappers. Tuck them around the mixture to form momo shapes and seal the edges. Spritz the momos with cooking spray and AirFry them for 9-11 minutes, flipping once.

Spanish Chorizo with Brussels Sprouts

INGREDIENTS (4 Servings)

4 Spanish chorizo sausages, halved
1 lb Brussels sprouts, trimmed and halved
2 tbsp olive oil

Salt and black pepper to taste
1 tsp garlic puree
1 thyme sprig, chopped

DIRECTIONS (Prep + Cook Time: 20 minutes)

Preheat the air fryer to 390 F. In a bowl, mix olive oil, garlic puree, salt, and black pepper. Add the Brussels sprouts and toss to coat. Arrange chorizo and Brussels sprouts on the greased frying basket and AirFry for 11-14 minutes, tossing once halfway through cooking. Top with thyme to serve.

Cheesy Sausage Balls

INGREDIENTS (4 Servings)

1 lb ground pork sausage meat
1 ¼ cups cheddar cheese, shredded
1 cup flour, sifted
¾ tsp baking soda
2 eggs

½ cup sour cream
½ tsp dried oregano
½ tsp smoked paprika
½ tsp garlic powder
2 tbsp coconut oil

DIRECTIONS (Prep + Cook Time: 25 minutes + chilling time)

Heat coconut oil in a pan over medium heat and brown the sausage meat for 3-4 minutes. Mix flour with baking soda in a bowl. Whisk eggs, sour cream, oregano, paprika, and garlic in another bowl.

Combine egg and flour mixtures using a spatula. Mix in the cheese and sausage meat; let cool slightly. Mold out balls out of the batter and refrigerate for 15 minutes. Remove from the fridge and brush them with the sausage fat. Place the balls in the basket and AirFry for 12-14 minutes at 400 F, shaking once.

Baked Potatoes with Bacon

INGREDIENTS (4 Servings)

4 potatoes, scrubbed, halved, cut lengthwise
1 tbsp olive oil

Salt and black pepper to taste
4 oz bacon, chopped

DIRECTIONS (Prep + Cook Time: 35 minutes)

Preheat the air fryer to 390 F. Brush the potatoes with olive oil and season with salt and black pepper. Arrange them in the greased frying basket, cut-side down. Bake for 15 minutes, flip them, top with bacon and bake for 12-15 minutes or until the potatoes are golden and the bacon is crispy. Serve.

Chive Roasted Red Potatoes

INGREDIENTS (4 Servings)

4 red potatoes, cut into wedges
1 tbsp garlic powder
Salt and black pepper to taste

2 tbsp chives, chopped
3 tbsp butter, melted

DIRECTIONS (Prep + Cook Time: 30 minutes)

Preheat the air fryer to 380 F. In a bowl, mix butter, garlic powder, salt, and pepper. Add the potatoes and shake to coat. Place them in the frying basket and Bake for 12 minutes, remove the basket, shake and continue to cook for another 8-10 minutes until golden brown. Serve warm topped with chives.

Feta French Fries

Ingredients (4 Servings)

6 russet potatoes, cut into strips
2 tbsp olive oil

4 oz feta cheese, grated
Salt and black pepper to taste

Directions (Prep + Cook Time: 35 minutes)

Preheat the air fryer to 400 F. Drizzle the potatoes with olive oil and toss to coat. Place in the frying basket and AirFry for 20 minutes, shaking once halfway through. Sprinkle the potatoes with freshly grated feta cheese and enjoy.

Crispy Hasselback Potatoes

INGREDIENTS (4 Servings)

2 tbsp lard, melted
1 lb russet potatoes
1 tbsp olive oil

Salt and black pepper to taste
1 garlic clove, crushed
1 tbsp fresh dill, chopped

DIRECTIONS (Prep + Cook Time: 25 minutes)

Preheat the air fryer to 400 F. On the potatoes, make thin vertical slits, around 1/5 inch apart. Make sure to cut the potatoes 3/4-the way down, so that they can hold together. Mix together the lard, olive oil, and garlic in a bowl. Brush the potatoes with some of the mixture.

Season with salt and pepper and place them in the greased frying basket. AirFry for 25-30 minutes, brushing once halfway through so they don't dry during cooking, until golden and crispy around the edges. Sprinkle with dill. Serve and enjoy!

Sweet Potato Boats

INGREDIENTS (4 Servings)

4 sweet potatoes, boiled and halved lengthwise
2 tbsp olive oil
1 shallot, chopped

1 cup canned mixed beans
¼ cup mozzarella cheese, grated
Salt and black pepper to taste

DIRECTIONS (Prep + Cook Time: 25 minutes)

Preheat the air fryer to 400 F. Grease the frying basket with olive oil.

Scoop out the flesh from the potatoes, so shells are formed. Chop the potato flesh and put it in a bowl. Add in shallot, mixed beans, salt, and pepper; mix to combine. Fill the potato shells with the mixture and top with the cheese. Arrange on the basket and place inside the fryer. Bake for 10-12 minutes.

Thyme & Garlic Sweet Potato Wedges

INGREDIENTS (2 Servings)

½ lb sweet potatoes, cut into wedges
1 tbsp coconut oil
¼ tsp salt
¼ tsp chili powder

¼ tsp garlic powder
¼ tsp smoked paprika
¼ tsp dried thyme
¼ tsp cayenne pepper

DIRECTIONS (Prep + Cook Time: 30 minutes)

In a bowl, mix coconut oil, salt, chili and garlic powders, paprika, thyme, and cayenne pepper. Toss in the potato wedges. Arrange the wedges on the frying basket and AirFry for 23-25 minutes at 380 F, shaking a few times through cooking until golden. Serve and enjoy!

Prosciutto & Cheese Stromboli

INGREDIENTS (4 Servings)

1 (13-oz) pizza crust
4 (1-oz) fontina cheese slices
8 slices prosciutto
12 cherry tomatoes, halved

4 fresh basil leaves, chopped
½ tsp dried oregano
Salt and black pepper to taste

DIRECTIONS (Prep + Cook Time: 30 minutes)

Roll out the pizza crust on a lightly floured work surface; slice into 4 squares. Top each one with a slice of fontina cheese, 2 slices of prosciutto, 3 halved cherry tomatoes, oregano, and basil. Season with salt and black pepper. Close the rectangles by folding in half, press, and seal the edges with a fork. Spritz with cooking spray and transfer to the greased frying basket. Bake for 15 minutes, turning once.

Fava Bean Falafel Bites

INGREDIENTS (4 Servings)

1 tbsp olive oil
1 can (15.5-oz) fava beans, drained
1 red onion, chopped
2 tsp chopped fresh cilantro
1 tsp ground cumin

Salt to taste
1 garlic clove, minced
3 tbsp flour
4 lemon wedges to serve

DIRECTIONS (Prep + Cook Time: 20 minutes)

Preheat the air fryer to 380 F. In a food processor, pulse all the ingredients until a thick paste is formed. Shape the mixture into ping pong-sized balls. Brush with olive oil and insert in the greased frying basket. AirFry for 12 minutes, turning once halfway through. Plate and serve with lemon wedges.

Plum & Pancetta Bombs

INGREDIENTS (4-6 Servings)

1 ¼ cups soft goat cheese, crumbled
1 tbsp fresh rosemary, finely chopped
1 cup almonds, chopped

Salt and black pepper to taste
15 dried plums, soaked and chopped
15 pancetta slices

DIRECTIONS (Prep + Cook Time: 20 minutes)

Line the frying basket with baking paper. In a bowl, add goat cheese, rosemary, almonds, salt, black pepper, and plums; stir well. Roll into balls and wrap with a pancetta slice. Place them into the fryer and AirFry for 10 minutes at 400 F, shaking once. Let cool for a few minutes. Serve with toothpicks.

Fried Sausage Ravioli

INGREDIENTS (6 Servings)

2 (18-oz) packages of fresh sausage ravioli
1 cup flour
1 cup marinara sauce

4 eggs, beaten in a bowl
2 cups breadcrumbs
2 tbsp Parmesan cheese, grated

DIRECTIONS (Prep + Cook Time: 15 minutes)

Preheat the air fryer to 400 F. In a bowl, mix breadcrumbs with Parmesan cheese. Dip sausage ravioli into the flour, then into the eggs, and finally in the breadcrumb mixture. Arrange the coated ravioli on the greased frying basket in an even layer and spritz them with cooking spray. AirFry for 10-12 minutes, turning once halfway through cooking until nice and golden. Serve hot with the marinara sauce.

Roasted Hot Chickpeas

INGREDIENTS (4 Servings)

1 (19-oz) can chickpeas, drained and rinsed
2 tbsp olive oil
½ tsp ground cumin
¼ tsp mustard powder

¼ tsp onion powder
½ tsp chili powder
¼ tsp cayenne pepper
¼ tsp salt

DIRECTIONS (Prep + Cook Time: 25 minutes)

Preheat the air fryer to 385 F. In a mixing bowl, thoroughly combine the olive oil, cumin, mustard powder, onion powder, chili powder, cayenne pepper, and salt. Add in the chickpeas.

Toss them until evenly coated. Transfer the chickpeas to the frying basket and Air Fry, shaking the basket every 2-3 minutes. Cook until they're as crunchy as you like them, about 15-20 minutes. Serve.

Paprika Baked Parsnips

INGREDIENTS (4 Servings)

½ tbsp paprika
1 lb parsnips, peeled and halved
4 tbsp avocado oil
2 tbsp fresh cilantro, chopped

2 tbsp Parmesan cheese, grated
1 tsp garlic powder
Salt and black pepper to taste

DIRECTIONS (Prep + Cook Time: 20 minutes)

Preheat the air fryer to 390 F.

In a bowl, mix paprika, avocado oil, garlic, salt, and black pepper. Toss in the parsnips to coat. Arrange them on the greased frying basket and Bake for 14-16 minutes, turning once halfway through cooking, until golden and crunchy. Remove and sprinkle with Parmesan cheese and cilantro. Serve.

Air-Fried Cheesy Broccoli with Garlic

INGREDIENTS (2 Servings)

2 tbsp butter, melted
1 egg white
1 garlic clove, grated

Salt and black pepper to taste
½ lb broccoli florets
⅓ cup grated Parmesan cheese

DIRECTIONS (Prep + Cook Time: 20 minutes)

In a bowl, whisk together butter, egg white, garlic, salt, and black pepper. Toss in the broccoli to coat. Arrange them in a single layer in the greased frying basket and AirFry for 10 minutes at 360 F, shaking once. Remove to a plate and sprinkle with Parmesan cheese. Serve immediately.

Roasted Coconut Carrots

INGREDIENTS (4 Servings)

1 tbsp coconut oil, melted
1 lb horse carrots, sliced

Salt and black pepper to taste
½ tsp chili powder

DIRECTIONS (Prep + Cook Time: 15 minutes)

Preheat the air fryer to 400 F.

In a bowl, mix the carrots with coconut oil, chili powder, salt, and black pepper. Place them in the fryer and AirFry for 7 minutes. Shake the basket and cook for another 5 minutes until golden brown. Serve.

Pumpkin Wedges

INGREDIENTS (4 Servings)

1 lb pumpkin, washed and cut into wedges
1 tbsp paprika
2 tbsp olive oil
1 lime, juiced

1 tbsp balsamic vinegar
Salt and black pepper to taste
1 tsp turmeric

DIRECTIONS (Prep + Cook Time: 20 minutes)

Preheat the air fryer to 400 F. Add the pumpkin wedges to the greased frying basket and AirFry for 10-12 minutes, flipping once. In a bowl, mix olive oil, lime juice, balsamic vinegar, turmeric, salt, black pepper, and paprika. Drizzle the dressing over the pumpkin and fry for 5 more minutes. Serve warm.

Baked Butternut Squash

INGREDIENTS (4 Servings)

2 cups butternut squash, cubed
2 tbsp olive oil
Salt and black pepper to taste

¼ tsp dried thyme
1 tbsp fresh parsley, finely chopped

DIRECTIONS (Prep + Cook Time: 25 minutes)

In a bowl, add squash, olive oil, salt, black pepper, and thyme; toss to coat. Place the squash in the air fryer and AirFry for 12-14 minutes at 360 F, shaking once or twice. Serve sprinkled with fresh parsley.

Cheesy Mushrooms

INGREDIENTS (2 Servings)

2 tbsp olive oil
Salt and black pepper to taste
10 button mushroom caps

2 tbsp mozzarella cheese, grated
2 tbsp cheddar cheese, grated
1 tsp Italian seasoning

DIRECTIONS (Prep + Cook Time: 20 minutes)

Preheat the air fryer to 390 F. In a bowl, mix olive oil, salt, black pepper, and Italian seasoning. Toss in the mushrooms to coat. Mix the cheeses in a separate bowl. Stuff the mushrooms with the cheese mixture and place them in the frying basket. Bake for 10-12 minutes until golden on top. Serve warm.

Walnut & Cheese Filled Mushrooms

INGREDIENTS (4 Servings)

4 large portobello mushroom caps
⅓ cup walnuts, finely chopped
1 tbsp canola oil

½ cup mozzarella cheese, shredded
2 tbsp fresh parsley, chopped

DIRECTIONS (Prep + Cook Time: 20 minutes)

Preheat the air fryer to 350 F. Grease the frying basket with cooking spray.

Rub the mushrooms with canola oil and fill them with mozzarella cheese. Top with walnuts and arrange them in the greased frying basket. Bake for 10-12 minutes or until golden on top. Remove and let cool for a few minutes. Sprinkle with freshly chopped parsley and serve.

Paprika Serrano Peppers

INGREDIENTS (4 Servings)

4 serrano peppers, halved and seeds removed
3 oz ricotta cheese, crumbled
1 cup breadcrumbs

1 tsp paprika
1 tbsp chives, chopped
1 tbsp olive oil

DIRECTIONS (Prep + Cook Time: 20 minutes)

Preheat the air fryer to 380 F. Grease the frying basket with cooking spray. In a bowl, combine ricotta cheese, paprika, and chives. Spoon the mixture into the pepper halves and top with breadcrumbs. Drizzle with olive oil. Place in the basket and Bake for 10-12 minutes. Serve warm.

Chili Edamame

INGREDIENTS (4 Servings)

1 (16-oz) bag frozen edamame in pods
1 red chili, finely chopped
1 tbsp olive oil

½ tsp garlic salt
½ tsp red pepper flakes
Black pepper to taste

DIRECTIONS (Prep + Cook Time: 20 minutes)

Preheat the air fryer to 380 F. In a mixing bowl, combine olive oil, garlic salt, red pepper flakes, and black pepper and mix well. Add in the edamame and toss to coat.

Transfer to the frying basket in a single layer and AirFry for 10 minutes, shaking once. Cook until lightly browned and just crispy. Work in batches if needed. Serve topped with the red chili.

Brie Cheese Croutons with Herbs

INGREDIENTS (2 Servings)

2 tbsp olive oil
1 tbsp french herbs

6 oz brie cheese, chopped
2 slices bread, halved

DIRECTIONS (Prep + Cook Time: 15 minutes + cooling time)

Preheat the air fryer to 340 F. Brush the bread slices with olive oil and sprinkle with herbs. Top with brie cheese. Place in the greased frying basket and Bake for 10-12 minutes. Let cool, then cut into cubes.

Super Cabbage Canapes

INGREDIENTS (2 Servings)

1 whole cabbage, cut into rounds
½ cup mozzarella cheese, shredded
½ carrot, cubed

¼ onion, cubed
¼ bell pepper, cubed
1 tbsp fresh basil, chopped

DIRECTIONS (Prep + Cook Time: 20 minutes)

Preheat the air fryer to 360 F. In a bowl, mix onion, carrot, bell pepper, and mozzarella cheese. Toss to coat evenly. Add the cabbage rounds to the greased frying basket, top with the cheese mixture, and Bake for 5-8 minutes. Garnish with basil and serve.

Broccoli Cheese Quiche

INGREDIENTS (3 Servings)

1 head broccoli, cut into florets
¼ cup Parmesan cheese, grated
½ cup heavy cream

Salt and black pepper to taste
5 eggs

DIRECTIONS (Prep + Cook Time: 30 minutes)

Preheat the air fryer to 340 F. Beat the eggs with the heavy cream. Season with salt and black pepper. In a greased baking dish, lay the florets and cover with the egg mixture. Spread Parmesan cheese on top and place inside the frying basket. Bake for 10-12 minutes until golden brown on top. Serve warm.

Easy Parmesan Sandwich

INGREDIENTS (1 Serving)

4 tbsp Parmesan cheese, shredded
2 scallions

1 tbsp butter, softened
2 bread slices

DIRECTIONS (Prep + Cook Time: 20 minutes)

Preheat the air fryer to 360 F. Spread only one side of the bread slices with butter. Cover one of the buttered slices with Parmesan and scallions and top with the buttered side of the other slice to form a sandwich. Place in the frying basket and Bake for 10-12 minutes. Cut into 4 triangles and serve.

Salty Carrot Cookies

INGREDIENTS (4 Servings)

6 carrots, boiled and mashed
Salt and black pepper to taste
½ tsp parsley

1 ¼ oz oats
1 whole egg, beaten
½ tsp thyme

DIRECTIONS (Prep + Cook Time: 25 minutes)

Preheat the air fryer to 360 F. In a bowl, combine carrots, salt, black pepper, egg, oats, thyme, and parsley; mix well to form batter. Shape into cookie shapes. Place the cookies in the greased frying basket and Bake for 14-16 minutes, flipping once halfway through. Serve.

Mini Cheese Scones

INGREDIENTS (4 Servings)

1 cup flour
A pinch of salt
1 tsp baking powder
2 oz butter, cubed

1 tsp fresh chives, chopped
1 egg
¼ cup milk
½ cup cheddar cheese, shredded

DIRECTIONS (Prep + Cook Time: 30 minutes)

Preheat the air fryer to 360 F. Sith the flour in a bowl and mix in butter, baking powder, and salt until a breadcrumb mixture is formed. Add cheese, chives, milk, and egg, and mix to get a sticky dough.

Roll the dough into small balls. Place the balls in the greased frying basket and AirFry for 18-20 minutes, shaking once or twice. Serve warm.

Cheddar Cheese Biscuits

INGREDIENTS (4 Servings)

½ cup butter, softened
1 tbsp melted butter
1 tsp salt
2 cups flour

½ cup buttermilk
½ cup cheddar cheese, grated
1 egg, beaten

DIRECTIONS (Prep + Cook Time: 30 minutes + cooling time)

Preheat the air fryer to 360 F. In a bowl, mix salt, flour, butter, cheese, and buttermilk to form a batter. Shape into balls and flatten them into biscuits. Arrange them on a greased frying basket and brush with the beaten egg. Drizzle with melted butter and Bake in the fryer for 18-20 minutes, flipping once.

Cauliflower & Tofu Croquettes

Ingredients (4 Servings)

1 lb cauliflower florets
2 eggs
½ cup tofu, crumbled
½ cup mozzarella cheese
⅓ cup breadcrumbs

1 tsp dried thyme
¼ tsp ground cumin
½ tsp onion powder
Salt and black pepper to taste
1 cup chipotle aioli

Directions (Prep + Cook Time: 30 minutes)

Place the cauliflower florets in your food processor and pulse until it resembles rice. Microwave the resulting "rice" in a heatproof dish for 4-6 minutes until it have softened completely. Let cool.

Preheat the air fryer to 390 F. Add the eggs, tofu, mozzarella cheese, breadcrumbs, thyme, cumin, onion powder, salt, and pepper to the cauliflower rice and mix to combine. Form the mixture into croquettes and arrange them on the greased frying basket. Spritz with cooking spray. AirFry for 14-16 minutes, turning once, until golden brown. Serve warm with the chipotle aioli.

Cheesy Mushroom & Cauliflower Balls

INGREDIENTS (4 Servings)

½ lb mushrooms, diced
3 tbsp olive oil + some more for brushing
1 small red onion, chopped
3 garlic cloves, minced
3 cups cauliflower, chopped

1 cup breadcrumbs
1 cup Grana Padano cheese, grated
2 sprigs fresh thyme, chopped
Salt and black pepper to taste

DIRECTIONS (Prep + Cook Time: 25 minutes + cooling time)

Heat 3 tbsp olive oil in a skillet over medium heat and sauté garlic and onion for 3 minutes. Add in mushrooms and cauliflower and stir-fry for 5 minutes. Add in Grana Padano cheese, black pepper, thyme, and salt. Turn off and let cool. Make small balls out of the mixture and refrigerate for 30 minutes.

Preheat the air fryer to 350 F. Remove the balls from the refrigerator and roll in the breadcrumbs. Brush with olive oil and place in the frying basket without overcrowding. Bake for 14-16 minutes, tossing every 4-5 minutes. Serve with sautéed zoodles and tomato sauce, if desired.

Spicy Cheese Lings

INGREDIENTS (4 Servings)

½ cup grated cheddar cheese + extra for rolling
1 cup flour + extra for kneading
¼ tsp chili powder

½ tsp baking powder
3 tsp butter, melted
A pinch of salt

DIRECTIONS (Prep + Cook Time: 20 minutes)

In a bowl, mix the cheese, flour, baking powder, chili powder, butter, and salt. Add some water and mix well to get a dough. Remove the dough onto a flat, floured surface. Using a rolling pin, roll out into a thin sheet and cut into lings' shape. Add the cheese lings to the greased frying basket and AirFry for 10-12 minutes at 350 F, flipping once halfway through. Serve with ketchup if desired.

Cocktail Meatballs

Ingredients (4 Servings)

½ lb ground beef
½ lb ground pork
2 oz bacon, chopped
1 egg

Salt and black pepper to taste
¼ tsp cayenne pepper
2 oz cheddar cheese, shredded
1 cup jalapeño tomato ketchup

Directions (Prep + Cook Time: 30 MINUTES)

Preheat the air fryer to 400 F. In a bowl, thoroughly mix all ingredients. Form the mixture into 1-inch balls using an ice cream scoop. Place them into the greased frying basket and spray with cooking oil. AirFry for 8-10 minutes, turning once. Serve with toothpicks and jalapeño tomato ketchup on the side.

French Beans with Toasted Almonds

INGREDIENTS (4 Servings)

1 lb French beans, trimmed
Salt and black pepper to taste
½ tbsp onion powder

2 tbsp olive oil
½ cup toasted almonds, chopped

DIRECTIONS (Prep + Cook Time: 15 minutes)

Preheat air fryer to 400 F. In a bowl, drizzle the beans with olive oil. Add onion powder, salt, and pepper and toss to coat. AirFry for 10-12 minutes, shaking once. Sprinkle with almonds and serve.

Cheddar Black Bean Burritos

INGREDIENTS (4 Servings)

4 tortillas
1 cup cheddar cheese, grated

1 can (8 oz) black beans, drained
1 tsp taco seasoning

DIRECTIONS (Prep + Cook Time: 10 minutes)

Preheat the air fryer to 350 F. Mix the beans with the taco seasoning. Divide the bean mixture between the tortillas and top with cheddar cheese. Roll the burritos and arrange them on the greased frying basket. Place in the air fryer and Bake for 4-5 minutes, flip, and cook for 3 more minutes. Serve warm.

Smoky Hazelnuts

INGREDIENTS (4-6 Servings)

2 cups almonds
2 tbsp liquid smoke

Salt to taste
1 tbsp molasses

DIRECTIONS (Prep + Cook Time: 20 minutes)

Preheat the air fryer to 360 F. In a bowl, add salt, liquid smoke, molasses, and almonds; toss to coat. Place the hazelnuts in the greased frying basket and Bake for 5-8 minutes, shaking once. Serve warm.

Spiced Almonds

INGREDIENTS (4 Servings)

½ tsp ground cinnamon
½ tsp smoked paprika
1 cup almonds

1 egg white
Sea salt to taste

DIRECTIONS (Prep + Cook Time: 15 minutes)

Preheat the air fryer to 310 F. Grease the frying basket with cooking spray. In a bowl, whisk the egg white with cinnamon and paprika and stir in the almonds. Spread the almonds in the frying basket and AirFry for 12-14 minutes, shaking once or twice. Remove and sprinkle with sea salt to serve.

Roasted Pumpkin Seeds with Cardamom

INGREDIENTS (4 Servings)

1 cup pumpkin seeds, pulp removed, rinsed
1 tbsp butter, melted
1 tbsp brown sugar

1 tsp orange zest
½ tsp cardamom
½ tsp salt

DIRECTIONS (Prep + Cook Time: 25 minutes)

Preheat air fryer to 320 F. Place the pumpkin seeds in a greased baking dish and place the dish in the fryer. AirFry for 4-5 minutes to avoid moisture. In a bowl, whisk butter, sugar, zest, cardamom, and salt.

Add the seeds to the bowl and toss to coat well. Transfer the seeds to the baking dish inside the fryer and Bake for 13-15 minutes, shaking the basket every 5 minutes, until lightly browned. Serve warm.

Masala Cashew Nuts

INGREDIENTS (2 Servings)

1 cup cashew nuts
Salt and black pepper to taste

½ tsp ground coriander
1 tsp garam masala

DIRECTIONS (Prep + Cook Time: 10 minutes)

Preheat the air fryer to 360 F. In a bowl, mix coriander, garam masala, salt, and pepper. Add cashews and toss to coat. Place in a greased baking dish and AirFry in the fryer for 5-8 minutes, shaking once.

Sweet Mixed Nuts

INGREDIENTS (5 Servings)

½ cup pecans
½ cup walnuts
½ cup almonds
A pinch of cayenne pepper

1 tbsp sugar
2 tbsp egg whites
2 tsp ground cinnamon
Cooking spray

DIRECTIONS (Prep + Cook Time: 15 minutes)

Add cayenne pepper, sugar, and cinnamon to a bowl and mix well; set aside. In another bowl, mix pecans, walnuts, almonds, and egg whites. Add in the spice mixture and stir. Grease a baking dish with cooking spray. Pour in the nuts and place the dish in the fryer. Bake for 5-7 minutes. Stir the nuts using a wooden spoon and cook for 4-5 more minutes. Pour the nuts into the bowl and let cool slightly.

PORK, BEEF & LAMB

Honey & BBQ Spare Ribs

INGREDIENTS (4 Servings)

1 rack pork spareribs, fat trimmed
½ tsp ginger powder
Salt and black pepper to taste
2 garlic cloves, minced

1 tsp olive oil
1 tbsp honey + for brushing
4 tbsp barbecue sauce
1 tsp soy sauce

DIRECTIONS (Prep + Cook Time: 30 minutes + marinating time)

Chop the ribs into individual bones. In a large bowl, whisk all the remaining ingredients, reserving some of the honey. Add in the meat and mix to coat. Cover with a lid and place in the fridge for 1 hour.

Preheat the air fryer to 350 F. Place the ribs in the frying basket and AirFry for 8 minutes. Slide the basket out and brush the ribs with the reserved honey. AirFry for 12-14 minutes until golden and crispy.

Char Siew Pork Ribs

INGREDIENTS (4 Servings)

2 lb pork ribs
2 tbsp char siew sauce
2 tbsp minced ginger
2 tbsp hoisin sauce

2 tbsp sesame oil
1 tsp honey
4 garlic cloves, minced
1 tbsp soy sauce

DIRECTIONS (Prep + Cook Time: 35 minutes + marinating time)

Whisk together all the ingredients, except for the ribs, in a large bowl. Add in the ribs and toss to coat. Cover with a lid. Place the bowl in the fridge to marinate for 2 hours. Preheat the air fryer to 390 F.

Put the ribs in the greased frying basket and place in the fryer; do not throw away the liquid from the bowl. Bake for 15 minutes. Pour in the marinade and cook for 10-12 more minutes. Serve hot.

Memphis-Style Pork Ribs

INGREDIENTS (4 Servings)

1 ½ lb St. Louis–style pork spareribs
Salt and black pepper to taste
½ tsp sweet paprika
½ tsp dry mustard
1 tbsp brown sugar

1 tbsp cayenne pepper
1 tsp poultry seasoning
1 tsp shallot powder
1 tsp garlic powder
½ cup hot sauce

DIRECTIONS (Prep + Cook Time: 40 minutes)

Preheat the air fryer to 370 F. Cut the ribs individually. In a bowl, mix all the remaining ingredients, except for the hot sauce. Add the ribs to the bowl and rub the seasoning onto the meat. Place the ribs in the greased frying basket and Bake for 20 minutes, turn them over, and cook for 10 more minutes or until the ribs are tender inside and golden brown and crisp on the outside. Serve with hot sauce.

Roasted Pork Rack with Macadamia Nuts

INGREDIENTS (2 Servings)

1 lb pork rack
2 tbsp olive oil
1 clove garlic, minced
Salt and black pepper to taste

1 cup macadamia nuts, finely chopped
1 tbsp breadcrumbs
1 egg, beaten in a bowl
1 tbsp rosemary, chopped

DIRECTIONS (Prep + Cook Time: 65 minutes)

Mix the olive oil and garlic vigorously in a bowl to make garlic oil. Place the rack of pork on a chopping board and brush with the garlic oil. Sprinkle with salt and pepper. Preheat the fryer to 370 F.

In a bowl, add breadcrumbs, macadamia nuts, and rosemary. Brush the meat with the beaten egg on all sides and generously sprinkle with the nut mixture. Place the coated pork in the frying basket and Bake for 30 minutes. Flip over and cook further for 5-8 minutes. Remove the meat onto a chopping board and let it rest for 10 minutes before slicing. Serve with a salad or steamed rice.

Chinese Sticky Ribs

INGREDIENTS (4 Servings)

1 tbsp sesame oil
1 ½ lb pork ribs
½ tsp red chili flakes
2 tbsp light brown sugar
1-inch piece ginger, grated
1 tbsp sweet chili sauce
Salt and black pepper to taste

2 garlic cloves, minced
1 tbsp balsamic vinegar
½ tsp onion powder
½ tsp Chinese Five spice powder

2 scallions, chopped

DIRECTIONS (Prep + Cook Time: 45 minutes + marinating time)

In a bowl, mix the red chili flakes, brown sugar, ginger, garlic, vinegar, onion powder, Five spice powder, chili sauce, salt, and black pepper. Add in the ribs and toss to coat. Chill for at least 1 hour.

Preheat the air fryer to 370 F. Remove the ribs from the fridge and place them in the greased frying basket. Brush with sesame oil and Bake for 25-30 minutes, flipping once. Serve topped with scallions.

Pork Sausage with Butter Bean Ratatouille

INGREDIENTS (4 Servings)

4 pork sausages
For Ratatouille
1 red bell pepper, chopped
2 zucchinis, chopped
1 eggplant, chopped
1 medium red onion, chopped
2 tbsp olive oil

1 cup canned butter beans, drained
15 oz canned tomatoes, chopped
1 tbsp balsamic vinegar
2 garlic cloves, minced
1 red chili, minced

DIRECTIONS (Prep + Cook Time: 45 minutes)

Preheat the air fryer to 390 F. Add the sausages to the greased frying basket and AirFry for 12-15 minutes, turning once halfway through. Cover with foil to keep warm. Mix all ratatouille ingredients in the frying basket and Bake for 15-18 minutes, shaking once. Serve the sausages with ratatouille.

Maple Mustard Pork Balls

INGREDIENTS (4 Servings)

1 lb ground pork
1 large onion, chopped
½ tsp maple syrup
1 tsp yellow mustard

½ cup basil leaves, chopped
Salt and black pepper to taste
2 tbsp cheddar cheese, grated
1 cup marinara sauce

DIRECTIONS (Prep + Cook Time: 25 minutes)

In a bowl, add the ground pork, onion, maple syrup, mustard, basil leaves, salt, pepper, and cheddar cheese; mix well and form small balls. Place in the greased air fryer and AirFry for 12 minutes at 400 F. Slide the basket out and shake the meatballs. Cook further for 5 minutes. Serve with marinara sauce.

Pork Meatball Noodle Bowl

INGREDIENTS (4 Servings)

2 lb ground pork
2 eggs, beaten
1 tbsp cooking oil, for greasing
1cup panko breadcrumbs
1 shallot, chopped
2 tsp soy sauce
2 garlic cloves, minced

½ tsp ground ginger
2 cups rice noodles, cooked
1 gem lettuce, torn
1 carrot, shredded
1 cucumber, peeled, thinly sliced
1 cup Asian sesame dressing
1 lime, cut into wedges

DIRECTIONS (Prep + Cook Time: 30 minutes)

Preheat the air fryer to 390 F. Mix the ground pork, eggs, breadcrumbs, shallot, soy sauce, garlic, and ginger in a mixing bowl. Divide the mixture into 24 balls. Place them into the greased frying basket.

AirFry for 12-15 minutes, shaking the basket every 5 minutes to ensure even cooking. Cook until the meatballs are golden brown. Divide the rice noodles, lettuce, carrot, and cucumber between 4 bowls. Top with meatballs and drizzle with the sesame dressing. Serve with lime wedges and enjoy.

Traditional Swedish Meatballs

INGREDIENTS (4 Servings)

1 lb ground pork
1 tbsp fresh dill, chopped
½ tsp nutmeg
⅓ cup seasoned breadcrumbs
1 egg, beaten

Salt and white pepper to taste
2 tbsp butter
⅓ cup sour cream
2 tbsp flour

DIRECTIONS (Prep + Cook Time: 25 minutes)

Preheat the air fryer to 360 F. In a bowl, combine the ground pork, dill, nutmeg, breadcrumbs, egg, salt, and pepper and mix well. Shape the mixture into small balls. AirFry them in the greased frying basket for 12-14 minutes, flipping once.

Meanwhile, melt butter in a saucepan over medium heat and stir in the flour until lightly browned, about 2 minutes. Gradually pour 1 cup of water and whisk until the sauce thickens. Stir in sour cream and cook for 1 minute. Pour the sauce over the meatballs to serve.

Best Ever Pork Burgers

INGREDIENTS (2 Servings)

½ lb ground pork
½ medium onion, chopped
½ tsp herbs de Provence
½ tsp garlic powder
Assembling
½ red onion, sliced in 2-inch rings
1 large tomato, sliced in 2-inch rings

½ tsp dried basil
½ tsp mustard
Salt and black pepper to taste
2 bread buns, halved

½ lettuce leaves, torn
4 slices cheddar cheese

DIRECTIONS (Prep + Cook Time: 30 minutes)

In a bowl, combine the ground pork, onion, herbs de Provence, garlic powder, basil, mustard, salt, and pepper and mix evenly. Form 2 patties out of the mixture and place on a flat plate.

Preheat the air fryer to 370 F. Place the pork patties in the greased frying basket and Bake for 10-12 minutes. Slid the basket out and turn the patties. Continue cooking for 5 more minutes. Lay lettuce on bun bottoms, add the patties, followed by a slice of onion, tomato, and cheddar cheese, and cover with the bun tops. Serve with ketchup and french fries if desired.

Pork & Pear Blue Cheese Patties

INGREDIENTS (2 Servings)

½ lb ground pork
1 pear, peeled and grated
1 cup breadcrumbs

2 oz blue cheese, crumbled
½ tsp ground cumin
Salt and black pepper to taste

DIRECTIONS (Prep + Cook Time: 20 minutes)

In a bowl, add the ground pork, pear, breadcrumbs, cumin, blue cheese, salt, and black pepper, and mix with your hands. Shape into 2 even-sized burger patties. Arrange the patties on the greased frying basket and AirFry for 12-14 minutes at 380 F, turning once halfway through. Serve warm.

Serbian Pork Skewers with Yogurt Sauce

INGREDIENTS (4 Servings)

1 lb pork sausage meat
Salt and black pepper to taste
1 onion, chopped
½ tsp garlic puree

1 tsp ground cumin
1 cup Greek yogurt
2 tbsp walnuts, finely chopped
1 tbsp fresh dill, chopped

DIRECTIONS (Prep + Cook Time: 25 minutes)

Preheat the air fryer to 340 F. In a bowl, mix the sausage meat, onion, garlic puree, ground cumin, salt, and pepper. Knead until everything is well incorporated. Form patties out the mixture, about ½ inch thick, and thread them onto flat skewers. Lay them on the greased frying basket.

AirFry for 14-16 minutes, turning them over once or twice until golden. Whisk the yogurt, walnuts, garlic, dill, and salt in a small bowl to obtain a sauce. Serve the skewers with the yogurt sauce.

Italian Fennel & Pork Balls

INGREDIENTS (4 Servings)

1 lb pork sausage meat
1 whole egg, beaten
1 onion, chopped
2 tbsp fresh sage, chopped

2 tbsp ground almonds
¼ head fennel bulb, chopped
1 cup passata di pomodoro (tomato sauce)
Salt and black pepper to taste

DIRECTIONS (Prep + Cook Time: 30 minutes)

Preheat the air fryer to 350 F. In a bowl, place the sausage meat, onion, almonds, fennel, egg, salt, and pepper. Mix with hands until well combined. Shape the mixture into balls. Add them to the greased frying basket and Bake for 14-16 minutes, shaking once. Top with sage and serve with passata sauce.

Mediterranean Pork Kabobs

INGREDIENTS (4 Servings)

1 lb pork tenderloin, cubed
Salt and black pepper to taste
1 green bell pepper, cut into chunks
8 pearl onions, halved

½ tsp Italian seasoning mix
½ tsp smoked paprika
1 zucchini, cut into chunks

DIRECTIONS (Prep + Cook Time: 30 minutes)

Preheat the air fryer to 350 F. In a bowl, mix the pork, paprika, salt, and pepper. Thread alternating the vegetables and the pork cubes onto bamboo skewers. Spray with cooking spray and transfer to the frying basket. Bake for 15-18 minutes, flipping once halfway through. Serve sprinkled with Italian mix.

Sausage Sticks Rolled in Bacon

INGREDIENTS (4 Servings)

Sausage:
8 bacon strips

8 pork sausages

Relish:
8 large tomatoes, chopped

Salt and black pepper to taste

1 clove garlic, peeled

2 tbsp sugar

1 small onion, peeled

1 tsp smoked paprika

3 tbsp fresh parsley, chopped

1 tbsp white wine vinegar

DIRECTIONS (Prep + Cook Time: 40 minutes + chilling time)

Pulse the tomatoes, garlic, and onion in a food processor until the mixture is pulpy. Transfer to a saucepan over medium heat and add vinegar, salt, and pepper; simmer for 10 minutes. Stir in the smoked paprika, parsley, and sugar and cook for 10 more minutes until it thickens. Let cool for 1 hour.

Neatly wrap each sausage in a bacon strip and stick in a bamboo skewer at the end of the sausage to secure the bacon ends. Place in a greased frying basket and AirFry for 12-14 minutes at 350 F, turning once halfway through. Serve the sausages with the cooled relish.

Veggies & Pork Pinchos

INGREDIENTS (4 Servings)

1 lb pork tenderloin, cubed

1 tsp ground fennel seeds

2 tbsp olive oil

½ tsp ground cumin

1 lime, juiced and zested

Salt and white pepper to taste

2 cloves garlic, minced

1 red pepper, cut into chunks

1 tsp chili powder

½ cup mushrooms, quartered

DIRECTIONS (Prep + Cook Time: 25 minutes+ marinating time)

In a bowl, mix half of the olive oil, lime zest and juice, garlic, chili, ground fennel, cumin, salt, and white pepper. Add in the pork and stir to coat. Cover with cling film and place in the fridge for 1 hour.

Preheat the air fryer to 380 F. Season the mushrooms and red pepper with salt and black pepper and drizzle with the remaining olive oil. Thread alternating the pork, mushroom and red pepper pieces onto short skewers. Place in the greased frying basket and AirFry for 15 minutes, turning once. Serve hot.

Spicy Tricolor Pork Kebabs

INGREDIENTS (4 Servings)

1 lb pork steak, cut into cubes

1 tsp garlic salt

¼ cup soy sauce

1 tsp red chili flakes

2 tsp smoked paprika

1 tbsp white wine vinegar

1 tsp chili powder

3 tbsp steak sauce

Skewing:
1 green pepper, cut into cubes

1 green squash, seeded and cut into cubes

1 red pepper, cut into cubes

Salt and black pepper to taste

1 yellow squash, seeded and cut into cubes

A bunch of skewers

DIRECTIONS (Prep + Cook Time: 25 minutes + marinating time)

In a mixing bowl, add the pork cubes, soy sauce, smoked paprika, chili powder, garlic salt, red chili flakes, wine vinegar, and steak sauce. Mix with a spoon and marinate for 1 hour in the fridge.

Preheat the air fryer to 370 F. On each skewer, stick the pork cubes and vegetables alternating them. Arrange the skewers on the greased frying basket and Bake them for 12-14 minutes, flipping once.

Sweet Pork Tenderloin

INGREDIENTS (4 Servings)

1 lb pork tenderloin, sliced
2 tbsp quince preserve
1 orange, juiced and zested

2 tbsp olive oil
1 tbsp soy sauce
Salt and black pepper to taste

DIRECTIONS (Prep + Cook Time: 30 minutes)

Brush the sliced tenderloin with 1 tbsp of olive oil and season with salt and black pepper. Put them into the greased frying basket and Bake for 13-15 minutes at 380 F, turning once halfway through.

Heat the remaining olive oil in a skillet over low heat and add in orange juice, soy sauce, orange zest, and quince preserve. Simmer until the sauce thickens slightly, about 2-3 minutes. Season to taste. Arrange the sliced pork on a platter and pour the quince sauce over. Serve immediately.

Stuffed Pork Tenderloin

INGREDIENTS (4 Servings)

16 bacon slices
1 lb pork tenderloin, butterflied
Salt and black pepper to taste
1 cup spinach
3 oz cream cheese

1 small onion, sliced
1 tbsp olive oil
1 clove garlic, minced
½ tsp dried thyme
½ tsp dried rosemary

DIRECTIONS (Prep + Cook Time: 45 minutes)

Place the tenderloin on a chopping board, cover it with a plastic wrap and pound it using a kitchen hammer to a 2-inches flat and square piece. Trim the uneven sides with a knife to have a perfect square; transfer to a plate. On the same chopping board, place and weave the bacon slices into a square the size of the pork. Place the pork on the bacon weave and set aside.

Heat olive oil in a skillet over medium heat and sauté onion and garlic until transparent, 3 minutes. Add in the spinach, rosemary, thyme, salt, and pepper and cook until the spinach wilts. Stir in the cream cheese until the mixture is even. Turn the heat off. Preheat the air fryer to 360 F.

Spread the spinach mixture onto the pork loin. Roll up the bacon and the pork over the spinach stuffing. Secure the ends with toothpicks and place in the greased air fryer. Bake for 15 minutes, turn them over, and cook for 5 more minutes or until golden. Let cool slightly before slicing.

Pork Lettuce Cups

INGREDIENTS (4 Servings)

1 tbsp sesame oil
1 lb pork tenderloin, sliced
½ white onion, sliced
2 tbsp sesame seeds, toasted
2 Little Gem lettuces, leaves separated

1 cup radishes, cut into matchsticks
1 tsp red chili flakes
2 tbsp teriyaki sauce
1 tsp honey
Salt and black pepper to taste

DIRECTIONS (Prep + Cook Time: 30 minutes + marinating time)

In a bowl, whisk teriyaki sauce, red chili flakes, honey, sesame oil, salt, and black pepper. Add in the pork and toss to coat. Cover with a lid and leave in the fridge to marinate for 30 minutes.

Preheat the air fryer to 360 F. Remove the pork from the marinade and place it in the greased frying basket, reserving the marinade liquid. AirFry for 11-13 minutes, turning once halfway through.

Arrange the lettuce leaves on a serving platter and divide the pork between them. Top with onion, radishes, and sesame seeds. Drizzle with the reserved marinade and serve.

Sage-Rubbed Pork Tenderloin

INGREDIENTS (4 Servings)

1 lb boneless pork tenderloin
1 tbsp olive oil
1 tbsp lime juice
½ tbsp soy sauce

½ tbsp chili powder
1 garlic clove, minced
2 tbsp fresh sage, minced
½ tsp ground coriander

DIRECTIONS (Prep + Cook Time: 45 minutes + marinating time)

Combine the lime juice, olive oil, soy sauce, chili powder, garlic, sage, and ground coriander in a bowl. Add in the pork and toss to coat. Cover with foil and refrigerate for at least 1 hour.

Preheat the air fryer to 390 F. Remove the pork from the bag, shaking off any extra marinade. Place in the greased frying basket and AirFry for 15 minutes. Flip it over and cook for another 5-7 minutes. Remove and let sit for 10 minutes so before cutting. Serve warm with steamed veggies or rice.

Zesty Breaded Pork Chops

INGREDIENTS (4 Servings)

4 lean pork chops
Salt and black pepper to taste
2 eggs
1 cup breadcrumbs
½ tsp garlic powder

1 tsp paprika
½ tsp dried oregano
½ tsp cayenne pepper
¼ tsp dry mustard
1 lemon, zested

DIRECTIONS (Prep + Cook Time: 30 minutes)

In a bowl, whisk the eggs with 1 tbsp of water. In another bowl, add the breadcrumbs, salt, black pepper, garlic powder, paprika, oregano, cayenne pepper, lemon zest, and dry mustard and mix evenly.

Preheat the air fryer to 380 F. In the egg mixture, dip each pork chop and then dip in the crumb mixture. Place in a greased frying basket and AirFry for 10 minutes. Flip and cook for another 5 minutes or until golden. Remove the chops to a chopping board and let them rest for 3 minutes before slicing.

Hungarian-Style Pork Chops

INGREDIENTS (4 Servings)

1 lb pork chops, boneless
2 tbsp olive oil
2 tsp Hungarian paprika
¼ tsp ground bay leaf
½ tsp dried thyme

1 tsp garlic powder
Salt and black pepper to taste
¼ cup yogurt
2 garlic cloves, minced

DIRECTIONS (Prep + Cook Time: 30 minutes)

Preheat the air fryer to 380 F. Spray the frying basket with non-stick cooking spray. Mix the Hungarian paprika, ground bay leaf, thyme, garlic powder, salt, and black pepper in a bowl. Rub the pork with the mixture, drizzle with some olive oil, and place the chops in the fryer to AirFry for 14-16 minutes, turning once. Mix yogurt with the remaining oil, garlic, and salt. Serve the chops drizzled with the sauce.

Pork Chops with Mustard-Apricot Glaze

INGREDIENTS (4 Servings)

4 pork chops, ½-inch thick
Salt and black pepper to taste
1 tbsp apricot jam

1 ½ tbsp minced, finely chopped
2 tbsp wholegrain mustard

DIRECTIONS (Prep + Cook Time: 25 minutes)

In a bowl, add apricot jam, garlic, mustard, salt, and black pepper; mix well. Add the pork chops and toss to coat. Place the chops in the greased frying basket and Bake for 10 minutes at 350 F. Turn the chops with a spatula and cook further for 6-8 minutes until golden and crispy. Once ready, remove the chops to a serving platter and serve with a side of steamed green veggies if desired.

Southeast-Asian Pork Chops

INGREDIENTS (4 Servings)

4 pork chops
2 garlic cloves, minced
½ tbsp sugar
4 stalks lemongrass, trimmed and chopped
2 shallots, chopped

2 tbsp olive oil
1 ¼ tsp soy sauce
1 ¼ tsp fish sauce
Salt and black pepper to taste

DIRECTIONS (Prep + Cook Time: 25 minutes + marinating time)

In a bowl, add garlic, sugar, lemongrass, shallots, olive oil, soy sauce, fish sauce, salt, and pepper; mix well. Add in the pork chops, coat them with the mixture and marinate for 2 hours in the fridge.

Preheat the air fryer to 400 F. Remove the chops from the marinade and place them in the frying basket. Bake for 14-16 minutes, flipping once, until golden. Serve with sautéed asparagus if desired.

Mexican Pork Chops with Black Beans

INGREDIENTS (4 Servings)

4 pork chops
1 lime, juiced
Salt and black pepper to taste
1 tsp garlic powder
1 tsp onion powder
2 tbsp olive oil
½ cup tomato sauce

1 onion, chopped
3 garlic cloves, minced
½ tsp oregano
1 tsp chipotle chili pepper
1 cup long-grain rice
2 tbsp butter
1 cup canned black beans, drained

DIRECTIONS (Prep + Cook Time: 45 minutes + marinating time)

In a bowl, whisk the onion powder, garlic powder, chipotle pepper, oregano, lime juice, olive oil, salt, and pepper. Coat the pork with the mixture. Cover and place in fridge and marinate for at least 1 hour.

Melt the butter in a saucepan over medium heat. Sauté the onion and garlic for 3 minutes. Stir in the rice for 1 minute and pour in the tomato sauce and 2 cups of water. Season with salt and pepper and bring to a boil. Reduce the heat and simmer for 16 minutes or until the rice is tender. Stir in the beans.

Preheat the air fryer to 350 F. Remove the meat from the marinade and place the chops in the greased air fryer. Bake for 15-18 minutes, flipping once halfway through. Serve with rice and black beans.

Roasted Pork Chops with Mushrooms

INGREDIENTS (4 Servings)

1 lb boneless pork chops
2 carrots, cut into sticks
1 cup mushrooms, sliced
2 tbsp olive oil

2 garlic cloves, minced
1 tsp cayenne pepper
1 tsp dried thyme
Salt and black pepper to taste

DIRECTIONS (Prep + Cook Time: 25 minutes)

Preheat the air fryer to 360 F. Season the chops with cayenne pepper, thyme, salt, and black pepper. In a bowl, combine carrots, garlic, olive oil, mushrooms, and salt. Place the veggies in the greased frying basket, top with the pork chops, and Bake for 15-18 minutes, turning the chops once. Serve hot.

Italian-Style Apple Pork Chops

INGREDIENTS (4 Servings)

1 small onion, sliced
3 tbsp olive oil
2 tbsp apple cider vinegar
½ tsp thyme
¼ tsp brown sugar

1 apple, sliced
½ tsp rosemary
¼ tsp smoked paprika
4 pork chops
Salt and black pepper to taste

DIRECTIONS (Prep + Cook Time: 30 minutes)

Preheat the air fryer to 350. Heat 2 tbsp olive oil in a skillet over medium heat and stir-fry onion, apple slices, 1 tbsp apple cider vinegar, brown sugar, thyme, and rosemary for 4 minutes; set aside.

In a bowl, mix remaining olive oil, remaining vinegar, paprika, salt, and pepper. Add in the chops and toss to coat. Place them in the air fryer and Bake for 10 minutes, flipping once halfway through. When cooked, top with the sautéed apples, return to the fryer, and cook for 5 more minutes. Serve warm.

Sweet French Pork Chops with Blue Cheese

INGREDIENTS (4 Servings)

2 tsp olive oil
1 tsp butter, softened
¼ cup blue cheese, crumbled

2 tbsp hot mango chutney
4 thin-cut pork chops
1 tbsp fresh thyme, chopped

DIRECTIONS (Prep + Cook Time: 30 minutes+ marinating time)

Preheat the air fryer to 390 F. In a bowl, whisk together butter, mango chutney, and blue cheese; set aside. Season the chops with salt and pepper and drizzle with olive oil. Place the chops in the frying basket and AirFry for 14-16 minutes, flipping once. Remove to a plate and spread the blue cheese mixture on each pork chop. Let sit covered with foil for 5 minutes. Sprinkle with fresh thyme and serve.

Spicy-Sweet Pork Chops

INGREDIENTS (4 Servings)

4 thin boneless pork chops
3 tbsp brown sugar
½ tsp cayenne pepper
½ tsp ancho chili powder

½ tsp garlic powder
1 tbsp olive oil
½ cup Cholula hot sauce
Salt and black pepper to taste

DIRECTIONS (Prep + Cook Time: 25 minutes)

Preheat your Air Fryer to 375 F.

To make the marinade, mix brown sugar, olive oil, cayenne pepper, garlic powder, salt, and pepper in a small bowl. Dip each pork chop into the marinade, shaking off, and placing them in the frying basket in a single layer. AirFry for 7 minutes. Slide the basket out, turn the chops, and brush them with marinade. Cook for another 5 to 8 minutes until golden brown. Plate and top with hot sauce to serve.

Juicy Double Cut Pork Chops

INGREDIENTS (4 Servings)

4 pork chops
½ cup green mole sauce
2 tbsp tamarind paste
1 garlic clove, minced
2 tbsp corn syrup

1 tbsp olive oil
2 tbsp molasses
4 tbsp southwest seasoning
2 tbsp ketchup
2 tbsp water

DIRECTIONS (Prep + Cook Time: 25 minutes + marinating time)

In a bowl, mix all ingredients, except for the pork chops and mole sauce. Add in the pork chops and toss to coat. Let them marinate for 30 minutes. Preheat the air fryer to 350 F. Place the chops in the greased frying basket. Bake for 16-18 minutes, turning once. Serve the chops drizzled with mole sauce.

Stuffed Pork Chops

INGREDIENTS (4 Servings)

4 thick pork chops
½ cup mushrooms, sliced
1 shallot, chopped
Salt and black pepper to taste

1 tbsp olive oil
2 tbsp butter
2 garlic cloves, minced
2 tbsp sage, chopped

DIRECTIONS (Prep + Cook Time: 35 minutes)

Melt the butter in a skillet over medium heat. Add and sauté the shallot, garlic, mushrooms, sage, salt, and black pepper for 4-5 minutes until tender. Preheat the air fryer to 350 F.

Cut a pocket into each pork chop to create a cavity. Fill the chops with the mushroom mixture and secure with toothpicks. Season the stuffed chops with salt and pepper and brush with olive oil. Place them in the frying basket and Bake for 18-20 minutes, turning once. Remove the toothpicks and serve.

Pork Escalopes with Beet & Cabbage Salad

INGREDIENTS (4 Servings)

2 eggs, beaten
4 boneless pork chops
1 tbsp olive oil
½ cup panko breadcrumbs
½ tsp garlic powder

Salt and black pepper to taste
1 cup white cabbage, shredded
1 red beet, grated
1 apple, sliced into matchsticks
2 tbsp Italian dressing

DIRECTIONS (Prep + Cook Time: 35 minutes)

In a mixing bowl, combine the cabbage, beet, and apple. Pour the Italian dressing all over and toss to coat. Keep in the fridge until ready to use. Preheat the air fryer to 390 F.

Divide the pork chops between two sheets of plastic wrap. Pound with a meat mallet or rolling pin until thin, about ¼ inch in thickness. In a shallow bowl, combine the breadcrumbs and garlic powder. In a second shallow bowl, whisk the eggs with salt and black pepper. First, coat the pork chop in the egg mixture. Shake off, dredge in the breadcrumbs. Lay the chops in a single layer in the greased frying basket, spray them with a little bit of olive oil, and AirFry for 8 minutes. Turn the chops over, spray again with some oil, and cook for another 4-7 minutes. Serve with the beet-cabbage salad.

Bavarian-Style Crispy Pork Schnitzel

INGREDIENTS (4 Servings)

4 pork chops, center-cut
1 egg, beaten
1 tsp chili powder
2 tbsp flour

2 tbsp sour cream
Salt and black pepper to taste
½ cup breadcrumbs
2 tbsp olive oil

DIRECTIONS (Prep + Cook Time: 25 minutes)

Preheat the air fryer to 380 F. Using a meat tenderizer, pound the chops until ¼-inch thickness. Whisk the egg and sour cream in a bowl. Mix the breadcrumbs with chili powder, salt, and pepper in another bowl. Coat the chops with flour, then egg mixture, and finally in breadcrumbs. Brush with olive oil and arrange them on the frying basket. AirFry for 13-15 minutes, turning once until golden brown. Serve.

Italian Pork Scallopini

INGREDIENTS (4 Servings)

4 pork loin thin steaks
Salt and black pepper to taste

¼ cup Parmesan cheese, grated
2 tbsp Italian breadcrumbs

DIRECTIONS (Prep + Cook Time: 20 minutes)

Preheat the air fryer to 390 F. Spritz the frying basket with cooking spray.

In a bowl, mix Italian breadcrumbs and Parmesan cheese. Season the pork steaks with salt and black pepper. Roll them in the breadcrumb mixture and spray them with cooking spray. Transfer to the frying basket and AirFry for 14-16 minutes, turning once halfway through. Serve immediately.

Provençal Pork Medallions

INGREDIENTS (4 Servings)

1 lb pork medallions
1 tbsp olive oil
1 tbsp herbs de Provence

½ cup dry white wine
½ lemon, juiced and zested
Salt and black pepper to taste

DIRECTIONS (Prep + Cook Time: 30 minutes + marinating time)

Preheat the air fryer to 360 F. Season the pork medallions with salt and black pepper and drizzle with olive oil. Place them in the frying basket and AirFry for 12-14 minutes, flipping once.

Place a saucepan over medium heat and add white wine and 2 tbsp of water; bring to a boil. Reduce the heat and add in the lemon zest and juice and herbs de Provence; season with salt and pepper. Simmer until the sauce thickens, about 2-3 minutes. Pour the sauce over the medallions and serve.

Thyme Pork Escalopes

INGREDIENTS (4 Servings)

4 pork loin steaks
2 tbsp olive oil
Salt and black pepper to taste

2 eggs
1 cup breadcrumbs
1 tbsp fresh thyme, chopped

DIRECTIONS (Prep + Cook Time: 30 minutes + marinating time)

In a bowl, mix olive oil, salt, and pepper to form a marinade. Place the pork in the marinade and let sit for 15 minutes. Preheat the fryer to 400 F. Beat the eggs in a separate bowl and add the breadcrumbs to a plate. Dip the meat into the eggs and then roll in the crumbs. Place the steaks in the greased frying basket and Bake for 16-18 minutes, shaking every 5 minutes. Sprinkle with thyme to serve.

Pork Belly the Philippine Style

INGREDIENTS (4 Servings)

2 lb pork belly, cut in half, blanched
1 bay leaf, crushed
2 tbsp soy sauce
3 garlic cloves, minced

1 tbsp peppercorns
1 tbsp peanut oil
½ tsp salt

DIRECTIONS (Prep + Cook Time: 50 minutes + marinating time)

Take a mortar and pestle and place in the bay leaf, garlic, salt, peppercorns, and peanut oil. Smash until paste-like consistency forms. Whisk the paste with soy sauce. Pierce the belly skin with a fork.

Rub the mixture onto the meat, wrap the pork with a plastic foil and refrigerate for 2 hours. Preheat the fryer to 350 F and grease the basket. AirFry the pork for 30 minutes, flipping once halfway through.

Pork Sandwiches with Bacon & Cheddar

INGREDIENTS (2 Servings)

½ lb pork steak
1 tsp steak seasoning
Salt and black pepper to taste
5 thick bacon slices

½ cup cheddar cheese, grated
½ tbsp Worcestershire sauce
2 burger buns, halved

DIRECTIONS (Prep + Cook Time: 40 minutes)

Preheat the air fryer to 400 F. Season the pork steak with black pepper, salt, and steak seasoning. Place in the greased frying basket and Bake for 20 minutes, turning at the 14-minute mark.

Remove the steak to a chopping board, let cool slightly, and using two forks, shred into small pieces. Place the bacon in the frying basket and AirFry at 370 F for 5-8 minutes. Chop the bacon and transfer to a bowl. Mix in the pulled pork, Worcestershire sauce, and cheddar cheese. Adjust the seasoning and spoon the mixture into the halved buns. Serve and enjoy.

Herbed Pork Belly

INGREDIENTS (4 Servings)

1 ½ lb pork belly, boiled
½ tsp garlic powder
½ tsp coriander powder
Salt and black pepper to taste

½ tsp dried thyme
½ tsp dried oregano
½ tsp cumin powder
1 lemon, halved

DIRECTIONS (Prep + Cook Time: 45 minutes)

In a bowl, add the garlic powder, coriander powder, salt, black pepper, thyme, oregano, and cumin powder. Poke holes all around the belly using a fork. Smear the herbs, rub thoroughly on all sides of the meat with your hands, and squeeze the lemon juice all over. Let sit for 5 minutes.

Preheat the air fryer to 330 F. Put the pork in the greased frying basket and Bake for 15 minutes. Flip, increase the temperature to 350 F, and cook for 14-16 more minutes. Remove to a chopping board. Let sit for 4-5 minutes before slicing. Serve the pork with sautéed asparagus and hot sauce if desired.

Beef Steak Strips with Tomato Sauce

INGREDIENTS (4 Servings)

1 lb beef steak, cut into strips
1 tbsp olive oil
½ cup flour
½ cup panko breadcrumbs
¼ tsp cayenne pepper
2 eggs, beaten

½ cup milk
Salt and black pepper to taste
1 lb tomatoes, chopped
1 tbsp tomato paste
1 tsp honey
1 tbsp white wine vinegar

DIRECTIONS (Prep + Cook Time: 40 minutes)

Place the tomatoes, tomato paste, honey, and vinegar in a deep skillet over medium heat. Cook for 6-8 minutes, stirring occasionally until the sauce thickens. Set aside to cool. Preheat the air fryer to 390 F.

Spray the frying basket with olive oil. In a shallow bowl, thoroughly combine the flour, salt, black pepper, and cayenne pepper. In a second shallow bowl, whisk the eggs and milk until well combined.

Dredge the steak strips in the flour mixture, then dip in the egg mixture, and finally turn in the breadcrumbs until completely coated. Arrange the strips in a single layer in the frying basket and spray with olive oil. AirFry for 8 minutes. Turn them and spray with a little bit of olive oil. Continue to cook for another 5-7 minutes until golden and crispy. Spoon into paper cones and serve warm with the tomato sauce. Enjoy!

Effortless Beef Short Ribs

INGREDIENTS (4 Servings)

1 ½ lb bone-in beef short ribs
½ cup soy sauce
¼ cup white wine vinegar
1 brown onion, chopped
1 tbsp ginger powder

2 garlic cloves, minced
1 tbsp olive oil
2 tbsp chives, chopped
Salt and black pepper to taste

DIRECTIONS (Prep + Cook Time: 15 minutes + marinating time)

In a shallow bowl, mix the short ribs, soy sauce, wine vinegar, onion, ginger powder, garlic, olive oil, salt, and pepper. Cover and marinate in the fridge for at least 2 hours. Preheat the air fryer to 390 F.

Arrange the ribs on the frying basket and Bake for 12 minutes. Slide the basket out, flip, and cook for another 7-8 minutes until browned and crispy. Serve sprinkled with freshly chopped chives.

Ginger-Garlic Beef Ribs with Hot Sauce

INGREDIENTS (2 Servings)

1 rack rib steak
Salt and white pepper to taste
½ tsp garlic powder

½ tsp red pepper flakes
½ tsp ginger powder
3 tbsp hot sauce

DIRECTIONS (Prep + Cook Time: 25 minutes)

Preheat the air fryer to 360 F. Season the rib rack with salt, garlic powder, ginger powder, white pepper, and red pepper flakes. Place in the greased frying basket and Bake for 10 minutes, turn and cook further for 5-7 minutes. Let sit for 3 minutes before slicing. Drizzle with hot sauce and serve.

Beef Koftas in Tomato Sauce

INGREDIENTS (4 Servings)

1 lb ground beef
1 medium onion, chopped
1 egg
4 tbsp breadcrumbs

1 tbsp fresh parsley, chopped
½ tbsp thyme leaves, chopped
10 oz tomato sauce
Salt and black pepper to taste

DIRECTIONS (Prep + Cook Time: 25 minutes)

Preheat the air fryer to 380 F. Mix all the ingredients, except for the tomato sauce, into a bowl. Shape the mixture into palm sized balls. Place the meatballs in the greased frying basket and AirFry for 12-14 minutes, shaking once. Pour the tomato sauce in a deep saucepan over medium heat and simmer for 2 minutes or until heated through. Add in the meatballs and stir with a wooden spoon to coat. Serve.

Beef Meatballs with Cranberry Sauce

INGREDIENTS (4 Servings)

1 small onion, chopped
1 lb grounded beef
1 tbsp fresh parsley, chopped
½ tbsp fresh thyme leaves, chopped

1 whole egg, beaten
3 tbsp breadcrumbs
Salt and black pepper to taste
1 cup cranberry sauce

DIRECTIONS (Prep + Cook Time: 25 minutes)

Preheat the air fryer to 390 F. In a bowl, mix all the ingredients, except for the cranberry sauce. Roll the mixture into 10-12 balls. Place the balls in the greased frying basket and Bake in the fryer for 8 minutes. Place the cranberry sauce in a saucepan over medium heat and stir for 2-3 minutes until heated through. Pour the sauce over the meatballs and serve.

Greek-Style Beef Meatballs

INGREDIENTS (4 Servings)

1 lb ground beef
2 tbsp olive oil
1 tsp ground cumin
¼ cup Kalamata olives, chopped
1 red onion, chopped

1 garlic clove, minced
1 egg, beaten
1 lb tomatoes, chopped
½ cup feta cheese, crumbled
Salt and black pepper to taste

DIRECTIONS (Prep + Cook Time: 40 minutes)

Preheat the air fryer to 350 F. Mix the ground beef, red onion, garlic, Kalamata olives, and egg in a bowl. Season with cumin, salt, and black pepper. Shape the meat mixture into golf-sized balls. Place them in the greased frying basket and AirFry for 11-13 minutes, shaking once halfway through.

Warm the olive oil in a saucepan over medium heat and add in the tomatoes, salt, and pepper. Bring to a boil and simmer for 8-10 until the sauce starts to thicken. Reduce the heat to low and gently stir in the meatballs; cook for 2 minutes. Transfer to a plate and scatter with the feta cheese all over to serve.

Mexican Beef Cabbage Wraps

INGREDIENTS (4 Servings)

1 lb ground beef
8 savoy cabbage leaves
1 small onion, chopped
1 tsp taco seasoning
1 tbsp cilantro-lime rotel

⅔ cup Mexican cheese, shredded
2 tbsp olive oil
Salt and black pepper to taste
2 garlic cloves, minced
1 tbsp fresh cilantro, chopped

DIRECTIONS (Prep + Cook Time: 30 minutes)

Preheat the air fryer to 400 F. Heat olive oil in a skillet over medium heat and sauté onion and garlic until fragrant, about 3 minutes. Add in the ground beef, salt, black pepper, and taco seasoning. Cook until the beef browns while breaking it with a vessel as it cooks. Add cilantro rotel and stir to combine.

Lay 4 savoy cabbage leaves on a flat surface and scoop ¼ of the beef mixture in the center; sprinkle with Mexican cheese. Wrap diagonally and double wrap with the remaining cabbage leaves.

Arrange the rolls on the greased frying basket and Bake for 8 minutes. Flip the rolls and cook for 5-6 more minutes. Remove to a plate, garnish with cilantro, and let cool before serving.

California-Style Street Beef Taco Rolls

INGREDIENTS (4 Servings)

2 tbsp olive oil
1 lb ground beef
1 onion, chopped
2 garlic cloves, minced
½ tbsp chili powder
2 tbsp creole seasoning

1 (15-oz) can diced tomatoes
4 taco shells
1 cup cheddar cheese, shredded
Salt and black pepper to taste
½ cup Pico de gallo
2 tbsp fresh cilantro, chopped

DIRECTIONS (Prep + Cook Time: 35 minutes)

Heat the olive oil in a pan over medium heat. Sauté garlic and onion for 3 minutes until soft. Add the ground beef and stir-fry for 6 minutes until no longer pink. Season with chili powder, creole seasoning, salt, and pepper. Pour in the tomatoes and stir-fry for another 5-6 minutes. Mix in the cheddar cheese.

Divide the meat mixture between taco shells and roll up them, sealing the edges. Spray each roll with cooking spray and place them in the greased frying basket. Bake for 10-12 minutes at 390 F, turning once halfway through. Garnish with Pico de gallo and fresh cilantro. Serve immediately.

Smoked Beef Burgers with Hoisin Sauce

INGREDIENTS (4 Servings)

1 lb ground beef
Salt and black pepper to taste
¼ tsp liquid smoke
2 tsp onion powder
1 tsp garlic powder
1 ½ tbsp hoisin sauce

4 buns, halved
4 trimmed lettuce leaves
4 tbsp mayonnaise
1 large tomato, sliced
4 cheddar cheese slices

DIRECTIONS (Prep + Cook Time: 30 minutes)

Preheat the air fryer to 370 F. In a bowl, combine the ground beef, salt, pepper, liquid smoke, onion powder, garlic powder, and hoisin sauce and mix with your hands. Form 4 patties out of the mixture.

Place the patties in the greased frying basket, making sure to leave enough space between them. Bake for 10 minutes, turn and cook further for 5-6 minutes until cooked through. Assemble the burgers in the buns with lettuce, mayonnaise, cheddar cheese, tomato slices, and the patties. Serve and enjoy!

South American Arepas with Cilantro Sauce

INGREDIENTS (4 Servings)

1 ½ lb ground beef
1 Fresno chili pepper, chopped
2 tbsp fresh cilantro, chopped
Salt and black pepper to taste

4 cheese arepas (buns), halved
½ red onion, sliced
1 cup mayonnaise
2 tbsp fresh lime juice

DIRECTIONS (Prep + Cook Time: 25 minutes)

In a small bowl, mix the mayonnaise with lime juice and cilantro. Season with salt and set aside.

Preheat the air fryer to 350 F. In a bowl, combine the ground beef, Fresno chili, salt, and black pepper. Mold the mixture into 4 patties. Spray them lightly on both sides with cooking spray and place in the frying basket. AirFry for 8 minutes, flip them, and cook for another 4-6 minutes or until browned and cooked through. Serve on cheese arepas with red onion and cilantro lime mayo sauce.

Healthy Burgers

INGREDIENTS (4 Servings)

1 ½ lb ground beef
½ tsp onion powder
Salt and black pepper to taste
½ tsp dried oregano

1 tbsp Worcestershire sauce
½ tsp garlic powder
1 tsp Maggi seasoning sauce
1 tbsp olive oil

DIRECTIONS (Prep + Cook Time: 25 minutes)

Preheat the air fryer to 350 F. In a bowl, combine Worcestershire and Maggi sauces, onion and garlic powders, oregano, salt, and pepper. Add in the ground beef and mix until well combined. Divide the meat mixture into 4 equal pieces and flatten to form patties. Brush with olive oil and place the patties in the frying basket. AirFry for 14-16 minutes, turning once halfway through. Serve immediately.

Classic Beef Meatloaf

INGREDIENTS (4 Servings)

1 lb ground beef
2 eggs, lightly beaten
½ cup breadcrumbs
2 garlic cloves, minced

1 onion, finely chopped
2 tbsp ketchup
1 tsp mixed dried herbs

DIRECTIONS (Prep + Cook Time: 35 minutes + cooling time)

Line a loaf pan that fits in the air fryer with baking paper. In a bowl, mix ground beef, eggs, breadcrumbs, garlic, onion, and mixed herbs. Gently press the mixture into the pan and top with ketchup. Place in the frying basket and Bake for 25 minutes at 380 F. Let cool for 10-15 minutes before slicing. Serve warm.

"Stefania" Beef Meatloaf

INGREDIENTS (4 Servings)

1 cup tomato basil sauce
1 ½ lb ground beef
1 diced onion
2 garlic cloves, minced
2 tbsp ginger, minced
½ cup breadcrumbs

3 hardboiled eggs, peeled
Salt and black pepper to taste
1 tsp paprika
½ tsp dried basil
2 tbsp fresh parsley, chopped
2 egg whites

DIRECTIONS (Prep + Cook Time: 40 minutes)

Preheat the air fryer to 360 F. In a bowl, add the beef, onion, garlic, ginger, breadcrumbs, paprika, salt, pepper, basil, parsley, and egg whites; mix well. Shape half of the mixture into a long oblong form. Arrange the boiled eggs in a row at the center. Cover the eggs with the remaining meat dough. Scoop the meat mixture into a greased baking pan. Shape the meat into the pan while pressing firmly. Brush the tomato sauce onto the meat. Place the pan in the frying basket and Bake for 25 minutes.

Homemade Hot Beef Satay

INGREDIENTS (4 Servings)

2 lb flank steaks, cut into long strips
2 tbsp fish sauce
2 tbsp soy sauce
2 tbsp sugar
1 ½ tsp garlic powder

1 ½ tsp ground ginger
2 tsp hot sauce
2 tbsp fresh cilantro, chopped
½ cup roasted peanuts, chopped

DIRECTIONS (Prep + Cook Time: 25 minutes)

Preheat the air fryer to 400 F. In a Ziploc bag, add the beef strips, fish sauce, sugar, garlic powder, soy sauce, ginger, and hot sauce. Seal the bag and shake thoroughly.

Open the bag, remove the beef strips, shake off the excess marinade, and place in the frying basket in a single layer. Avoid overlapping. AirFry for 6 minutes, turn the beef, and cook further for 6 minutes. Dish the meat and garnish with roasted peanuts and freshly chopped cilantro.

Argentinian Beef Empanadas

INGREDIENTS (4 Servings)

1 lb ground beef
½ onion, diced
1 garlic clove, minced
¼ cup tomato salsa
4 empanada shells

1 egg yolk
2 tsp milk
½ tsp cumin
Salt and black pepper to taste
2 tbsp olive oil

DIRECTIONS (Prep + Cook Time: 30 minutes)

Heat olive oil in a pan over medium heat and cook the ground beef, onion, cumin, garlic, salt, and black pepper for 5-6 minutes, stirring occasionally. Stir in tomato salsa and cook for 3 minutes; set aside.

Preheat the air fryer to 350 F. In a bowl, whisk the egg yolk with milk. Divide the beef mixture between empanada shells, fold the shells and seal the ends with a fork. Brush with the egg mixture. Place the empanadas in the greased frying basket and AirFry for 10-12 minutes, flipping once. Serve warm.

Mexican Chorizo & Beef Empanadas

INGREDIENTS (4 Servings)

2 garlic cloves, minced
½ cup green bell peppers, chopped
1 red onion, chopped
4 oz chorizo, chopped
½ lb ground beef

4 dough discs
1 cup Mexican blend cheese, shredded
2 tbsp vegetable oil
¼ cup chunky salsa
Salt and black pepper to taste

DIRECTIONS (Prep + Cook Time: 35 minutes)

Warm the vegetable oil in a pan over medium heat and sauté bell peppers, garlic, and onion for 4 minutes until tender. Add the ground beef and chorizo and stir-fry for 5-6 minutes. Season with salt and pepper. Pour in the chunky salsa and cook, stirring occasionally, until the sauce thickens, 5 minutes.

Preheat the air fryer to 390 F. Divide the meat mixture and cheese between the dough discs. Fold them in half over the filling; press and seal the edges with a fork. Spritz with cooking spray and transfer to the air fryer. Bake for 12-15 minutes, turning once until golden. Let cool slightly before serving.

Cheesy Italian Beef Meatloaf

INGREDIENTS (4 Servings)

1 lb ground beef
2 tbsp fresh basil, chopped
1 onion, diced
1 tbsp Worcestershire sauce

2 tbsp tomato paste
Salt and black pepper to taste
1 cup breadcrumbs
3 tbsp mozzarella cheese, grated

DIRECTIONS (Prep + Cook Time: 35 minutes)

Preheat the air fryer to 350 F. In a bowl, add all ingredients except for the cheese. Mix with hands until well combined. Place in a greased baking dish and shape into a loaf. Place in the frying basket and Bake for 15-18 minutes. Top with the cheese 3-4 minutes before it's cooked. Let cool slightly and slice.

Mini Beef Sausage Rolls

INGREDIENTS (4 Servings)

1 lb beef sausage meat
3 green onions, thinly sliced
8 mini puff pastry squares

1 cup flour
1 egg, beaten

DIRECTIONS (Prep + Cook Time: 30 minutes)

Preheat the air fryer to 360 F. Grease the frying basket with cooking spray.

In a bowl, mix the meat with green onions. Lay the pastry squares on a floured surface and divide the sausage mixture at the center of the pastry squares. Brush the edges with some of the beaten egg. Fold the squares and seal them. Transfer to the frying basket and brush the top of the rolls with the remaining egg. AirFry for 18-20 minutes, flipping once, until crisp and golden. Serve warm.

Garlic Steak with Mexican Salsa

INGREDIENTS (4 Servings)

2 rib-eye steaks
1 tbsp olive oil
Garlic salt and black pepper to taste
½ cup heavy cream
1 avocado, roughly chopped
7 oz canned sweetcorn

½ red onion, sliced
10 cherry tomatoes, quartered
2 tbsp fresh cilantro, chopped
1 green chili, minced
1 lime, zested and juiced
½ cup heavy cream

DIRECTIONS (Prep + Cook Time: 25 minutes)

Preheat your air fryer to 390 F. In a bowl, whisk the olive oil, garlic salt, and black pepper. Massage the mixture onto the rib-eye steaks to coat on all sides. Lay the steaks in the greased frying basket and AirFry for 16-18 minutes, turning once halfway through. Remove to a plate.

In a bowl, mix the avocado, corn, cherry tomatoes, red onion, cilantro, chili, lime juice, and lime zest. Season to taste. Serve the steaks with the Mexican salsa and a dollop of heavy cream on the side.

Beef Steak with Mustard Sauce

Ingredients (2 Servings)

2 (8-oz) beef sirloin steaks
Garlic salt and black pepper to taste
1 tbsp olive oil

½ cup sour cream
1 tbsp Dijon mustard
½ lemon, juiced and zested

Directions (Prep + Cook Time: 40 minutes + marinating time)

In a bowl, whisk the olive oil with garlic salt and black pepper. Add in the beef and toss to coat. Cover and let sit for 1 hour at room temperature.

Place a small saucepan over medium heat and add in the sour cream, Dijon mustard, lemon zest, salt, and pepper. Bring to a simmer for 2-3 minutes. Remove and pour in the lemon juice; stir and set aside.

Preheat the air fryer to 380 F. Place the beef in the greased frying basket and AirFry the beef for 6 minutes, turn over, and cook further for 6 minutes or until medium-rare. For well-done, add 1 more minute per side. Spoon the sauce over the beef and serve.

Chipotle Rib-Eye Steak with Avocado Salsa

INGREDIENTS (4 Servings)

1 ½ lb rib-eye steak
2 tsp olive oil
1 tbsp chipotle chili pepper

Salt and black pepper to taste
1 avocado, diced
Juice from ½ lime

DIRECTIONS (Prep + Cook Time: 30 minutes + marinating time)

Place the steak on a chopping board. Drizzle with olive oil and sprinkle with chipotle pepper, salt, and black pepper. Rub the spices onto the meat. Let it sit to incorporate flavors for 30 minutes.

Preheat the air fryer to 400 F. Pull out the frying basket and place the meat inside. Bake for 10 minutes. Turn the steak and continue cooking for 6 minutes. Remove the steak, cover with foil, and let it sit for 5 minutes before slicing. Mash avocado in a bowl and mix with the lime juice. Serve with the sliced beef.

Gorgonzola Rib Eye Steak

INGREDIENTS (4 Servings)

1 ½ lb rib-eye steak
1 tsp garlic powder
1 cup heavy cream
1 cup gorgonzola cheese, crumbled

2 tbsp fresh chives, chopped
2 tbsp olive oil
Salt and black pepper to taste

DIRECTIONS (Prep + Cook Time: 25 minutes)

Preheat the air fryer to 400 F. In a bowl, combine olive oil, garlic powder, salt, and pepper. Rub the steak with the seasoning and place it in the frying basket. Bake for 14-16 minutes, flipping once.

Warm the heavy cream in a skillet over medium heat. Add the gorgonzola cheese and chives; stir until you obtain a smooth sauce, and the cheese is melted, 3 minutes. Drizzle the sauce over the steaks.

Chimichurri New York Steak

INGREDIENTS (4 Servings)

½ cup chimichurri salsa
1 tbsp olive oil
1 ½ lb New York strip steak

1 tbsp smoked paprika
Salt and black pepper to taste
1 jar (16-oz) roasted peppers, sliced

DIRECTIONS (Prep + Cook Time: 25 minutes + cooling time)

Preheat the air fryer to 380 F. Rub the steak with smoked paprika, salt, and black pepper. Drizzle with olive oil and Bake in the air fryer for 12-14 minutes, turning once halfway through. Transfer to a cutting board and let it sit for 5 minutes. Slice, drizzle with chimichurri salsa, and serve with roasted peppers.

Tender Rib Eye Steak

INGREDIENTS (2 Servings)

2 beef rib-eye steaks
1 tbsp balsamic vinegar
½ tbsp Italian seasoning

2 tbsp olive oil
Salt and black pepper to taste

DIRECTIONS (Prep + Cook Time: 25 minutes + marinating time)

In a bowl, combine all ingredients and toss to coat. Refrigerate for 30 minutes. Preheat the air fryer to 360 F. Transfer the beef to the frying basket and Bake for 18-20 minutes, flipping once. Serve hot.

Parsley Crumbed Beef Strips

INGREDIENTS (2 Servings)

2 tbsp vegetable oil
½ tsp fresh parsley, chopped
1 cup breadcrumbs

1 whole egg, whisked
1 thin beef sirloin steak, cut into strips
1 lemon, juiced

DIRECTIONS (Prep + Cook Time: 25 minutes)

Preheat the air fryer to 370 F. In a bowl, add breadcrumbs, parsley, and vegetable oil and stir well to get a loose mixture. Dip the beef in the egg, then coat in the crumbs mixture. Place the strips in the greased frying basket and AirFry for 14-16 minutes, flipping once. Serve with a drizzle of lemon juice.

Pesto Beef Steaks

INGREDIENTS (4 Servings)

4 boneless beef steaks
1 tbsp smoked paprika

Salt and black pepper to taste
4 tbsp pesto sauce

DIRECTIONS (Prep + Cook Time: 25 minutes + marinating time)

Season the steaks with paprika, salt, and black pepper, and let sit for 20 minutes. Preheat the air fryer to 390 F. Place the steaks in the greased frying basket and Bake for 14-16 minutes, flipping once. Remove to a cutting board and let cool slightly before slicing. Top with pesto sauce and serve.

Delicious Beef with Rice & Broccoli

INGREDIENTS (4 Servings)

1 lb beef steak, cut into strips
Salt and black pepper to taste
2 cups cooked rice
1 ½ tbsp soy sauce
2 tsp sesame oil

2 tsp ginger, finely chopped
2 tsp vinegar
1 garlic clove, finely chopped
½ head steamed broccoli, chopped

DIRECTIONS (Prep + Cook Time: 40 minutes)

Season the beef with salt and black pepper. Preheat the air fryer to 400 F and grease the frying basket. Bake the beef for 12-14 minutes, turning once. Remove to a plate and cover with foil to keep it warm.

Warm sesame oil in a skillet over medium heat. Sauté the ginger and garlic for 3 minutes until tender. Add in vinegar, cooked rice, broccoli, garlic, and soy sauce. Stir-fry for 1 minute or until heated through. Serve the strips over a bed of the rice mixture.

French-Style Entrecote with Bordelaise Sauce

INGREDIENTS (2 Servings)

2 beef rib-eye steaks	¼ cup Merlot wine
1 tbsp butter, softened	½ cup beef stock
1 shallot, chopped	Salt and black pepper to taste

DIRECTIONS (Prep + Cook Time: 30 minutes)

Preheat the air fryer to 390 F. Rub the steaks with salt and pepper. Place them in the greased frying basket and Bake for 12-15 minutes, turning once halfway through. Let cool slightly before slicing.

Melt the butter in a saucepan over medium heat and sauté the shallot for 3 minutes. Pour in the wine and stock and simmer until reduced by half. Pour the sauce over the beef and serve with french fries.

Spicy Sweet Beef with Veggie Topping

INGREDIENTS (4 Servings)

2 beef steaks, sliced into thin strips	Juice of 1 lime
2 garlic cloves, minced	Salt and black pepper to taste
2 tsp maple syrup	1 cauliflower, cut into florets
1 tsp oyster sauce	2 carrots, cut into chunks
1 tsp cayenne pepper	1 cup green peas
½ tsp olive oil	

DIRECTIONS (Prep + Cook Time: 20 minutes)

Preheat the air fryer to 400 F. In a bowl, place the beef strips, garlic, maple syrup, oyster sauce, cayenne pepper, olive oil, lime juice, salt, and black pepper; stir to combine. Transfer the mixture to the frying basket. Top with the veggies. Transfer to the fryer and Bake for 12-14 minutes, shaking once.

Sausage-Stuffed Beef Rolls

INGREDIENTS (4 Servings)

½ lb beef sausage, sliced	2 tbsp Worcestershire sauce
1 tbsp olive oil	½ tbsp garlic powder
1 ½ lb sirloin steaks, sliced	½ tbsp onion powder
2 bell peppers, cut into thin strips	Salt and black pepper to taste

DIRECTIONS (Prep + Cook Time: 60 minutes + marinating time)

Pound the steaks very thin using a meat mallet. Mix the Worcestershire sauce, garlic powder, and onion powder in a bowl. Add in the steaks and stir to coat. Cover with foil and refrigerate for at least 30 minutes. While the steaks are marinating, soak 8 toothpicks in water, about 15-20 minutes.

Preheat the air fryer to 390 F. Remove the steaks from the fridge. Place the bell peppers and beef sausage in the middle of the steaks, then sprinkle with salt and black pepper. Roll up the beef tightly and secure using toothpicks. Generously spray the frying basket with olive oil. Place the beef rolls in the frying basket with the toothpick side down; do not overlap. AirFry for 10 minutes. Turn the rolls and cook for another 7-10 minutes or until nice and crispy. Serve warm.

Thai Roasted Beef

INGREDIENTS (4 Servings)

1 lb beef steak, sliced
Salt and black pepper to taste
2 tbsp soy sauce
1 tbsp fresh ginger, minced
2 chilies, seeded and chopped
2 garlic cloves, chopped
1 tsp brown sugar

Juice of 1 lime
2 tbsp mirin
1 tbsp fresh cilantro, chopped
1 tbsp fresh basil, chopped
2 tbsp sesame oil
2 tbsp fish sauce

DIRECTIONS (Prep + Cook Time: 20 minutes + marinating time)

Place all ingredients, except for the beef, in a blender and process until smooth. Transfer to a zipper bag and add in the beef. Seal the bag, shake to combine, and refrigerate for 1 hour.

Preheat the air fryer to 350 F. Place the marinated beef in the greased frying basket and AirFry for 12-14 minutes. Let sit for a couple of minutes before serving.

Bloody Mary Beef Steak with Avocado

INGREDIENTS (4 Servings)

1 ½ lb flank steaks
2 tbsp tomato juice
1 lemon, juiced and zested
2 tbsp vodka

1 tsp Worcestershire sauce
1 tsp hot sauce
Celery salt and black pepper to taste

DIRECTIONS (Prep + Cook Time: 20 minutes + marinating time)

Combine tomato juice, vodka, Worcestershire sauce, hot sauce, lemon juice and zest, celery salt, and black pepper in a bowl. Add in the flank steaks and toss to coat. Marinate for 30 minutes.

Preheat the air fryer to 360 F. Remove the steaks from the marinade and place them in the greased frying basket. Bake for 14-16 minutes, turning once halfway through. Let them cool slightly before serving.

Mexican Beef Quesadillas

INGREDIENTS (4 Servings)

2 tbsp olive oil
8 soft round taco shells
1 lb beef steak, sliced
1 cup mozzarella cheese, grated

½ cup fresh cilantro, chopped
1 jalapeño chili, chopped
1 cup corn kernels, canned
Salt and black pepper to taste

DIRECTIONS (Prep + Cook Time: 30 minutes)

Heat olive oil in a skillet over medium heat. Brown the beef for 6 minutes, stirring occasionally. Place the cooked beef on each taco shell, top with mozzarella cheese, cilantro, jalapeño, corn, salt, and pepper. Fold in half and secure with toothpicks. Arrange the quesadillas in the greased frying basket. Bake in the preheated air fryer for 14-16 minutes at 380 F, turning once halfway through. Serve.

Korean Beef Bulgogi

INGREDIENTS (4 Servings)

1 lb flank steak
2 cups cooked brown rice
2 cups steamed broccoli florets
½ cup soy sauce
1 tbsp gochujang (hot pepper paste)
1 tbsp fresh ginger, grated

2 spring onion, sliced diagonally
2 tbsp brown sugar
2 tbsp red wine vinegar
1 tbsp olive oil
1 tbsp sesame oil
3 tsp slurry (2 tsp cornstarch mixed with 1 tsp water)

DIRECTIONS (Prep + Cook Time: 40 minutes + marinating time)

Slice the flank steak across the grain into about ¼-inch strips. Whisk the soy sauce, gochujang, ginger, brown sugar, vinegar, olive oil, and sesame oil in a large bowl. Add in the beef strips and toss to coat. Cover the bowl with plastic wrap and refrigerate for 1 hour.

Preheat your Air Fryer to 390 F. Remove the steak from the marinade. Set any leftover marinade aside. Put the steak in the greased frying basket in a single layer and AirFry for 10 minutes. Turn the meat pieces over and cook until they reach your desired level of doneness according to the internal temperature. Rare is 120 F, medium-rare is 130 F, the medium is 140 F, and medium well is 150 F.

Put the reserved marinade in a small saucepan over medium heat and bring to a boil. Pour the slurry into the saucepan and simmer until the sauce thickens, about 3 minutes. Add in the meat pieces and stir to coat. Remove from the heat. Divide the brown rice and steamed broccoli between 4 bowls. Top with the meat and sprinkle with spring onions. Serve immediately.

Beef Veggie Mix with Hoisin Sauce

INGREDIENTS (4 Servings)

Hoisin Sauce:
2 tbsp soy sauce
1 tbsp peanut butter
½ tsp sriracha sauce

1 tsp sugar
1 tsp rice vinegar
3 cloves garlic, minced

Beef Veggie Mix:
1 ½ lb beef sirloin steak, cut into strips
1 yellow pepper, cut into strips
1 green pepper, cut into strips
1 white onion, cut into strips
1 red onion, cut into strips
1 lb broccoli, cut into florets

1 tbsp soy sauce
2 tsp sesame oil
1 garlic clove, minced
1 tsp ground ginger
1 tbsp olive oil

DIRECTIONS (Prep + Cook Time: 60 minutes)

Place a pan over low heat and add all hoisin sauce ingredients. Bring to a simmer and cook until reduced, about 3-4 minutes; let cool. To the chilled hoisin sauce, add garlic, sesame oil, soy sauce, ginger, and ½ cup of water; mix well. Stir in the beef, cover, and refrigerate for 20 minutes to marinate.

Preheat the air fryer to 400 F. In the frying basket, combine broccoli, peppers, onions, and olive oil. Place in the fryer and Bake for 10 minutes, shaking once. Transfer to a plate; cover with foil to keep warm.

Remove the meat from the fridge and drain the liquid into a bowl. Add the beef to the heated frying basket. Bake for 10 minutes, shake, and cook for 7 more minutes. Transfer to the veggie plate, season with salt and pepper, and pour the hoisin sauce over. Serve immediately.

Beef Roast with Red Potatoes

INGREDIENTS (4 Servings)

2 tbsp olive oil
1 (2-lb) top round roast beef
Salt and black pepper to taste

½ tsp dried thyme
1 tsp fresh rosemary, chopped
1 lb red potatoes, halved

DIRECTIONS (Prep + Cook Time: 50 minutes)

Preheat the air fryer to 360 F. In a bowl, mix rosemary, salt, pepper, half of the oil, and thyme; rub onto the beef. Place the meat in the frying basket and Bake for 20 minutes. Give the meat a turn and cook for 10-15 more minutes until browned. Remove the meat to a plate and cover with foil to keep warm.

Season the potatoes with the remaining olive oil, salt, and black pepper. Bake in the air fryer for 20-25 minutes at 400 F, shaking the basket occasionally. Slice the beef and serve with potatoes.

Beef Steak Au Poivre

Ingredients (4 Servings)

2 tbsp butter
1 lb beef tenderloin steaks, 1 ½-inch thick
Salt to taste
2 tbsp whole peppercorns, crushed

1 tsp Dijon mustard
1 tsp olive oil
½ cup brandy
1 cup heavy cream

Directions (Prep + Cook Time: 30 minutes + marinating time)

Preheat air fryer to 400 F. Season the beef with salt and coat in the peppercorns. Transfer them to the greased frying basket. Drizzle with olive oil and AirFry the beef for 12-14 minutes, turning once.

Warm butter in a pan over medium heat. Remove the pan, add in the brandy, and shake the pan until it evaporates. Stir in mustard and heavy cream and return to the heat, 3 minutes. Pour over the beef to serve.

Fusion Flank Steak with Mexican Dressing

INGREDIENTS (4 Servings)

2 tbsp sesame oil
5 tbsp tamari sauce
3 tsp honey
1 tbsp grated fresh ginger
2 green onions, minced
2 garlic cloves, minced
¼ tsp crushed red pepper flakes

1 ¼ pounds flank steak
Salt to taste
1 Jalapeño pepper, minced
2 tbsp fresh cilantro, roughly chopped
2 tbsp chives, finely chopped
1 lime, juiced
3 tbsp olive oil

DIRECTIONS (Prep + Cook Time: 25 minutes + marinating time)

In a bowl, combine the jalapeño pepper with the cilantro, chives, lime juice, olive oil, and salt; set aside.

In another shallow bowl, mix the sesame oil, tamari sauce, honey, ginger, green onions, garlic, and pepper flakes. Stir until the honey is dissolved. Put the steak into the bowl and massage the marinade onto the meat to coat well. Cover the bowl with a lid and marinate for 2 hours in the fridge.

Preheat the air fryer to 390 F. Remove the steak from the marinade and place it in the air fryer. Bake for 6 minutes, flip, and cook further until it is done to your preference, 6-8 minutes. Let the steak rest for a few minutes and slice thinly against the grain. Serve topped with the Mexican dressing.

Pesto Beef Rolls with Spinach

INGREDIENTS (4 Servings)

4 beefsteak slices
Salt and black pepper to taste
3 tbsp pesto

4 cheddar cheese slices
¾ cup spinach, chopped
1 bell pepper, seeded and sliced

DIRECTIONS (Prep + Cook Time: 30 minutes)

Preheat the air fryer to 400 F. Spread the steak slices with pesto and top with cheddar cheese, spinach, and bell pepper. Roll the slices up and secure them with toothpicks. Season with salt and pepper. Place the rolls in the greased frying basket and AirFry for 14-16 minutes, turning once halfway through. Serve.

Air Fried Beef with Veggies & Oyster Sauce

INGREDIENTS (4 Servings)

1 lb circular beef steak, cut into strips
½ cauliflower head, cut into florets
2 carrots, sliced into rings
⅓ cup oyster sauce

2 tbsp sesame oil
⅓ cup sherry
1 tsp soy sauce
1 tsp white sugar

1 tsp cornstarch
1 tbsp olive oil

1 garlic clove, minced
2 tbsp pine nuts, toasted

DIRECTIONS (Prep + Cook Time: 25 minutes)

Preheat the air fryer to 390 F. In a bowl, mix all ingredients, except for the beef, cauliflower, and carrots. Add in the beef and stir to coat. Bake in the fryer for 14-16 minutes, shaking once or twice. Blanch the cauliflower and carrots in salted water in a pot over medium heat for 3-4 minutes. Drain and place on a serving plate. Top with pine nuts. When the beef is ready, place it on the side of the veggies and serve.

Beer-Dredged Corned Beef

INGREDIENTS (4 Servings)

2 tbsp olive oil
1 white onion, chopped
2 carrots, julienned

1 (12-15 oz) bottle beer
1 cup chicken broth
1 lb corned beef

DIRECTIONS (Prep + Cook Time: 35 minutes + marinating time)

Preheat the air fryer to 380 F. Cover the beef with beer and let sit for 20 minutes. Heat olive oil in a pot over medium heat and sauté the carrots and onion for 3 minutes. Add in the drained beef and broth and bring to a boil. Then simmer for 5 minutes. Remove the meat with a slotted spoon and place it in the greased frying basket. AirFry for 12 minutes or until nicely browned. Serve with veggies and sauce.

Yummy London Broil with Parsley Butter

INGREDIENTS (4 Servings)

2 London broil steaks, cut into strips
1 tbsp brown sugar
½ tsp onion powder
2 garlic cloves, minced
½ sweet paprika
½ tsp mustard powder

1 tbsp Worcestershire sauce
2 tbsp canola oil
½ lemon, juiced
Salt and black pepper to taste
2 tbsp butter, softened
2 tbsp parsley, chopped

DIRECTIONS (Prep + Cook Time: 30 minutes + marinating time)

In a bowl, mix brown sugar, onion powder, garlic, paprika, mustard powder, Worcestershire sauce, canola oil, lemon juice, salt, and pepper. Add in the steaks and toss to coat. Refrigerate for 1 hour. Preheat the air fryer to 400 F. Place the beef in the greased frying basket and AirFry for 12-15 minutes, shaking once. Mix the butter with parsley, salt, and pepper. Spread on the beef slices and serve hot.

Lamb Meatballs with Roasted Veggie Bake

INGREDIENTS (2 Servings)

½ lb ground lamb
1 shallot, chopped
½ tsp garlic powder
1 egg, beaten
1 potato, chopped
¼ red onion, sliced

1 carrot, sliced diagonally
½ small beetroot, sliced
1 cup cherry tomatoes, halved
2 tbsp olive oil
Salt and black pepper to taste
Parmesan shavings

DIRECTIONS (Prep + Cook Time: 25 minutes)

Preheat the air fryer to 370 F. In a bowl, mix red onion, potato, cherry tomatoes, carrot, beetroot, salt, and olive oil. Transfer to the frying basket and Bake for 10 minutes, shaking once. In another bowl, mix the ground lamb, egg, shallot, garlic powder, salt, and black pepper. Shape the mixture into balls. Place them over the vegetables in the air fryer, and AirFry for 12-14 minutes, flipping once. Remove the dish and top with Parmesan shavings to serve.

Simple Roasted Beef with Herbs

INGREDIENTS (2 Servings)

2 tsp olive oil
1 lb beef roast
½ tsp dried rosemary

½ tsp dried thyme
½ tsp dried oregano
Salt and black pepper to taste

DIRECTIONS (Prep + Cook Time: 35 minutes)

Preheat the air fryer to 400 F. Drizzle olive oil all over the beef and sprinkle with salt, black pepper, and herbs. Massage the meat with your hands. Place in the air fryer and Bake for 15 minutes for medium-rare and 18 minutes for well-done. Check halfway through cooking and flip to ensure it cooks evenly. Remove from the fryer, wrap in foil for 10 minutes, to reabsorb the juices and serve sliced.

Herby Roast Beef

INGREDIENTS (4 Servings)

2 lb beef loin
Salt and black pepper to taste
½ tsp dried thyme
½ tsp dried rosemary

½ tsp dried oregano
½ tsp garlic powder
1 tsp onion powder
2 tbsp olive oil

DIRECTIONS (Prep + Cook Time: 25 minutes)

Preheat the air fryer to 380 F. In a bowl, combine all the ingredients, except for the beef. Rub the mixture onto the meat. Place it in the air fryer and Bake for 8-10 minutes. Turn the meat over and cook for 7-8 more minutes until well roasted. Let cool before slicing. Serve with steamed veggies if desired.

Crunchy Beef Escalopes

INGREDIENTS (4 Servings)

4 beef bottom round steaks, thinly cut
½ cup flour, sifted
2 eggs, beaten
Salt and black pepper to taste

1 cup breadcrumbs
2 tbsp olive oil
2 butter slices

DIRECTIONS (Prep + Cook Time: 25 minutes)

Preheat the air fryer to 360 F. Coat the steaks in the sifted flour and shake off any excess. Dip into the beaten eggs, season with salt and black pepper, and toss into the breadcrumbs to coat well. Brush with olive oil and AirFry for 16 minutes, turning once halfway through. Serve topped with butter slices.

Traditional Lamb Kabobs

INGREDIENTS (4 Servings)

1 ½ lb ground lamb
1 green onion, chopped
2 tbsp mint leaves, chopped
3 garlic cloves, minced
1 tsp paprika
2 tsp coriander seeds
½ tsp cayenne pepper

1 tsp salt
1 tbsp fresh parsley, chopped
1 tsp cumin
½ tsp ground ginger
1 red bell pepper, cut into 2-inch pieces
1 sweet onion, cut into wedges
1 cup whole small mushrooms

DIRECTIONS (Prep + Cook Time: 35 minutes)

Preheat the air fryer to 380 F. Combine all ingredients, except for the bell pepper, sweet onion, and mushrooms, in a bowl. Mix well with your hands until the herbs and spices are evenly distributed. Form the mixture into sausage shapes. Thread the shapes and vegetables onto the skewers, alternately, and place them in the greased frying basket. AirFry for 14-16 minutes, turning once. Serve hot.

Wiener Beef Schnitzel

INGREDIENTS (1 Serving)

1 (½ inch thick) top sirloin steak
1 egg, beaten
2 oz panko breadcrumbs
2 tbsp flour, sifted

Lemon slices
¼ tsp garlic powder
1 parsley butter slice
Salt and black pepper to taste

DIRECTIONS (Prep + Cook Time: 20 minutes)

Preheat the air fryer to 350 F. Combine the breadcrumbs, garlic, salt, and pepper in a bowl. Dredge the steak in the flour, then dip in the egg, and finally toss it into the crumbs mixture. Place in the greased frying basket and AirFry for 12 minutes, turning once. Top with parsley butter and lemon slices.

Beef Liver with Onions

INGREDIENTS (2 Servings)

1 lb beef liver, sliced
2 onions, sliced
1 tbsp black truffle oil

Salt and black pepper to taste
1 garlic clove, minced
1 tbsp fresh parsley, chopped

DIRECTIONS (Prep + Cook Time: 25 minutes)

Preheat the air fryer to 360 F. Season the liver with salt and pepper; brush with the oil. Spread the onion slices on a greased frying basket. Bake in the fryer for 5 minutes. Arrange the liver on top of the onions and Bake further for 12-14 minutes, turning once halfway through cooking. Serve with garlic and parsley.

African Minty Lamb Kofta

INGREDIENTS (4 Servings)

1 lb ground lamb
1 tsp cumin
2 tbsp mint, chopped
1 tsp garlic powder
1 tsp onion powder

1 tbsp ras el hanout
½ tsp dried coriander
4 bamboo skewers
Salt and black pepper to taste

DIRECTIONS (Prep + Cook Time: 25 minutes + marinating time)

In a bowl, mix ground lamb, cumin, garlic and onion powders, mint, ras el hanout, coriander, salt, and black pepper. Mold into sausage shapes and place onto skewers. Let sit for 15 minutes in the fridge.

Preheat the air fryer to 380 F. Grease the frying basket with cooking spray. Arrange the skewers in the basket and AirFry for 10-12 minutes, turning once halfway through. Serve with yogurt dip if desired.

Lamb Chops with Lemony Couscous

INGREDIENTS (4 Servings)

4 lamb chops
2 tbsp olive oil
2 garlic cloves, minced
Salt and black pepper to taste

2 tbsp fresh thyme, chopped
1 cup couscous
1 lemon, zested and juiced

DIRECTIONS (Prep + Cook Time: 25 minutes)

Preheat the air fryer to 400 F. Rub the lamb chops with olive oil, garlic, salt, and black pepper. Place them in the greased frying basket. AirFry for 14-16 minutes, turning once halfway through cooking.

Meanwhile, place the couscous in a heatproof bowl and pour over 1½ cups of salted boiling water. Cover and let it sit for 8-12 minutes until all the water is absorbed. Gently stir in the lemon juice and lemon zest and fresh thyme with a fork. Serve the lamb on a bed of couscous and enjoy!

Easy Lamb Chop Bites

INGREDIENTS (4 Servings)

1 lb lamb loin chops
1 egg
¼ cup buttermilk

1 cup corn flakes, crushed
Salt and black pepper to taste

DIRECTIONS (Prep + Cook Time: 25 minutes)

In a bowl, whisk the egg with buttermilk. Add in the lamb and stir to coat. On a plate, spread the corn flakes and mix them with salt and pepper. Coat the lamb chops in the cornflakes and arrange them on the greased frying basket. AirFry for 12-16 minutes at 360 F, turning once halfway through. Serve.

Sweet & Sour Lamb Strips

INGREDIENTS (4 Servings)

1 cup cornflour
1 tsp garlic powder
1 tsp allspice
For the sauce
6 tbsp ketchup
½ lemon, juiced

Salt and black pepper to taste
2 eggs
1 lb lean lamb, cut into strips

1 tsp honey
2 tbsp soy sauce

DIRECTIONS (Prep + Cook Time: 20 minutes)

Preheat the air fryer to 350 F. In a bowl, whisk all the sauce ingredients with ½ cup of water until smooth; reserve. In another bowl, mix the garlic powder, cornflour, allspice, salt, and black pepper.

In a third bowl, beat the eggs with a pinch of salt. Coat the lamb in the cornflour mixture, then dip in the eggs, then again in the cornflour mixture. Spray with cooking spray and place in the frying basket. AirFry for 14-16 minutes, shaking once halfway through. Serve drizzled with the prepared sauce.

Thyme Lamb Chops with Asparagus

INGREDIENTS (4 Servings)

1 lb lamb chops
2 tbsp olive oil
2 tsp fresh thyme, chopped

1 garlic clove, minced
Salt and black pepper to taste
1 lb asparagus spears, trimmed

DIRECTIONS (Prep + Cook Time: 25 minutes)

Preheat the air fryer to 400 F. Drizzle the asparagus with some olive oil and sprinkle with salt. Season the chops with salt and pepper. Brush with the remaining olive oil and place in the frying basket. AirFry for 10 minutes, turn and add the asparagus. Cook for another 4-6 minutes. Serve topped with thyme.

Lamb Taquitos

INGREDIENTS (4 Servings)

1 lb lamb meat, sliced into strips
2 tbsp olive oil
2 tsp fresh cilantro, chopped

2 tsp fire-roasted green chilies
2 tbsp queso fresco, crumbled
4 corn tortillas

DIRECTIONS (Prep + Cook Time: 25 minutes)

Warm olive oil in a skillet over medium heat and stir-fry the lamb for 5-6 minutes. Remove and stir in green chilies. Preheat the air fryer to 400 F. Divide the mixture between tortillas and roll up them. Spritz with cooking spray and AirFry for 8 minutes, turning once. Top with queso fresco and cilantro to serve.

POULTRY

Spice-Rubbed Jerk Chicken Wings

INGREDIENTS (4 Servings)

2 lb chicken wings
2 tbsp olive oil
3 garlic cloves, minced
1 tbsp chili powder
½ tbsp cinnamon powder
½ tsp allspice
1 habanero pepper, seeded

1 tbsp soy sauce
½ tbsp lemon pepper
¼ cup red wine vinegar
3 tbsp lime juice
½ tbsp ginger, grated
½ tbsp fresh thyme, chopped
⅓ tbsp sugar

DIRECTIONS (Prep + Cook Time: 30 minutes + marinating time)

In a bowl, add olive oil, garlic, chili powder, cinnamon powder, allspice, habanero pepper, soy sauce, lemon pepper, red wine vinegar, lime juice, ginger, thyme, and sugar; mix well. Add the chicken wings to the mixture and toss to coat. Cover and refrigerate for 1 hour.

Preheat the air fryer to 380 F. Remove the chicken from the fridge, drain all the liquid, and pat dry with paper towels. Working in batches, cook the wings in the greased frying basket for 16 minutes in total. Shake once halfway through. Remove to a serving platter and serve with a blue cheese dip if desired.

Sticky Chicken Wings with Coleslaw

INGREDIENTS (2 Servings)

10 chicken wings
2 tbsp hot chili sauce
½ tbsp balsamic vinegar
1 tbsp pomegranate molasses
1 tsp brown sugar
1 tsp tomato paste
Salt and black pepper to taste

4 tbsp mayonnaise
½ cup yogurt
1 tbsp lemon juice
½ white cabbage, shredded
1 carrot, grated
1 green onion, sliced
2 tbsp fresh parsley, chopped

DIRECTIONS (Prep + Cook Time: 30 minutes + marinating time)

Mix hot chili sauce, balsamic vinegar, pomegranate molasses, brown sugar, tomato paste, salt, and pepper in a bowl. Coat the chicken wings with the mixture, cover, and refrigerate for 30 minutes.

In a salad bowl, combine the cabbage, carrot, green onion, and parsley; mix well. In another bowl, whisk the mayonnaise, yogurt, lemon juice, salt, and black pepper. Pour over the coleslaw and mix to combine. Keep in the fridge until ready to use.

Preheat the air fryer to 350 F. Put the chicken wings in the greased frying basket and AirFry for 14-16 minutes, turning once halfway through. Serve with the chilled coleslaw and enjoy!

Sweet Chili & Ginger Chicken Wings

INGREDIENTS (4 Servings)

1 lb chicken wings
1 tsp ginger root powder

1 tbsp tamarind powder
¼ cup sweet chili sauce

DIRECTIONS (Prep + Cook Time: 20 minutes)

Preheat the air fryer to 390 F. Rub the chicken wings with tamarind and ginger root powders. Spray with cooking spray and place in the fryer. AirFry for 6 minutes. Slide the basket out and cover the wings with sweet chili sauce; cook for 6-8 more minutes until nice and crispy. Serve warm.

Crispy Chicken Wings with Buffalo Sauce

INGREDIENTS (4 Servings)

1 lb chicken wings
Salt and white pepper to taste
1 tsp garlic powder
½ tsp chili powder

½ tsp ground nutmeg
2 tbsp butter, melted
½ cup red hot sauce
1 tbsp sugar

DIRECTIONS (Prep + Cook Time: 30 minutes)

Preheat the air fryer to 390 F. In a bowl, add the garlic powder, chili powder, nutmeg, salt, and white pepper. Rub the chicken wings with the mixture and transfer them to the greased frying basket. Brush with some butter and AirFry for 20-22 minutes, flipping once, or until crispy and golden brown. In a bowl, whisk the remaining butter, hot sauce, and sugar. Serve the wings with the sauce.

Italian Parmesan Wings with Herbs

INGREDIENTS (4 Servings)

1 lb chicken wings
¼ cup butter
¼ cup Parmesan cheese, grated
2 cloves garlic, minced

½ tsp dried oregano
½ tsp dried rosemary
Salt and black pepper to taste
¼ tsp paprika

DIRECTIONS (Prep + Cook Time: 30 minutes)

Preheat the air fryer to 370 F. Season the wings with salt and pepper and place them in the greased frying basket. AirFry for 12-14 minutes, flipping once. Remove to a the greased frying basket.

Melt the butter in a skillet over medium heat and cook the garlic for 1 minute. Stir in paprika, oregano, and rosemary for another minute. Spread the mixture over the chicken wings, sprinkle with Parmesan cheese, and Bake in the air fryer for 5 minutes or until the cheese is bubbling. Serve immediately.

Greek-Style Chicken Wings

INGREDIENTS (4 Servings)

1 lb chicken wings
1 tbsp fresh parsley, chopped
Salt and black pepper to taste
1 tbsp cashew butter
1 garlic clove, minced

1 tbsp yogurt
1 tsp honey
½ tbsp vinegar
½ tbsp garlic chili sauce

DIRECTIONS (Prep + Cook Time: 25 minutes)

Preheat the air fryer to 360 F. Season the wings with salt and pepper and spritz with cooking spray. AirFry for 14-16 minutes, shaking once. In a bowl, mix the remaining ingredients. Transfer the wings to the greased frying basket, top with the sauce, and cook in the air fryer for 5 more minutes. Serve.

Hot Chili Chicken Wings

INGREDIENTS (2 Servings)

8 chicken wings
1 cup cornflour
½ cup white wine

1 tsp chili paste
1-inch fresh ginger, grated
1 tbsp olive oil

DIRECTIONS (Prep + Cook Time: 25 minutes + marinating time)

In a bowl, mix wine, chili paste, and ginger. Add in the chicken wings and marinate for 30 minutes. Preheat the air fryer to 360 F. Remove the chicken, drain, and coat in cornflour. Brush with olive oil and place in the frying basket. AirFry for 14-16 minutes, shaking once until crispy. Serve and enjoy!

One-Tray Parmesan Chicken Wings

INGREDIENTS (4 Servings)

8 chicken wings
1 tsp Dijon mustard
Salt and black pepper to taste

2 tbsp olive oil
4 tbsp Parmesan cheese, grated
2 tsp fresh parsley, chopped

DIRECTIONS (Prep + Cook Time: 25 minutes)

Preheat the air fryer to 380 F. Season the wings with salt and pepper. Brush them with mustard. Coat the chicken wings with 2 tbsp of Parmesan cheese, drizzle with olive oil, and place in the greased frying basket. AirFry for 14-16 minutes, turning once. When cooked, sprinkle with the remaining Parmesan cheese and top freshly chopped parsley.

Korean-Style Chicken Wings

INGREDIENTS (4 Servings)

8 chicken wings
2 tbsp sesame oil
1 tbsp honey
3 tbsp light soy sauce

2 crushed garlic clove
1 small knob fresh ginger, grated
2 tbsp black sesame seeds, toasted
1green onion, sliced

DIRECTIONS (Prep + Cook Time: 30 minutes + marinating time)

Add all ingredients to a Ziploc bag, except for the sesame seeds. Seal up and massage the ingredients until the wings are well coated. Let them marinate for 30 minutes in the fridge.

Preheat the air fryer to 400 F. Place the wings in the frying basket and AirFry for 10 minutes, flip, and cook for 8-10 more minutes until golden. Sprinkle with sesame seeds and green onion and serve.

Thai Tom Yum Wings

INGREDIENTS (2 Servings)

8 chicken wings
2 tbsp tom yum paste
1 tbsp water

½ cup flour
2 tbsp cornstarch
½ tbsp baking powder

DIRECTIONS (Prep + Cook Time: 30 minutes + marinating time)

Whisk the tom yum paste and water in a small bowl. Place the wings in a large bowl, pour the tom yum mixture over, and brush to coat well. Cover the bowl with foil and refrigerate for 2 hours.

Preheat the air fryer to 370 F. In a shallow bowl, mix the flour, baking powder, and cornstarch. Dredge the chicken wings in the flour mixture, shaking off, and place them in the greased frying basket. Spritz with cooking spray and AirFry them for 7-8 minutes. Flip and cook for another 5-6 minutes until crispy.

Homemade Chicken Patties

INGREDIENTS (4 Servings)

1 lb ground chicken
½ onion, chopped
2 garlic cloves, chopped
1 egg, beaten
½ cup breadcrumbs

½ tsp cumin
½ tbsp paprika
½ tbsp coriander seeds, crushed
Salt and black pepper to taste

DIRECTIONS (Prep + Cook Time: 25 minutes)

Preheat the air fryer to 360 F. In a bowl, mix the ground chicken, onion, garlic, egg, breadcrumbs, cumin, paprika, coriander seeds, salt, and black pepper. Shape the mixture into 4 patties. Arrange them on the greased frying basket and Bake for 10-12 minutes, turning once halfway through. Serve.

Authentic Mongolian Chicken Wings

INGREDIENTS (4 Servings)

1 lb chicken wings
1 cup flour
1 cup breadcrumbs
2 eggs, beaten
2 tbsp canola oil
Salt and black pepper to taste

2 tbsp sesame seeds
2 tbsp red pepper paste
1 tbsp apple cider vinegar
1 tbsp honey
1 tbsp soy sauce

DIRECTIONS (Prep + Cook Time: 35 minutes)

Preheat the air fryer to 350 F. Separate the chicken wings into winglets and drummettes. In a bowl, mix the canola oil, salt, and black pepper. Coat the chicken with flour, dip in the beaten eggs, and then in the crumbs. Place the chicken in the greased frying basket. AirFry for 14-16 minutes, shaking once.

Whisk the red pepper paste, vinegar, soy sauce, honey, and ¼ cup of water in a saucepan over medium heat. Simmer for 5-7 minutes until the sauce thickens. Pour the sauce over the chicken and sprinkle with sesame seeds. Serve and enjoy!

Chicken Fingers with Red Mayo Dip

INGREDIENTS (4 Servings)

1 lb chicken breasts, cut into finger-sized strips
1 tbsp olive oil
½ tsp paprika
½ tsp garlic powder
½ cup seasoned breadcrumbs
1 tsp dried parsley

Salt and black pepper to taste
½ cup mayonnaise
2 tbsp ketchup
½ tsp garlic powder
½ tsp sweet chili sauce

DIRECTIONS (Prep + Cook Time: 35 minutes)

Preheat the air fryer to 375 F. Add the chicken with salt, black pepper, paprika, and garlic powder in a bowl, mix to coat. Mix the breadcrumbs and parsley in another bowl. Dredge the chicken strips in the crumbs mixture, brush them with olive oil and place them in the fryer. AirFry for 10 minutes.

Shake or toss the strips, spray with olive oil, and cook for 8-10 more minutes or until golden and crisp. In a bowl, whisk the mayonnaise, ketchup, garlic powder, sweet chili sauce, salt, and black pepper. Pour the dip into a serving bowl and serve with the chicken fingers. Enjoy!

Chicken Kebabs with Sriracha Dipping Sauce

INGREDIENTS (4 Servings)

1 lb ground chicken
½ tsp garlic powder
Salt and black pepper to taste
Sauce
½ cup mayonnaise
1 lemon, juiced

1 tbsp fresh oregano
¼ tsp cayenne powder
¼ tsp paprika

2 tsp sriracha sauce
1 tsp ketchup

DIRECTIONS (Prep + Cook Time: 30 minutes)

Preheat the air fryer to 390 F. Place ground chicken, garlic powder, cayenne powder, paprika, oregano, salt, and black pepper in a large bowl. Gently mix with hands until well combined. Form the mixture into cylinder shapes and AirFry them in the greased frying basket for 15 minutes, flipping once, until evenly browned on the outside. Place all the sauce ingredients in a bowl and stir well. Taste and adjust the seasoning. Serve the chicken kebabs with the sauce on the side.

Chicken Meatballs with Farfalle Pasta

INGREDIENTS (6 Servings)

1 ½ lb ground chicken
3 tbsp olive oil
4 oz fresh spinach, chopped
½ cup panko bread crumbs
¼ tsp garlic powder

1 egg, beaten
⅓ cup feta cheese, crumbled
8 oz farfalle pasta, cooked
2 cups marinara sauce
Salt and black pepper to taste

DIRECTIONS (Prep + Cook Time: 30 minutes)

Preheat the air fryer to 360 F. Mix the breadcrumbs, salt, black pepper, and garlic powder in a bowl. Add the egg, ground chicken, spinach, and feta and stir to combine. Shape the mixture into balls.

Arrange them in a single layer in the greased frying basket and spray with the remaining olive oil. AirFry for 7 minutes, flip them, and cook for another 5-8 minutes or until golden. Serve the chicken meatballs on farfalle pasta and spoon over the marinara sauce.

Mexican Jalapeño Quesadillas

INGREDIENTS (4 Servings)

8 tortillas
2 cups Monterey Jack cheese, shredded
½ cup cooked chicken, shredded

1 cup canned fire-roasted jalapeño peppers, chopped
1 beaten egg, to seal tortillas

DIRECTIONS (Prep + Cook Time: 20 minutes)

Preheat the air fryer to 390 F. Divide the chicken, Monterey Jack cheese, and jalapeño peppers between 4 tortillas. Seal the tortillas with the beaten egg. Grease with cooking spray. Bake the quesadillas in the air fryer for 12-14 minutes, turning once halfway through. Work in batches. Serve with green salsa.

Crispy Breaded Chicken Bites

Ingredients (4 Servings)

4 chicken breasts, sliced
1 cup panko breadcrumbs
¼ cup grated Parmesan cheese

2 large eggs
¼ cup flour
½ cup ketchup

Directions (Prep + Cook Time: 20 minutes + marinating time)

Preheat the fryer to 360 F. In a bowl, mix Parmesan with breadcrumbs. Whisk the eggs in another bowl, and pour the flour in a third bowl. Dip the chicken slices into the flour, then into the eggs, and finally roll them in the cheese crumbs; press lightly to coat. Put the chicken in the greased frying basket and spritz with cooking oil. Bake for 14-16 minutes, flipping once until crispy. Serve with ketchup.

Spiced Chicken Tacos

INGREDIENTS (6 Servings)

1 tbsp buffalo sauce
2 cups shredded cooked chicken
6 oz cream cheese, softened
2 oz sharp cheese, grated

1 tbsp olive oil
1 tsp ground cumin
½ tsp smoked paprika
12 flour tortillas

DIRECTIONS (Prep + Cook Time: 20 minutes)

Preheat air fryer to 360 F. Stir the cheeses and Buffalo sauce in a bowl, then add the chicken and stir some more. On a clean workspace, lay the tortillas and spoon 2-3 tablespoons of the chicken mixture at the center of each tortilla. Sprinkle with cumin and paprika. Roll them up and put them in the air fryer, seam side down. Spray each tortilla with olive oil and AirFry for 8-10 minutes or until golden and crisp.

Spanish-Style Crusted Chicken Fingers

INGREDIENTS (2 Servings)

2 chicken breasts, cut into strips
Salt and black pepper to taste
1 tsp garlic powder
3 tbsp cornstarch

4 tbsp breadcrumbs
4 tbsp Manchego cheese, grated
1 egg, beaten

DIRECTIONS (Prep + Cook Time: 25 minutes + marinating time)

Combine salt, garlic, and black pepper in a bowl. Add in the chicken strips and stir to coat. Marinate for 1 hour in the fridge. Mix the breadcrumbs with Manchego cheese in another bowl.

Preheat the air fryer to 350 F. Remove the chicken from the fridge, lightly toss in cornstarch, dip in egg and coat the strips in the cheese mixture. Place them in the greased frying basket and AirFry for 14-16 minutes, shaking once, until nice and crispy. Serve with a side of vegetable fries. Yummy!

Quinoa Chicken Nuggets

INGREDIENTS (4 Servings)

2 chicken breasts, cut into large chunks
½ cup cooked quinoa, cooled
1 cup flour

2 eggs, beaten
½ tsp cayenne pepper
Salt and black pepper to taste

DIRECTIONS (Prep + Cook Time: 25 minutes)

In a bowl, beat the egg with salt and black pepper. Spread the flour on a plate and mix in the cayenne pepper. Coat the chicken in the flour, then dip in the eggs, shake off, and coat in the quinoa. Press firmly so the quinoa sticks on the chunks. Spritz with cooking spray and AirFry the nuggets in the fryer for 14-16 minutes at 360 F, turning once halfway through cooking. Serve hot.

Rice Krispies Chicken Goujons

INGREDIENTS (2 Servings)

2 chicken breasts, cut into strips
Salt and black pepper to taste
½ tsp dried tarragon
½ cup rice Krispies

1 egg, beaten
½ cup plain flour
1 tbsp butter, melted

DIRECTIONS (Prep + Cook Time: 20 minutes)

Preheat the air fryer to 390 F. Line the frying basket with baking paper. Season the chicken with salt and pepper. Roll the strips in flour, then dip in egg, and finally coat in the rice Krispies. Place the strips in the fryer, drizzle with butter, and AirFry for 12-14 minutes, shaking once. Top with tarragon to serve.

San Antonio Taco Chicken Strips

INGREDIENTS (4 Servings)

3 mixed bell peppers, cut into chunks
1 red onion, sliced
1 lb chicken tenderloins, cut into strips

1 tbsp olive oil
2 tbsp cilantro, chopped
1 tbsp taco seasoning

DIRECTIONS (Prep + Cook Time: 25 minutes)

Preheat the air fryer to 375 F. Mix the strips, bell peppers, onion, olive oil, and taco seasoning in a large bowl and stir until the strips are coated. Place the strips and veggies in the greased fryer basket and AirFry for 7 minutes. Shake the basket, and cook for 5-8 more minutes, until the chicken is thoroughly cooked, and the veggies are starting to char. Serve topped with cilantro.

Harissa Chicken Sticks

INGREDIENTS (4 Servings)

4 chicken tenders, cut into strips
½ tsp ground cumin seeds
1 tbsp harissa powder

Salt and black pepper to taste
4 cup panko breadcrumbs
2 large eggs, beaten

DIRECTIONS (Prep + Cook Time: 20 minutes)

Preheat the air fryer to 400 F. In a bowl, mix the breadcrumbs, harissa powder, cumin, salt, and black pepper. Dip the chicken strips in eggs and dredge in the harissa-crumb mixture. Place in the greased frying basket and AirFry for 14-16 minutes, flipping once halfway through. Serve immediately. Yummy!

South Asian Chicken Strips

INGREDIENTS (4 Servings)

1 lb chicken breasts, cut into strips
2 tomatoes, cubed
1 green chili pepper, cut into stripes
½ tsp cumin
2 green onions, sliced

2 tbsp olive oil
1 tbsp yellow mustard
½ tsp ginger powder
2 tbsp fresh cilantro, chopped
Salt and black pepper to taste

DIRECTIONS (Prep + Cook Time: 30 minutes)

Warm the olive oil in a pan over medium heat. Sauté the green onions and chili pepper for 2-3 minutes. Stir in tomatoes, mustard, ginger powder, cumin, cilantro, and salt for 2 minutes; set aside.

Preheat the air fryer to 380 F. Season the chicken with salt and pepper and place the strips in the greased frying basket. AirFry for 14-16 minutes, shaking once. Top with the tomato sauce and serve.

Crunchy Coconut Chicken Dippers

INGREDIENTS (4 Servings)

2 cups coconut flakes
4 chicken breasts, cut into strips
½ cup cornstarch

Salt and black pepper to taste
2 eggs, beaten

DIRECTIONS (Prep + Cook Time: 25 minutes)

Preheat the air fryer to 350 F. Mix salt, pepper, and cornstarch in a bowl. Dip the strips in the cornstarch, then into the eggs, and finally, coat in the coconut flakes. Place the chicken strips in the greased frying basket and AirFry for 14-16 minutes, flipping once until crispy. Serve with berry sauce if desired.

Popcorn Chicken Tenders

INGREDIENTS (4 Servings)

1 lb chicken tenders, cut into strips
½ cup cooked popcorn
½ cup panko breadcrumbs
2 eggs

½ cup cornflour
½ tsp dried oregano
2 tbsp butter, melted
Salt and black pepper to taste

DIRECTIONS (Prep + Cook Time: 25 minutes)

Preheat the air fryer to 400 F. Pulse the popcorn in a blender until crumbs-like texture. In a bowl, combine the cornflour, oregano, salt, and black pepper. In another bowl, beat the eggs with some salt.

In a third bowl, mix the breadcrumbs with the popcorn crumbs. Dip the chicken strips in the cornflour, then in the eggs, and then coat in the crumbs. Place in the greased frying basket. Drizzle with butter and AirFry for 12-14 minutes, shaking once or twice during cooking, until nice and crispy. Serve hot.

Chicken Skewers with Yogurt Dip

INGREDIENTS (4 Servings)

1 lb chicken tenderloins
1 tsp ground ginger
¼ cup soy sauce
1 tbsp white vinegar
1 tbsp honey
1 tbsp toasted sesame oil

1 lime, zested and juiced
2 tsp toasted sesame seeds
4 tbsp Greek yogurt
2 tbsp fresh cilantro, chopped
2 tbsp sweet chili sauce
8 wooden skewer, soaked in water for 30 minutes

DIRECTIONS (Prep + Cook Time: 30 minutes + marinating time)

In a small bowl, combine the Greek yogurt, cilantro, sweet chili sauce, and lime zest. Keep in the fridge until ready to use. Combine the ginger, soy sauce, vinegar, honey, sesame oil, and lime juice in a zip-top bag. Place the chicken in the bag, seal it, and shake to coat. Put it in the fridge for at least 2 hours.

Preheat the air fryer to 380 F. Thread each tenderloin onto a wooden skewer and sprinkle with sesame seeds. Keep the excess marinade. Put the skewers in a single layer in the greased fryer basket and AirFry for 6 minutes, flip the tenderloins, baste with more marinade, and cook for 5-8 more minutes or until golden brown. Serve the skewers with the yogurt dip.

Chicken Pinchos with Salsa Verde

INGREDIENTS (4 Servings)

4 chicken breasts, cut into large cubes
Salt to taste
1 tsp chili powder
1 tbsp maple syrup
½ cup soy sauce
Salsa Verde
1 garlic clove
2 tbsp olive oil
Zest and juice from 1 lime

2 red peppers, cut into sticks
1 green pepper, cut into sticks
8 mushrooms, halved
2 tbsp sesame seeds

¼ cup fresh parsley, chopped
A bunch of skewers

DIRECTIONS (Prep + Cook Time: 35 minutes)

In a bowl, mix chili powder, salt, maple syrup, soy sauce, and sesame seeds and coat in the chicken. Start stacking up the ingredients, alternately, on skewers: red pepper, green pepper, a chicken cube, and a mushroom half until the skewer is fully loaded. Repeat the process for all the ingredients.

Preheat the air fryer to 330 F. Brush the pinchos with the soy sauce mixture and place them into the greased frying basket. AirFry for 20 minutes, flipping once halfway through.

Blend all salsa verde ingredients in a food processor until you obtain a chunky paste. Taste and season with salt. Arrange the pinchos on a platter and serve with the salsa verde

Ranch Cheesy Chicken Tenders

INGREDIENTS (4 Servings)

2 tbsp olive oil
¾ cup breadcrumbs
2 tbsp Ranch dressing spice blend

½ cup Parmesan cheese, grated
2 tbsp cheddar cheese, grated
1 lb chicken tenders

DIRECTIONS (Prep + Cook Time: 30 minutes)

Preheat the air fryer to 390 F. In a bowl, mix Parmesan cheese, cheddar cheese, breadcrumbs, and ranch dressing. Add in the tenders and coat well. Drizzle with olive oil and transfer the tenders in the greased frying basket. AirFry for 8-10 minutes. Toss the tenders and cook for 6-8 minutes until crispy.

Crispy Chicken Tenders with Hot Aioli

INGREDIENTS (4 Servings)

1 lb chicken breasts, cut into strips
4 tbsp olive oil
1 cup breadcrumbs
Salt and black pepper to taste
½ tbsp garlic powder

½ tbsp cayenne pepper
½ cup mayonnaise
2 tbsp lemon juice
½ tbsp ground chili

DIRECTIONS (Prep + Cook Time: 20 minutes)

Preheat the air fryer to 390 F. Mix the crumbs, salt, black pepper, garlic powder, and cayenne pepper in a bowl. Brush the strips with some olive oil. Coat them in the crumbs mixture and arrange them in the greased frying basket in an even layer. AirFry for 12-14 minutes, turning once halfway through. To prepare the hot aioli: add the mayo, lemon juice and ground chili in a small bowl and whisk to combine. Serve with the chicken tenders and enjoy!

Juicy Chicken Fillets with Peppers

INGREDIENTS (2 Servings)

2 chicken fillets, cubed
Salt and black pepper to taste
1 cup flour
2 eggs
½ cup apple cider vinegar
½ tbsp ginger paste
½ tbsp garlic paste

1 tbsp sugar
1 red chili, minced
1 tbsp tomato puree
1 tbsp paprika
4 tbsp water
1 red bell pepper, seeded, cut into strips
1 green bell pepper, seeded, cut into strips

DIRECTIONS (Prep + Cook Time: 35 minutes)

Preheat the air fryer to 350 F. Sift the flour in a bowl and whisk in the eggs, salt, and pepper. Coat the chicken cubes in the flour mixture. Place them in the frying basket. Spray with cooking spray and AirFry for 8 minutes. Shake the basket, and cook for 6-8 more minutes until golden and crispy.

In a bowl, add apple cider vinegar, ginger paste, garlic paste, sugar, red chili, tomato puree, paprika, and water and mix well with a fork. Place a skillet over medium heat and spritz with cooking spray. Stir in the pepper strips and stir-fry until sweaty but still crunchy. Pour the chili mixture over, stir, and simmer for 10 minutes. Serve the chicken drizzled with the pepper-chili sauce.

Effortless Chicken Scallopini

INGREDIENTS (4 Servings)

4 chicken breasts
3 oz breadcrumbs
2 tbsp Parmesan cheese, grated
1 cup + 1 tbsp flour
2 eggs, beaten

2 tbsp fresh dill, chopped
2 tbsp butter
2 tbsp lemon juice
2 tbsp capers
½ cup chicken broth

DIRECTIONS (Prep + Cook Time: 30 minutes)

Preheat the air fryer to 370 F. Place some plastic wrap underneath and on top of the breasts. Using a rolling pin, beat the breasts until they become skinny. In a bowl, mix Parmesan and breadcrumbs. Dip the chicken in the eggs, then in the flour, and finally in the crumbs. AirFry for 14-16 minutes, flipping once.

Melt the butter in a saucepan and stir in 1 tbsp of flour for 1-2 minutes. Pour in the lemon juice and chicken broth and simmer for 2-3 minutes until the sauce thickens. Remove and stir in the capers and dill. Pour the sauce over the chicken and serve.

Balsamic Chicken with Green Beans

INGREDIENTS (4 Servings)

1 lb chicken breasts, sliced
¾ cup balsamic vinegar
1 lb green beans, trimmed

1 garlic clove, minced
1 lb cherry tomatoes, halved
2 tbsp olive oil

DIRECTIONS (Prep + Cook Time: 40 minutes + marinating time)

In a bowl, add ½ cup of balsamic vinegar and the chicken; stir to coat. Refrigerate for at least 1 hour.

Preheat the air fryer to 375 F. Mix the green beans, garlic, cherry tomatoes, and the remaining balsamic vinegar in a bowl and toss to coat. Put the veggies in the greased frying basket and AirFry for 8 minutes. Shake the basket and fry further for 5-7 minutes until the beans are crisp and tender and the tomatoes are soft and slightly charred. Remove and cover with foil to keep warm.

Spray the frying basket with olive oil. Add in the chicken in a single layer and AirFry for 7 minutes. Turn and cook for 5-8 more minutes until golden. Serve the chicken with the veggies.

Cajun Chicken Tenders

INGREDIENTS (4 Servings)

1 lb chicken breasts, sliced
3 eggs
1 cup flour
2 tbsp olive oil

½ tbsp garlic powder
Salt and black pepper to taste
1 tbsp Cajun seasoning
¼ cup milk

DIRECTIONS (Prep + Cook Time: 25 minutes)

Sprinkle the chicken slices with garlic powder and Cajun seasoning. Pour the flour on a plate. In a bowl, whisk the eggs along with milk and olive oil. Season with salt and black pepper.

Preheat the air fryer to 370 F. Dip the chicken slices into the egg mixture, and then coat in the flour. Arrange them on the greased frying basket and AirFry for 12-14 minutes, flipping once until crispy.

Crispy Chicken Tenderloins

INGREDIENTS (4 Servings)

8 chicken tenderloins
2 eggs, beaten

2 tbsp butter, melted
1 cup seasoned breadcrumbs

DIRECTIONS (Prep + Cook Time: 20 minutes)

Preheat the air fryer to 380 F. Dip the chicken in the eggs, then coat in the seasoned crumbs. Drizzle the frying basket with some butter and place in the chicken. Brush it with the remaining butter and AirFry for 14-16 minutes, shaking once halfway through. Serve with your favorite dip.

Almond-Fried Crispy Chicken

INGREDIENTS (4 Servings)

4 chicken breasts, cubed
2 cups almond meal
3 whole eggs

½ cup cornstarch
Salt and black pepper to taste
1 tbsp cayenne pepper

DIRECTIONS (Prep + Cook Time: 25 minutes)

Preheat the air fryer to 350 F. In a bowl, mix the cornstarch, salt, black pepper, and cayenne pepper and toss in the chicken. In another bowl, beat the eggs. In a third bowl, pour the almond meal. Dredge the chicken in the eggs, then in almond meal. AirFry for 14-16 minutes, shaking once or twice. Serve.

Jerusalem Matzah & Chicken Schnitzels

INGREDIENTS (4 Servings)

4 chicken breasts
1 cup panko breadcrumbs
2 tbsp Parmesan cheese, grated

6 sage leaves, chopped
½ cup fine matzah meal
2 beaten eggs

DIRECTIONS (Prep + Cook Time: 25 minutes)

Pound the chicken to ¼-inch thickness using a rolling pin. In a bowl, mix Parmesan cheese, sage, and breadcrumbs. Coat the chicken in matzah meal, dip it in the eggs, then coat in the crumbs' mixture.

Preheat the air fryer to 390 F. Spritz the chicken breasts with cooking spray and AirFry them for 14-16 minutes, turning once halfway through, until golden and crispy. Serve warm.

Chicken Fillets with Sweet Chili Adobo

INGREDIENTS (4 Servings)

2 chicken breasts, halved
Salt and black pepper to taste

¼ cup sweet chili sauce
1 tsp turmeric

DIRECTIONS (Prep + Cook Time: 20 minutes)

Preheat the air fryer to 390 F. In a bowl, place the sweet chili sauce, salt, black pepper, and turmeric; mix well. Lightly brush the chicken with the mixture and place them in the greased frying basket. AirFry for 12-14 minutes, turning once halfway through. Serve with a side of steamed greens if desired.

Chicken Schnitzel with Gypsy Sauce

INGREDIENTS (2 Servings)

2 chicken breasts
2 eggs, beaten
1 cup flour
1 cup breadcrumbs
2 tbsp olive oil

1 onion, sliced
1 cup canned tomatoes, diced
2 green and red bell peppers, sliced
½ cup red wine
1 cup chicken stock

DIRECTIONS (Prep + Cook Time: 25 minutes)

Place the chicken between 2 plastic sheets; flatten out using a rolling pin. Place the eggs, flour, and crumbs in 3 different bowls. Coat the chicken in flour, then in the eggs, and finally in the crumbs.

Preheat the air fryer to 350 F. Place the chicken in the greased frying basket and AirFry for 14-16 minutes, flipping once. Warm the olive oil in a saucepan over medium heat and sauté the onion and peppers until tender, 5 minutes. Pour in the wine to deglaze and add the stock and tomatoes. Bring to a boil and simmer for 6-8 minutes until it thickens slightly. Pour the sauce over the schnitzel and serve.

Gluten-Free Crunchy Chicken

INGREDIENTS (4 Servings)

2 garlic cloves, minced
1 lb chicken breasts, sliced
½ tsp dried thyme
1 cup potato flakes

Salt and black pepper to taste
½ cup cheddar cheese, grated
½ cup mayonnaise
1 lemon, zested

DIRECTIONS (Prep + Cook Time: 30 minutes)

Preheat the air fryer to 350 F. In a bowl, mix the garlic, potato flakes, cheddar cheese, thyme, lemon zest, salt, and pepper. Brush the chicken slices with mayonnaise, then roll in the potato mixture. Place in the greased frying basket and AirFry for 18-20 minutes, flipping once halfway through. Serve warm.

Sweet Curried Chicken Cutlets

INGREDIENTS (4 Servings)

1 lb chicken breasts, halved crosswise
2 tbsp garlic mayonnaise
½ tsp chili powder

½ tsp curry powder
½ tsp brown sugar
2 tbsp soy sauce

DIRECTIONS (Prep + Cook Time: 25 minutes + marinating time)

Put the chicken halves between 2 pieces of plastic wrap and gently pound them to ¼-inch thickness using a rolling pin. In a bowl, mix the chili powder, curry powder, brown sugar, and soy sauce. Add in the chicken and toss to coat. Cover with plastic wrap and refrigerate for 1 hour.

Preheat the air fryer to 350 F. Remove the chicken from the marinade and place it in the greased frying basket. AirFry for 8 minutes, flip, and cook further for 6-8 minutes until crispy. Serve with garlic mayo.

Jamaican Chicken Fajitas

INGREDIENTS (4 Servings)

1 lb chicken tenderloins
1 cup Jamaican jerk seasoning
2 tbsp lime juice
2 tbsp olive oil
4 large tortilla wraps

1 cup julienned carrots
1 cucumber, peeled, sliced
1 cup shredded lettuce
1 cup coleslaw mix
½ cup mango chutney

DIRECTIONS (Prep + Cook Time: 30 minutes + marinating time)

Whisk the olive oil, jerk seasoning, and lime juice in a bowl. Add in the chicken and toss to coat. Put in the fridge for 1 hour. Remove the chicken from the fridge, setting the leftover marinade aside.

Preheat the air fryer to 380 F. Arrange the chicken tenderloins in the greased frying basket in a single layer. AirFry for 8 minutes. Flip them and brush with some more marinade. Fry for 5-7 more minutes.

Divide the coleslaw mix, carrots, cucumber, lettuce, and mango chutney between the tortilla wraps. Add the chicken tenderloins on top and roll the tortillas up. Serve warm or cold and enjoy!

Greek Chicken Gyros

INGREDIENTS (4 Servings)

2 chicken breasts, cut into strips
Salt and black pepper to taste
1 cup flour
1 egg, beaten

½ cup breadcrumbs
4 flatbreads
2 cups white cabbage, shredded
3 tbsp Greek yogurt dressing

DIRECTIONS (Prep + Cook Time: 20 minutes)

Preheat the air fryer to 380 F. Season the chicken with salt and black pepper. Pour the breadcrumbs in one bowl, the flour in another, and the egg in a third bowl. Dredge the strips in flour, then in the egg, and finally in the crumbs. Spray with cooking oil and transfer to the fryer. AirFry for 12-14 minutes, flipping once halfway through. Serve the "pitas" filled with the strips, cabbage, and yogurt dressing.

Swiss-Style Breaded Chicken

INGREDIENTS (4 Servings)

½ cup seasoned breadcrumbs
¼ cup Gruyere cheese, grated
1 lb chicken breasts
½ cup flour

2 eggs, beaten
Salt and black pepper to taste
4 lemon slices

DIRECTIONS (Prep + Cook Time: 20 minutes)

Preheat the air fryer to 370 F. Spray the frying basket with cooking spray.

Mix the breadcrumbs with Gruyere cheese in a bowl, beat the eggs in another bowl, and pour the flour into a third bowl. Toss the chicken in the flour, then in the eggs, and finally in the breadcrumbs mixture.

Place in the frying basket and AirFry for 12-14 minutes. Turn the chicken over at the 6-minute mark. Once golden brown, remove to a plate and serve topped with lemon slices.

Chicken Teriyaki

INGREDIENTS (4 Servings)

1 lb chicken tenderloins
⅓ cup soy sauce
⅓ cup honey
3 tbsp white vinegar
1 ½ tsp dried thyme
½ tsp cayenne pepper

½ tsp ground allspice
2 cups cooked brown rice
2 cups steamed broccoli florets
1 tsp ground black pepper
1 tbsp fresh cilantro, chopped
2 green onions, chopped

DIRECTIONS (Prep + Cook Time: 25 minutes + marinating time)

Mix soy sauce, honey, white vinegar, thyme, black pepper, cayenne pepper, and allspice in a bowl to make a marinade. Toss the tenderloins in the marinade and coat. Cover and refrigerate for 30 minutes.

Preheat the air fryer to 380 F. Remove the chicken from the marinade; keep the marinade for later. Put the chicken in a single layer in the greased frying basket and AirFry for 6 minutes. Turn the chicken and brush with the remaining marinade. Cook for 5-7 more minutes or until crispy. Divide the rice, broccoli, and chicken tenderloins between 4 bowls. Top with cilantro and green onions and serve.

Chicken Breasts with Avocado-Mango Salsa

INGREDIENTS (2 Servings)

½ lb chicken breasts, sliced
2 tbsp olive oil
½ tsp cayenne pepper powder
Salt and black pepper to taste

1 mango, chopped
1 avocado, chopped
1 red pepper, chopped
1 tbsp balsamic vinegar

DIRECTIONS (Prep + Cook Time: 20 minutes + marinating time)

In a bowl, mix the olive oil, cayenne pepper, salt, and black pepper. Add in the breasts, toss to coat, and marinate for 1 hour. Preheat the air fryer to 360 F. Place the chicken in the frying basket and AirFry for 12-14 minutes, flipping once. Meanwhile, mix the avocado, mango, red pepper, balsamic vinegar, and salt in a large bowl. Spoon the salsa over the chicken slices and serve.

Lemony Chicken Breast

INGREDIENTS (2 Servings)

1 chicken breast
2 lemon, juiced and rind reserved
1 tbsp chicken seasoning

1 tbsp garlic puree
Salt and black pepper to taste

DIRECTIONS (Prep + Cook Time: 25 minutes)

Preheat the air fryer to 350 F. Place a silver foil sheet on a flat surface. Add all seasonings along with the lemon rind. Lay the chicken breast onto a chopping board and trim any fat.

Season each side with the seasoning. Place in the silver foil sheet, seal, and flatten with a rolling pin. Place the breast in the frying basket and AirFry for 14-16 minutes, flipping once halfway through.

Prosciutto-Wrapped Chicken Breasts

INGREDIENTS (2 Servings)

2 chicken breasts
1 tbsp olive oil
Salt and black pepper to taste

4 sun-dried tomatoes, sliced
2 brie cheese slices
4 thin prosciutto slices

DIRECTIONS (Prep + Cook Time: 25 minutes)

Preheat the air fryer to 370 F. Put the chicken breasts on a chopping board and cut a small incision deep enough to make stuffing possible. Insert 1 slice of brie cheese and 4-5 tomato slices into each cut.

Lay the prosciutto on the chopping board. Put the chicken on one side and roll the prosciutto over the breast, making sure that both ends of the prosciutto meet under the chicken.

Brush with olive oil and sprinkle with salt and black pepper. Place the chicken in the frying basket and AirFry for 14-16 minutes, turning once halfway through. Slice each chicken breast in half and serve.

French-Style Sweet Chicken Breasts

INGREDIENTS (4 Servings)

1 tsp yellow mustard
1 tbsp apricot jam
2 garlic cloves, minced

Salt and black pepper to taste
1 lb chicken breasts
3 tbsp butter, melted

DIRECTIONS (Prep + Cook Time: 20 minutes)

Preheat the air fryer to 360 F. In a bowl, mix together mustard, butter, garlic, apricot jam, black pepper, and salt. Rub the chicken with the mixture and place them in the greased frying basket. AirFry for 10 minutes, flip, and cook them for 5-6 more minutes or until golden and crispy. Slice before serving.

Creamy Asiago Chicken

INGREDIENTS (4 Servings)

4 chicken breasts, cubed
½ tsp garlic powder
1 cup mayonnaise

½ cup Asiago cheese, grated
Salt and black pepper to taste
2 tbsp fresh basil, chopped

DIRECTIONS (Prep + Cook Time: 25 minutes)

Preheat the air fryer to 380 F. In a bowl, mix Asiago cheese, mayonnaise, garlic powder, black pepper, and salt. Add in the chicken and toss to coat. Place the coated chicken in the greased frying basket. AirFry for 14-16 minutes, shaking once or twice. Serve sprinkled with freshly chopped basil.

Chicken Parmigiana with Fresh Rosemary

INGREDIENTS (4 Servings)

1 lb chicken breasts, halved
1 cup seasoned breadcrumbs
½ cup Parmesan cheese, grated

Salt and black pepper to taste
2 eggs
2 sprigs rosemary, chopped

DIRECTIONS (Prep + Cook Time: 25 minutes)

Preheat the air fryer to 380 F. Put the chicken halves on a clean flat surface and cover with a clingfilm. Gently pound them to become thinner using a rolling pin. Beat the eggs in a bowl and season them with salt and black pepper. In a separate bowl, mix breadcrumbs with Parmesan cheese.

Dip the chicken in the eggs, then in the crumbs and spray with cooking spray. AirFry them for 6 minutes, flip and cook for 5-7 more minutes or until golden and crispy. Sprinkle with rosemary to serve.

Chicken Tikka Masala

INGREDIENTS (4 Servings)

2 chicken breasts, sliced
Salt and black pepper to taste
¼ tsp garlic powder
1 tbsp paprika
½ cup plain yogurt
1 tsp lemon juice
½ tsp ginger powder
1 tsp ground cumin
1 tbsp garam masala
2 cups basmati rice, cooked
2 tbsp fresh cilantro, chopped
1 cup red hot sauce

DIRECTIONS (Prep + Cook Time: 30 minutes + marinating time)

In a bowl, combine garlic powder, paprika, yogurt, lemon juice, ginger powder, cumin, garam masala, salt, and black pepper. Add in the chicken, toss to coat, cover and refrigerate for 1 hour.

Preheat the air fryer to 360 F. Line the frying basket with waxed paper and place in the chicken slices. AirFry them for 14-16 minutes, flipping once halfway through cooking. Remove the chicken to a bowl, and stir in the hot sauce. Sprinkle with fresh cilantro and serve over cooked basmati rice.

Easy Chicken Enchiladas

INGREDIENTS (4 Servings)

1 lb chicken breasts, cut into strips
1 cup mozzarella cheese, grated
½ cup salsa
1 can green chilies, chopped
8 flour tortillas
1 cup enchilada sauce

DIRECTIONS (Prep + Cook Time: 35 minutes)

Preheat the air fryer to 400 F. In a bowl, mix salsa and enchilada sauce. Toss in the chicken cubes to coat. Place the chicken in the greased frying basket and Bake for 14-18 minutes, shaking once.

Remove and divide between the tortillas. Top with mozzarella and green chilies and roll the tortillas up. Place in the greased frying basket and Bake for 8-10 minutes. Serve with guacamole if desired.

Caprese Chicken with Balsamic Sauce

INGREDIENTS (4 Servings)

4 chicken breasts, cubed
6 basil leaves, chopped
¼ cup balsamic vinegar
4 tomato slices
1 tbsp butter, melted
4 fresh mozzarella cheese slices

DIRECTIONS (Prep + Cook Time: 25 minutes + marinating time)

Preheat the air fryer to 400 F. Mix butter and balsamic vinegar and pour it over the chicken in a bowl. Let marinate for 30 minutes. Place the chicken in the greased frying basket and AirFry for 14-16 minutes, shaking once or twice. Serve topped with basil, tomato, and fresh mozzarella slices.

Texas BBQ Chicken Thighs

INGREDIENTS (4 Servings)

8 chicken thighs
Salt and black pepper to taste
2 tsp Texas BBQ Jerky seasoning
1 tbsp olive oil
2 tbsp fresh cilantro, chopped

DIRECTIONS (Prep + Cook Time: 30 minutes)

Preheat the air fryer to 380 F. Grease the frying basket with cooking spray. Drizzle the chicken with olive oil, season with salt and black pepper, and rub with BBQ seasoning. Place in the fryer and AirFry for 14-16 minutes in total, flipping once. Top with fresh cilantro and serve.

Spinach Loaded Chicken Breasts

INGREDIENTS (4 Servings)

1 cup spinach, chopped
4 tbsp cottage cheese, crumbled
2 chicken breasts

2 tbsp Italian seasoning
2 tbsp olive oil

DIRECTIONS (Prep + Cook Time: 25 minutes)

Preheat the air fryer to 390 F. Grease the basket with cooking spray. Mix spinach and cottage cheese in a bowl. Halve the breasts with a knife and flatten them with a meat mallet. Season with Italian seasoning. Divide the spinach/cheese mixture between the chicken pieces.

Roll them up to form cylinders and use toothpicks to secure them. Brush with olive oil and place them in the frying basket. Bake for 7-8 minutes, turn, and cook for 6 minutes or until golden brown. Serve.

Hawaiian-Style Chicken

INGREDIENTS (4 Servings)

4 chicken breasts, cubed
2 tbsp ketchup
½ tbsp ginger, minced
½ cup soy sauce

2 tbsp sherry
1 tbsp sriracha sauce
½ cup pineapple juice
½ cup brown sugar

DIRECTIONS (Prep + Cook Time: 35 minutes + marinating time)

In a bowl, mix ketchup, pineapple juice, brown sugar, soy sauce, sriracha sauce, sherry, and ginger. Add in the chicken and toss to coat. Cover and refrigerate for 8 hours or overnight.

Preheat the air fryer to 360 F. Remove the chicken from the fridge, drain from the marinade and place in the greased frying basket. AirFry for 18-22 minutes, shaking occasionally and brushing with the marinade every 4-5 minutes. Serve the chicken with grilled pineapple slices if desired.

Chicken Breasts "En Papillote"

INGREDIENTS (4 Servings)

1 lb chicken breasts
2 tbsp butter, melted

Salt and black pepper to taste
½ tsp dried marjoram

DIRECTIONS (Prep + Cook Time: 25 minutes)

Preheat the air fryer to 380 F. Place each chicken breast on a 12x12 inches aluminum foil wrap, and season with salt and pepper. Top with marjoram and butter. Wrap the foil around the breasts in a loose way to create a flow of air. Bake the in the fryer for 15 minutes. Unwrap, let cool slightly, and serve.

French-Style Chicken Thighs

INGREDIENTS (4 Servings)

1 tbsp herbs de Provence
1 lb bone-in, skinless chicken thighs
Salt and black pepper to taste
2 garlic cloves, minced

½ cup honey
¼ cup Dijon mustard
2 tbsp butter

DIRECTIONS (Prep + Cook Time: 20 minutes)

Preheat the air fryer to 390 F. In a bowl, mix herbs de Provence, salt, and pepper. Rub onto the chicken thighs. Transfer to the greased frying basket and Bake for 15 minutes, flipping once, until golden.

Meanwhile, melt butter in a saucepan over medium heat. Stir in honey, mustard, and garlic; cook until reduced to a thick consistency, 3 minutes. Serve the chicken drizzled with the honey-mustard sauce.

Air Fried Chicken Bowl with Black Beans

INGREDIENTS (4 Servings)

4 chicken breasts, cubed
1 can sweet corn
1 can black beans, rinsed and drained

1 cup red and green peppers, stripes, cooked
2 tbsp vegetable oil
1 tsp chili powder

DIRECTIONS (Prep + Cook Time: 20 minutes)

Preheat the air fryer to 380 F. Sprinkle the chicken with salt, black pepper, and a bit of oil. Place in the greased frying basket and AirFry for 14-16 minutes until golden and crispy. Meanwhile, in a deep skillet, pour the remaining oil and stir in chili powder, corn, peppers, and beans. Add a little bit of hot water and stir-fry for 3 minutes. Transfer the veggies to a serving platter and top with the fried chicken.

Ham & Cheese Chicken Breasts

INGREDIENTS (4 Servings)

4 chicken breasts
4 ham slices
4 Swiss cheese slices
3 tbsp all-purpose flour
4 tbsp butter

½ tbsp paprika
1 tbsp chicken bouillon granules
¼ cup dry white wine
1 cup heavy cream

DIRECTIONS (Prep + Cook Time: 25 minutes)

Preheat the air fryer to 380 F. Pound the chicken and put a slice of ham and cheese onto each one. Fold the edges over the filling and seal them with toothpicks. In a bowl, combine paprika and flour, and coat in the chicken. Transfer them to the greased frying basket and Bake for 15 minutes, turning once.

In a large skillet over medium heat, melt the butter and add the bouillon granules, wine, and heavy cream. Bring to a boil, reduce the heat to low, and simmer for 5 minutes. Serve the chicken with sauce.

Chicken Cheesy Divan Casserole

INGREDIENTS (4 Servings)

4 chicken breasts
Salt and black pepper to taste
1 cup cheddar cheese, shredded

1 broccoli head, cut into florets
½ cup cream of mushroom soup
½ cup croutons

DIRECTIONS (Prep + Cook Time: 30 minutes)

Preheat the air fryer to 390 F. Rub the chicken breasts with salt and black pepper and place them in the greased frying basket. Bake for 15 minutes, flipping once. Let cool a bit and cut into bite-size pieces.

In a bowl, add chicken pieces, broccoli florets, cheddar cheese, and mushroom soup cream; mix well. Scoop the mixture into a greased baking dish, add the croutons on top and spray with cooking spray. Put the dish in the frying basket and Bake for 8-10 minutes until golden. Serve with rice if desired.

Creamy Onion Chicken

INGREDIENTS (4 Servings)

4 chicken breasts, cubed
1 ½ cups onion soup mix

1 cup mushroom soup
½ cup heavy cream

DIRECTIONS (Prep + Cook Time: 20 minutes + marinating time)

Preheat the fryer to 400 F. Warm the soup, soup mix, and the heavy cream in a pan over low heat for 1 minute. Pour over the chicken in a bowl, and let sit for 25 minutes. Remove the chicken to the greased frying basket and AirFry for 15 minutes, shaking once. Drizzle with the remaining sauce to serve.

Restaurant-Style Chicken with Yogurt Sauce

INGREDIENTS (4 Servings)

½ cup breadcrumbs
2 whole eggs, beaten
½ cup all-purpose flour
Salt and black pepper to taste
2 tbsp olive oil

1 ¼ lb chicken tenders
1 cup Greek yogurt
1 tbsp lemon juice
1 tbsp fresh dill, chopped

DIRECTIONS (Prep + Cook Time: 25 minutes)

Preheat the air fryer to 380 F. Pour the crumbs, eggs, and flour into 3 separate bowls. Season the tenders with salt and pepper and dredge them first in the flour, then in eggs, and finally in the crumbs. AirFry them in the greased frying basket for 10 minutes. Flip and cook for 5 more minutes or until golden. Mix the yogurt with lemon juice, dill, salt, and pepper until smooth. Serve with the tenders.

Sweet Wasabi Chicken

INGREDIENTS (2 Servings)

2 tbsp wasabi
1 tbsp agave syrup
2 tsp black sesame seeds

Salt and black pepper to taste
2 chicken breasts, cut into large chunks

DIRECTIONS (Prep + Cook Time: 25 minutes)

Preheat the air fryer to 380 F. In a bowl, mix all ingredients and season to taste. Rub the mixture onto the chicken and arrange the chunks in a greased frying basket. Bake for 14-16 minutes, turning once.

Tasty Kiev-Style Chicken

INGREDIENTS (4 Servings)

1 lb chicken breasts
4 tbsp butter, softened
1 tbsp fresh dill, chopped
2 garlic cloves, minced
1 tbsp lemon juice

Salt and black pepper to taste
1 cup plain flour
2 eggs, beaten in a bowl
1 cup panko breadcrumbs

DIRECTIONS (Prep + Cook Time: 25 minutes)

Preheat the air fryer to 390 F. In a bowl, mix butter, dill, garlic, lemon juice, salt, and pepper until a smooth paste is formed. Using a sharp knife, make a deep cut of each breast to create a large pocket.

Stuff with the butter mixture and secure with toothpicks. Coat the breasts in the flour, then dip in the eggs, and finally in the breadcrumbs. Place the chicken in the greased frying basket and Bake for 10 minutes. Turn over and cook for 5-7 more minutes or until golden. Serve sliced.

Tropical Coconut Chicken Thighs

INGREDIENTS (4 Servings)

1 tbsp curry powder
4 tbsp mango chutney
Salt and black pepper to taste

¾ cup coconut, shredded
1 lb chicken thighs

DIRECTIONS (Prep + Cook Time: 20 minutes)

Preheat the air fryer to 400 F. In a bowl, mix curry powder, mango chutney, salt, and black pepper. Brush the thighs with the glaze and roll the thighs in the shredded coconut. Bake them in the greased frying basket for 12-14 minutes, turning once, until golden brown. Serve and enjoy!

Rosemary & Oyster Chicken Breasts

INGREDIENTS (2 Servings)

2 chicken breasts
1 tbsp ginger paste
1 tbsp soy sauce
1 tbsp olive oil

1 tbsp oyster sauce
2 fresh rosemary sprigs, chopped
1 tbsp brown sugar
2 lemon wedges

DIRECTIONS (Prep + Cook Time: 25 minutes + marinating time)

Place the ginger paste, soy sauce, and olive oil in a mixing bowl and stir well. Coat in the chicken breasts. Cover the bowl with a lid and refrigerate for 30 minutes.

Preheat the air fryer to 370 F. Transfer the marinated chicken to a baking dish and Bake in the fryer for 6 minutes. Mix oyster sauce, rosemary, and brown sugar in a bowl. Pour the sauce over the chicken. Return to the air fryer and Bake for 8-10 minutes. Remove the rosemary and serve with lemon wedges.

Cheesy Marinara Chicken

INGREDIENTS (2 Servings)

2 chicken fillets, ½-inch thick
2 eggs, beaten
½ cup breadcrumbs
2 tbsp marinara sauce

2 tbsp Grana Padano cheese, grated
2 mozzarella cheese slices
Salt and black pepper to taste

DIRECTIONS (Prep + Cook Time: 20 minutes)

Season the chicken with salt and black pepper. Dip the fillets in the eggs, then in the crumbs, and arrange them in the greased frying basket. AirFry for 7-8 minutes at 400 F. Turn, top with marinara sauce, Grana Padano and mozzarella cheeses, and bake further for 5-6 more minutes. Serve warm.

Garlicky Chicken Cubes On A Green Bed

INGREDIENTS (2 Serving)

1 chicken breast, cut into cubes
2 tbsp olive oil
1 garlic clove, minced
½ cup baby spinach

½ cup romaine lettuce, shredded
3 large kale leaves, chopped
1 tsp balsamic vinegar
Salt and black pepper to taste

DIRECTIONS (Prep + Cook Time: 20 minutes)

Preheat the air fryer to 390 F. In a bowl, add the chicken, 1 tbsp of olive oil, garlic, salt, and pepper; mix well. Pour the mixture into a baking dish that fits in the fryer. Bake for 14 minutes, shaking once. In a bowl, mix the greens, 1 tbsp of olive oil, and vinegar. Place the cooked chicken on top and serve.

Chicken Thighs with Herby Tomatoes

INGREDIENTS (2 Servings)

2 chicken thighs
2 ripe tomatoes, sliced
¼ tsp red pepper flakes
2 cloves garlic, minced

¼ tbsp dried tarragon
¼ tbsp olive oil
Salt and black pepper to taste

DIRECTIONS (Prep + Cook Time: 25 minutes)

Preheat the air fryer to 390 F. Add the tomatoes, red pepper flakes, garlic, tarragon, and olive oil to a bowl. Mix well. Season the chicken with salt and pepper and place the thighs in the greased frying basket. Bake for 8-10 minutes, flipping once. Top with the tomato mixture and Bake for 5 more minutes.

Chicken Thighs with Parmesan Crust

INGREDIENTS (4 Servings)

½ cup Italian breadcrumbs
2 tbsp Parmesan cheese, grated
1 tbsp butter, melted

4 chicken thighs
½ cup marinara sauce
½ cup sharp cheddar cheese, shredded

DIRECTIONS (Prep + Cook Time: 25 minutes)

Preheat the air fryer to 380 F. In a bowl, mix the breadcrumbs with cheddar cheese. Brush the thighs with butter. Dip each thigh into the crumbs mixture. Arrange them in the greased frying basket.

AirFry for 6-7 minutes, flip them over, top with shredded Parmesan cheese, and cook for another 4-6 minutes until crispy. Serve immediately with marinara sauce on the side.

Classic Buttermilk Chicken Thighs

INGREDIENTS (4 Servings)

1 ½ lb chicken thighs
½ tbsp cayenne pepper
Salt and black pepper to taste
1 cup flour

½ tsp paprika
½ tsp baking powder
2 cups buttermilk

DIRECTIONS (Prep + Cook Time: 25 minutes + marinating time)

Place the chicken thighs in a bowl. Stir in cayenne, salt, black pepper, and buttermilk. Refrigerate for 2 hours. Preheat the air fryer to 350 F. In another bowl, mix flour, paprika, salt, and baking powder. Dredge the chicken thighs in the flour and then place them in the greased frying basket. Bake them for 16-18 minutes, flipping once halfway through cooking. Serve hot.

Traditional Chicken Mole

INGREDIENTS (4 Servings)

1 lb chicken thighs, bone-in
Salt and garlic powder to taste
1 cup mole verde, Mexican sauce

2 cups long-grain rice, cooked
2 tbsp pumpkin seeds
2 tbsp fresh cilantro, chopped

DIRECTIONS (Prep + Cook Time: 35 minutes)

Preheat the air fryer to 390 F. Season the chicken thighs with salt and garlic powder and spritz with cooking spray. AirFry them in the greased frying basket for 18-22 minutes, turning once, until golden brown. Pour the mole sauce over and cook until thoroughly warmed, about 3-5 minutes. Sprinkle with pumpkin seeds and cilantro. Serve warm with rice and enjoy!

Chicken Drumsticks with Garlic-Butter Sauce

INGREDIENTS (4 Servings)

1 lb chicken drumsticks, skin removed
2 tbsp canola oil
½ tsp paprika
½ tsp garlic powder
½ tsp onion powder

Salt and black pepper to taste
3 garlic cloves, minced
½ cup butter
1 tbsp fresh lemon juice
2 tbsp fresh parsley, chopped

DIRECTIONS (Prep + Cook Time: 35 minutes + marinating time)

In a resealable bag, mix canola oil, paprika, garlic powder, onion powder, salt, and pepper. Add in the chicken and massage until well-coated. Marinate for 30 minutes. Preheat the air fryer to 380 F. Add the chicken to the greased frying basket and AirFry for 18-22 minutes, turning once halfway through.

Melt the butter in a saucepan over medium heat. Sauté the garlic for 1 minute, stirring constantly or until tender but not burn. Add the lemon juice and salt and stir-fry for 30 more seconds. Remove the butter from the heat and sprinkle with fresh parsley. Pour the sauce over the chicken and serve.

Enchilada Chicken Thighs

INGREDIENTS (4 Servings)

4 chicken thighs, boneless
2 garlic cloves, crushed
1 jalapeño pepper, finely chopped

4 tbsp green enchilada sauce
Salt and black pepper to taste

DIRECTIONS (Prep + Cook Time: 20 minutes)

Preheat the air fryer to 390 F. In a bowl, add the thighs, garlic, jalapeño pepper, enchilada sauce, salt, and pepper and stir to coat. Place the thighs in the greased frying basket in an even layer and AirFry them for 12-14 minutes, turning once, until golden. Serve warm.

Cauli-Oat Crusted Drumsticks

INGREDIENTS (4 Servings)

8 chicken drumsticks
½ tsp dried oregano
½ tsp dried thyme
2 oz oats

10 oz cauliflower florets, steamed
1 egg, beaten
1 tsp ground cayenne pepper
Salt and black pepper to taste

DIRECTIONS (Prep + Cook Time: 30 minutes)

Preheat the air fryer to 350 F. Rub the drumsticks with salt and black pepper. Place all the remaining ingredients, except for the egg, in a food processor. Pulse until smooth. Dip each drumstick in the egg first and then in the oat mixture. AirFry in the greased frying basket for 14-16 minutes, turning once.

Indonesian Sambal Chicken Drumsticks

INGREDIENTS (2 Servings)

2 chicken drumsticks, skin removed
2 tbsp sambal oelek chili paste
2 tsp honey

1 tbsp fish sauce
1 tbsp garlic paste
3 spring onions, finely sliced

DIRECTIONS (Prep + Cook Time: 30 minutes + marinating time)

Put the chicken drumsticks in a resealable bag and add sambal oelek, honey, garlic, and fish sauce; squish the bag until well-coated. Marinate in the fridge for at least 2 hours.

Preheat the air fryer to 400 F. Add the chicken drumsticks to the greased frying basket and Bake for 18-22 minutes, flipping once, until crispy and golden. Scatter with spring onions and serve.

Chicken & Baby Potato Traybake

INGREDIENTS (4 Servings)

1 lb chicken drumsticks, skin on and bone-in
3 shallots, quartered
Salt and black pepper to taste
1 tbsp cayenne pepper

1 lb baby potatoes, halved
½ tsp garlic powder
2 tbsp olive oil
1 cup cherry tomatoes

DIRECTIONS (Prep + Cook Time: 30 minutes)

Preheat the air fryer to 360 F. Place the chicken in a baking tray and add in shallots, potatoes, oil, garlic powder, cayenne, salt, and pepper; toss to coat. Place in the air fryer and Bake for 18-20 minutes, turning once. Slide the basket out and add in the cherry tomatoes. Cook for 5 minutes until charred.

Southern-Style Fried Chicken Drumsticks

INGREDIENTS (4 Servings)

1 lb chicken drumsticks
1 tbsp hot chili sauce
1 cup buttermilk
1 tsp turmeric
1 garlic clove, minced

1 tsp smoked paprika
½ cup flour
½ cup breadcrumbs
Salt and black pepper to taste
1 lemon, cut into wedges

DIRECTIONS (Prep + Cook Time: 40 minutes + marinating time)

In a large bowl, combine the buttermilk, hot sauce, garlic, salt, and black pepper. Add the chicken and toss to coat. Let it marinate in the fridge for at least 2 hours. Preheat the air fryer to 400 F.

Mix the flour, breadcrumbs, turmeric, and paprika into a large plate. Remove the chicken from the marinade and dip the chicken into the flour mixture to coat. Transfer to the greased frying basket. Spray with oil and AirFry for 18-22 minutes, flipping once, until golden brown. Serve with lemon wedges.

Crispy Drumsticks with Blue Cheese Sauce

INGREDIENTS (4 Servings)

Drumsticks:
1 lb drumsticks
3 tbsp butter
1 tsp paprika

¼ cup hot sauce
1 tsp onion powder
1 tsp garlic powder

Blue Cheese Sauce:
½ cup mayonnaise
1 cup blue cheese, crumbled
1 cup sour cream
½ tsp garlic powder
½ tsp onion powder

Salt and black pepper to taste
½ tsp cayenne pepper
1 ½ tsp white wine vinegar
2 tbsp buttermilk
1 ½ tsp Worcestershire sauce

DIRECTIONS (Prep + Cook Time: 35 minutes + marinating time)

Melt the butter in a skillet over medium heat and stir in the remaining drumstick ingredients, except for the drumsticks. Cook the mixture for 5 minutes or until the sauce reduces; then let cool. Place the drumsticks in a bowl, pour the cooled sauce over, and coat well. Refrigerate for 2 hours.

In a jug, add sour cream, blue cheese, mayonnaise, garlic powder, onion powder, buttermilk, cayenne pepper, white wine vinegar, Worcestershire sauce, black pepper, and salt. Using a stick mixer, blend the ingredients until well mixed with no large lumps. Taste and adjust the seasoning if needed.

Preheat the air fryer to 350 F. Remove the drumsticks from the fridge and place them in the greased frying basket. Bake for 14-16 minutes. Turn the drumsticks with tongs every 5 minutes to ensure they cook evenly. Serve with blue cheese sauce and a side of celery sticks.

Peri-Peri Chicken Legs

INGREDIENTS (4 Servings)

1 lb chicken legs
1 cup hot Peri-Peri Sauce
2 tbsp olive oil

1 lemon, cut into wedges
2 tbsp fresh parsley, chopped

DIRECTIONS (Prep + Cook Time: 40 minutes + marinating time)

In a large bowl, coat the chicken legs in Peri-Peri sauce. Cover and marinate in the fridge for 2 hours.

Preheat the air fryer to 360 F. Remove the chicken from the marinade and lay the legs in the greased frying basket. AirFry for 18-22 minutes, turning at least twice while brushing with the marinade. Cook until browned and charred. Sprinkle with fresh parsley and serve with lemon wedges.

Thyme Fried Chicken Legs

INGREDIENTS (4 Servings)

4 chicken legs
½ lemon, juiced
1 tbsp garlic powder

½ tsp dried thyme
⅓ cup olive oil
Salt and black pepper to taste

DIRECTIONS (Prep + Cook Time: 20 minutes)

Preheat the fryer to 350 F. In a bowl, mix olive oil, thyme, garlic, lemon juice, salt, and pepper. Brush the chicken legs with most of the mixture and arrange them in the frying basket. Bake the legs in the air fryer for 8 minutes, flip the legs and brush again. Bake for 6 more minutes or until crispy. Serve.

Thai Chicken Satay

INGREDIENTS (4 Servings)

1 lb chicken drumsticks
2 cloves garlic, minced
2 tbsp sesame oil
½ cup Thai peanut satay sauce

1 lime, zested and juiced
2 tbsp sesame seeds, toasted
4 scallions, chopped
1 red chili, sliced

DIRECTIONS (Prep + Cook Time: 25 minutes + marinating time)

In a bowl, mix the satay sauce, sesame oil, garlic, lime zest, and lime juice. Add in the chicken and toss to coat. Place in the fridge for 2 hours to marinate. Preheat the air fryer to 380 F. Transfer the marinated chicken to the frying basket and AirFry for 18-20 minutes, flipping once halfway through. Garnish with sesame seeds, scallions, and red chili and serve.

Chicken Asian Lollipop

INGREDIENTS (4 Servings)

1 lb mini chicken drumsticks
½ tbsp soy sauce
1 tbsp lime juice
Salt and black pepper to taste
1 tbsp cornstarch
1 garlic clove, minced

½ tbsp chili powder
½ tbsp garlic-ginger paste
1 tbsp plain vinegar
1 egg, beaten
1 tbsp flour
1 tbsp maple syrup

DIRECTIONS (Prep + Cook Time: 25 minutes)

Mix garlic-ginger paste, chili powder, maple syrup, soy sauce, vinegar, egg, garlic, salt, and black pepper in a bowl. Add the chicken and toss to coat. Mix cornstarch and flour in another bowl. Preheat the air fryer to 350 F. Roll the drumsticks into the flour mixture and AirFry in the greased frying basket for 5-7 minutes. Turn and cook for 5-7 more minutes or until golden. Serve drizzled with lime juice.

Chicken Quarters with Broccoli & Carrots

Ingredients (4 Servings)

4 chicken legs
1 carrot, sliced
1 cup broccoli florets

Salt and black pepper to taste
1 tsp red pepper flakes
2 tbsp olive oil

Directions (Prep + Cook Time: 35 minutes)

Preheat the air fryer to 390 F. Season the legs with salt and black pepper and drizzle with some olive oil. Place them in the greased frying basket and AirFry for 8 minutes. Slide the basket out, and flip the chicken. Pour the broccoli and carrot over and sprinkle with salt and pepper. Drizzle with the remaining olive oil and cook for 6-8 more minutes or until the vegetables are tender. Top with flakes and serve.

Asian Sticky Chicken Wingettes

INGREDIENTS (4 Servings)

1 ginger, minced
1 garlic clove, minced
½ tbsp chili sauce
½ tbsp honey
1 ½ tbsp soy sauce
1 tbsp fresh cilantro, chopped
½ tbsp apple cider vinegar
1 lb chicken wingettes
1 tbsp roasted peanuts, chopped
Salt and black pepper to taste

DIRECTIONS (Prep + Cook Time: 25 minutes)

Preheat the air fryer to 360 F. Season the wingettes with salt and black pepper. In a bowl, mix the ginger, garlic, chili sauce, honey, soy sauce, cilantro, and vinegar. Coat the chicken in the mixture. AirFry in the greased frying basket for 14-16 minutes, turning once. Serve sprinkled with peanuts.

Roasted Chicken with Pancetta & Thyme

INGREDIENTS (4 Servings)

1 (3,5 lb) whole chicken
1 lemon
4 slices pancetta, roughly chopped
1 onion, chopped
1 sprig fresh thyme, chopped
Salt and black pepper to taste

DIRECTIONS (Prep + Cook Time: 60 minutes)

In a bowl, mix pancetta, onion, thyme, salt, and black pepper. Insert the mixture into the chicken's cavity and press tight. Put the whole lemon in, and rub the top and sides of the chicken with salt and pepper. Transfer to the greased frying basket, breast side down, and Bake for 30 minutes at 360 F. Turn the chicken breast side up, and cook for 12-15 more minutes or until golden brown and crisp.

BBQ Whole Chicken

INGREDIENTS (4 Servings)

1 whole small chicken, cut into pieces
Salt to taste
½ tsp smoked paprika
½ tsp garlic powder
1 cup BBQ sauce

DIRECTIONS (Prep + Cook Time: 60 minutes)

Rub the chicken pieces with salt, paprika, and garlic powder. Place in the greased frying basket and Bake for 25 minutes at 400 F. Remove to a plate and brush with barbecue sauce. Wipe the fryer clean from the chicken fat, return the chicken to the fryer, skin-side up, and Bake for 8-10 more minutes.

Whole Chicken with Sage & Garlic

INGREDIENTS (4 Servings)

3 tbsp butter
4 cloves garlic, crushed
1 onion, chopped
2 eggs, beaten
⅓ cup sage, chopped
1 (3 lb) whole chicken
Salt and black pepper to taste

DIRECTIONS (Prep + Cook Time: 50 minutes)

Melt butter in a pan over medium heat and sauté garlic and onion until browned, about 5 minutes. Add in the eggs, sage, black pepper, and salt; mix well. Cook for 20 seconds and turn the heat off.

Fill the chicken cavity with the mixture. Tie the legs with a butcher's twine and brush with olive oil. Rub the top and sides of the chicken with salt and black pepper. Preheat the air fryer to 390 F. Place the chicken into the greased frying basket and Bake for 25 minutes.

Turn the chicken over and cook for 10-15 more minutes, checking regularly to ensure it doesn't dry or overcook. When done, wrap in aluminum foil and let rest for 10 minutes. Carve and serve.

Spanish Roasted Whole Chicken

INGREDIENTS (4 Servings)

1 (3 lb) whole chicken

Spanish seasoning
Salt and black pepper to taste
1 tsp cayenne chili powder
1 tsp garlic powder
1 tsp oregano

1 lime, juiced

1 tsp ground coriander
1 tsp cumin
2 tbsp olive oil
1 tsp paprika

DIRECTIONS (Prep + Cook Time: 60 minutes + marinating time)

In a bowl, mix the oregano, garlic powder, cayenne chili powder, coriander, paprika, cumin, black pepper, salt, and olive oil. Rub onto the chicken and refrigerate it for 20 minutes to marinate.

Preheat the air fryer to 350 F. Remove the chicken from the fridge, place it breast side down in the greased frying basket, and Bake for 30 minutes. Turn the chicken breast-side up and continue cooking for 10-15 minutes. When over, let it rest for 10 minutes, then drizzle with lime juice and serve.

Honey & Lemon-Glazed Stuffed Chicken

INGREDIENTS (4-6 Servings)

1 (3 lb) whole chicken

Stuffing
2 red onions, chopped
2 tbsp olive oil
2 dry apricots, soaked and chopped
1 zucchini, chopped

Glaze
5 oz honey
Juice from 1 lemon

1 apple, peeled and chopped
2 cloves finely chopped garlic
4 tbsp fresh thyme, chopped
Salt and black pepper to taste

2 tbsp olive oil
Salt and black pepper to taste

DIRECTIONS (Prep + Cook Time: 60 minutes)

In a bowl, mix together all the stuffing ingredients. Fill the cavity of the chicken with the stuffing, without packing it tightly. Place the chicken, breast-side down, in the air fryer and Bake for 30 minutes at 380 F.

Warm the olive oil, honey, and lemon juice in a large pan; season with salt and pepper. Slide the basket out and flip the chicken breast side up. Brush with some of the honey-lemon glaze and return to the fryer. Bake for another 13-15 minutes, brushing every 5 minutes with the glaze. Serve warm.

Greek-Style Whole Chicken

INGREDIENTS (4-6 Servings)

1 (3 lb) whole chicken, cut into pieces
3 garlic cloves, minced
2 tbsp olive oil
1 tbsp ouzo (anise-flavored aperitif)

1 tbsp fresh rosemary, chopped
1 tbsp fresh Greek oregano, chopped
Juice from 1 lemon
Salt and black pepper to taste

DIRECTIONS (Prep + Cook Time: 50 minutes)

Preheat the air fryer to 380 F. In a large bowl, combine garlic, ouzo, rosemary, olive oil, lemon juice, Greek oregano, salt, and black pepper. Mix well and rub the mixture onto the chicken.

Place the chicken in the frying basket, breast side down, and Bake for 30 minutes. Turn the chicken, breast side up, and Broil for 10-15 more minutes until golden. Let sit for a few minutes before carving.

Mediterranean-Style Whole Chicken

INGREDIENTS (4 Servings)

1 (3 lb) whole chicken
½ cup prunes, pitted
3 garlic cloves, minced
2 tbsp capers
2 bay leaves

2 tbsp red wine vinegar
2 tbsp olive oil
1 tbsp dried oregano
1 tbsp brown sugar
Salt and black pepper to taste

DIRECTIONS (Prep + Cook Time: 60 minutes)

Preheat the air fryer to 360 F. In a bowl, mix prunes, capers, garlic, olive oil, bay leaves, oregano, vinegar, salt, and pepper. Spread the mixture on the bottom of a baking dish and place the chicken breast side down on top. Bake for 30 minutes in the fryer, turn it breast side up, and sprinkle with brown sugar on top; bake further for 10-15 minutes until golden. Let sit for a few minutes before slicing.

Whole Chicken with Fresno Chili Sauce

INGREDIENTS (4 Servings)

1 chicken (around 3 lb)
2 tsp garlic powder
½ cup Greek yogurt
1 lemon, juiced
Fresno chili sauce
2 tbsp olive oil
2 Fresno peppers, chopped
1 garlic clove, peeled

2 tsp tomato paste
2 tsp ancho chili powder
2 tsp ground cinnamon
2 tsp sumac

2 tomatoes, chopped
1 Vidalia onion, halved
1 tbsp lemon juice

DIRECTIONS (Prep + Cook Time: 70 minutes)

Preheat the air fryer to 380 F. In a bowl, mix yogurt, garlic powder, lemon juice, tomato paste, ancho chili powder, cinnamon, and sumac. Brush the chicken with the mixture and place it in the greased frying basket. Bake for 50-55 minutes, turning once, or until cooked through and golden.

Warm the olive oil in a pan over medium heat and sauté the Fresno peppers, Vidalia onion, and garlic for 2 minutes. Add in the remaining ingredients and simmer for 2-3 more minutes. Transfer to a food processor and pulse until smooth. Remove the chicken from the fryer, cover and let it rest for 10 minutes. Then carve the chicken and serve with the chili sauce.

Moroccan Turkey Meatballs

INGREDIENTS (6 Servings)

½ cup couscous
1 cucumber, chopped
1 egg, beaten
1 lb ground turkey
2 garlic cloves, minced

½ cup panko breadcrumbs
1 tbsp soy sauce
2 tsp harissa powder, divided
1 tsp sriracha sauce
Salt and black pepper to taste

DIRECTIONS (Prep + Cook Time: 40 minutes)

In a bowl, mix couscous and 1 cup of boiling water. Cover and let sit for 8-10 minutes. Fluff with a fork.

Preheat the air fryer to 360 F. In a bowl, mix the ground turkey, breadcrumbs, egg, soy sauce, 1 tbsp of harissa, garlic, salt, and black pepper. Make small balls with a tablespoon. Combine the remaining harissa powder and sriracha sauce in a small bowl to make a glaze; set aside.

Arrange the meatballs on the greased frying basket in a single later and AirFry for 8 minutes. Slide the basket out and generously brush the meatballs with the glaze. Cook for 4-7 more minutes or to your liking. Season the couscous with salt and mix in the cucumber. Top with the meatballs and serve.

Honey-Glazed Turkey

INGREDIENTS (4 Servings)

1 to 1 ½ lb turkey tenderloin
¼ cup honey
2 tbsp Dijon mustard
½ tsp dried thyme
½ tsp garlic powder

½ onion powder
1 tbsp olive oil
½ tbsp spicy brown mustard
Salt and black pepper to taste

DIRECTIONS (Prep + Cook Time: 50 minutes)

Preheat the air fryer to 375 F. Combine the honey, mustard, thyme, garlic powder, and onion powder in a bowl to make a paste. Season the turkey with salt and pepper, then brush the paste all over.

Put the turkey in the frying basket and spray with olive oil. AirFry for 15 minutes. Turn the tenderloin over and spray again before frying for 10-15 more minutes until golden brown. Remove the turkey, cover loosely with foil and let stand 10 minutes before slicing. Serve and enjoy!

Turkey Burgers with Cabbage Slaw

INGREDIENTS (4 Servings)

1 lb ground turkey
¼ cup breadcrumbs
1 tbsp olive oil
¼ cup hoisin sauce

4 buns
2 green onions, sliced
1 cup cabbage slaw
1 cup cherry tomatoes, halved

DIRECTIONS (Prep + Cook Time: 30 minutes)

Preheat the air fryer to 375 F. Mix the ground turkey, breadcrumbs, and hoisin sauce in a bowl and create 4 equal patties. Put the patties in the greased frying basket, spray with olive oil, and AirFry for 10 minutes. Turn the patties, spray with oil again, and cook for 5-10 more minutes or until golden. Lay the patties on the buns and top with cherry tomatoes, green onions, and cabbage slaw. Serve.

Parmesan Turkey Meatballs

INGREDIENTS (4 Servings)

1 lb ground turkey
1 egg
½ cup breadcrumbs
1 tbsp garlic powder

1 tbsp Italian seasoning
1 tbsp onion powder
¼ cup Parmesan cheese, grated
Salt and black pepper to taste

DIRECTIONS (Prep + Cook Time: 25 minutes)

Preheat the air fryer to 400 F. In a bowl, mix ground turkey, egg, breadcrumbs, garlic powder, onion powder, Italian seasoning, Parmesan cheese, salt, and black pepper. Make bite-sized balls out of the mixture. Add the balls to the greased frying basket and AirFry for 12-14 minutes, shaking once. Serve.

Thyme Turkey Nuggets

INGREDIENTS (2 Servings)

½ lb ground turkey
1 egg, beaten
1 cup breadcrumbs

½ tsp dried thyme
½ tsp fresh parsley, chopped
Salt and black pepper to taste

DIRECTIONS (Prep + Cook Time: 20 minutes)

Preheat the air fryer to 350 F. In a bowl, mix ground turkey, thyme, parsley, salt, and pepper. Shape the mixture into nuggets. Dip them in the egg, and then in the breadcrumbs. Place the nuggets in the frying basket, spray with cooking spray and AirFry for 12-14 minutes, flipping once. Serve with garlic mayo.

Turkey & Veggie Skewers

INGREDIENTS (4 Servings)

1 lb turkey breast, cubed
2 tbsp fresh rosemary, chopped
Salt and black pepper to taste
1 green bell pepper, cut into chunks

1 red bell pepper, cut into chunks
1 cup cherry tomatoes
1 red onion, cut into wedges

DIRECTIONS (Prep + Cook Time: 35 minutes)

Preheat the air fryer to 350 F. Spray the frying basket with cooking spray.

Season the turkey with salt and black pepper. Thread the bell peppers, cherry tomatoes, onion, and turkey cubes alternately onto skewers. Spray with cooking spray and place them in the frying basket. Bake for 25-30 minutes, turning once halfway through. Serve sprinkled with fresh rosemary.

Turkey Strips with Cranberry Glaze

INGREDIENTS (4 Servings)

1 lb turkey breast, cut into strips
1 tbsp chicken seasoning

Salt and black pepper to taste
½ cup cranberry sauce

DIRECTIONS (Prep + Cook Time: 35 minutes)

Preheat the air fryer to 390 F. Season the turkey with chicken seasoning, salt, and black pepper. Spritz with cooking spray and AirFry for 20-25 minutes, shanking once or twice throughout cooking.

Put a saucepan over low heat, and add the cranberry sauce and ¼ cup of water. Simmer for 5 minutes, stirring continuously. Serve the turkey drizzled with cranberry sauce. Yummy!

Mediterranean-Rubbed Turkey Tenderloins

INGREDIENTS (4 Servings)

1 lb turkey breast, sliced
2 tbsp olive oil
½ tsp garlic powder

1 cup jellied cranberry sauce
Salt and black pepper to taste
2 tsp Mediterranean herb seasoning

DIRECTIONS (Prep + Cook Time: 40 minutes)

Preheat the air fryer to 360 F. In a bowl, whisk the olive oil, garlic powder, Mediterranean herbs, salt, and pepper. Add the turkey and toss to coat. AirFry them for 20-25 minutes, flipping once. Transfer the turkey to a serving plate, cover with foil, and let stand for 5 minutes. Serve with cranberry sauce.

Roasted Turkey with Brussels Sprouts

INGREDIENTS (4-6 Servings)

1 ½ - 2 lb turkey breast
2 garlic cloves, minced
1 tbsp olive oil
2 tsp Dijon mustard

½ tsp rosemary
½ tsp thyme
1 lb Brussels sprouts, halved
Salt and black pepper to taste

DIRECTIONS (Prep + Cook Time: 60 minutes)

Preheat the air fryer to 375 F. Mix the garlic, olive oil, Dijon mustard, rosemary, thyme, salt, and black pepper in a bowl to make a paste. Smear the paste all over the turkey breast.

Put the turkey breast in the greased frying basket and AirFry for 20 minutes. Turn it over and baste it with any drippings from the bottom drawer. Add in Brussels sprouts and fry for 16-20 more minutes. Let the turkey sit for 10 minutes before slicing. Serve with Brussels sprouts and a bed of rice if desired.

Turkey Tenderloins with Fattoush Salad

INGREDIENTS (4 Servings)

1 ½ lb turkey tenderloin
3 tbsp olive oil
½ tsp paprika
½ tsp garlic powder
½ tsp cayenne pepper
Salt and black pepper to taste
1 tbsp lemon juice

1 tbsp pomegranate molasses
½ lb Roma tomatoes, chopped
2 spring onions, sliced
2 tbsp fresh mint, chopped
6 radishes, thinly sliced
1 cucumber, deseeded and diced
5 oz pita crackers

DIRECTIONS (Prep + Cook Time: 50 minutes)

In a bowl, mix the lemon juice, 2 tbsp of olive oil, pomegranate molasses, and salt and whisk with a fork. Add in the tomatoes, spring onions, radishes, cucumber, fresh mint and toss to coat. Set aside.

Preheat your Air Fryer to 375 F. Combine the paprika, garlic powder, salt, pepper, and cayenne pepper in a bowl, then rub the mixture all over the turkey. Place the turkey in the greased frying basket and spray with olive oil. AirFry for 30-35 minutes, turning once until golden. Remove and let it sit for 5-8 minutes before slicing. Divide the fattoush salad between pita crackers and top with turkey slices.

Chipotle Buttered Turkey

INGREDIENTS (4 Servings)

1 lb turkey breast, sliced
2 cups panko breadcrumbs

Salt and chipotle powder to taste
1 stick butter, melted

DIRECTIONS (Prep + Cook Time: 25 minutes)

In a bowl, combine panko breadcrumbs and chipotle chili pepper. Sprinkle turkey with salt and brush with some butter. Coat the turkey with the crumbs mixture. Transfer to the frying basket and grease with some butter. AirFry for 10 minutes at 390 F. Flip the slices, drizzle with the remaining butter, and Bake for 4-7 more minutes, until nice and crispy. Serve and enjoy!

Mini Turkey Meatloaves with Hot Sauce

INGREDIENTS (4 Servings)

2 tbsp olive oil
1 lb ground turkey
¼ cup hot sauce

1 shallot, chopped
1 egg
Salt and black pepper to taste

DIRECTIONS (Prep + Cook Time: 35 minutes)

Preheat the air fryer to 360 F. In a bowl, mix the ground turkey, shallot, egg, salt, and pepper. Divide the mixture between 4 greased muffin cups. Spoon the hot sauce over the meatloaves. Bake in the fryer for 20-25 minutes. Insert a meat thermometer and it should display at least 165 F. Serve hot.

Turkey Stuffed Bell Peppers

INGREDIENTS (2 Servings)

1 tsp fresh cilantro, chopped
1 green onion, chopped
½ lb ground turkey

Salt and garlic powder to taste
4 mini bell peppers, halved lengthwise, seeded
2 tbsp mozzarella cheese, crumbled

DIRECTIONS (Prep + Cook Time: 30 minutes)

Preheat the air fryer to 360 F. Combine the ground turkey, onion, mozzarella cheese, garlic powder, and salt, then spoon the mixture into the bell peppers. Put the stuffed peppers in the greased frying basket and Bake for 10-15 minutes or until cooked through. Garnish with fresh cilantro and serve.

FISH & SEAFOOD

Herbed Crab Croquettes

INGREDIENTS (4 Servings)

1 ½ lb lump crabmeat
⅓ cup sour cream
⅓ cup mayonnaise
1 red pepper, finely chopped
⅓ cup red onion, chopped
½ celery stalk, chopped
1 tsp fresh tarragon, chopped
1 tsp fresh chives, chopped

1 tsp fresh parsley, chopped
1 tsp cayenne pepper
1 ½ cups breadcrumbs
2 tsp olive oil
1 cup flour
2 eggs, beaten
Salt to taste
Lemon wedges to serve

DIRECTIONS (Prep + Cook Time: 30 minutes)

Heat olive oil in a skillet over medium heat and sauté the red pepper, onion, and celery for 5 minutes or until sweaty and translucent. Turn off the heat. Pour the breadcrumbs and salt on a plate. In 2 separate bowls, add the flour and the beaten eggs, respectively, and set aside.

In a separate bowl, add crabmeat, mayonnaise, sour cream, tarragon, chives, parsley, cayenne pepper, and sautéed vegetables. Form bite-size oval balls out of the mixture and place the balls on a plate.

Preheat the air fryer to 390 F. Dip each crab meatball in the beaten eggs and press down in the breadcrumb mixture. Place the croquettes in the greased frying basket without overcrowding. AirFry for 10-12 minutes or until golden brown, turning once. Serve hot with lemon wedges.

Crab Fritters with Sweet Chili Sauce

INGREDIENTS (4 Servings)

1 lb jumbo crabmeat
1 lime, zested and juiced
1 tsp ginger paste
1 tsp garlic puree
1 tbsp fresh cilantro, chopped

1 red chili, roughly chopped
1 egg
¼ cup panko breadcrumbs
1 tsp soy sauce sauce
3 tbsp sweet chili sauce

DIRECTIONS (Prep + Cook Time: 25 minutes)

Preheat the air fryer to 400 F. In a bowl, mix crabmeat, lime zest, egg, ginger paste, and garlic puree. Form small cakes out of the mixture and dredge them in the breadcrumbs. Place in the greased frying basket and AirFry for 14-16 minutes, shaking once until golden brown. In a small bowl, mix the sweet chili sauce with lime juice and soy sauce. Serve the fritters topped with cilantro and the chili sauce.

Old Bay Crab Sticks with Garlic Mayo

INGREDIENTS (4 Servings)

1 lb crab sticks
1 tbsp old bay seasoning
⅓ cup panko breadcrumbs
2 eggs

½ cup mayonnaise
2 garlic cloves, minced
1 lime, juiced
1 cup flour

DIRECTIONS (Prep + Cook Time: 20 minutes)

Preheat the air fryer to 390 F. Beat the eggs in a bowl. In another bowl, mix the breadcrumbs with old bay seasoning. Pour the flour into a third bowl. Dip the sticks in the flour, then in the eggs, and finally in the breadcrumbs. Spray with cooking spray and AirFry for 12-14 minutes, flipping once, until golden. Mix the mayonnaise with garlic and lime juice. Serve as a dip along with crab sticks.

Crabmeat & Veggie Patties with Basil Dip

INGREDIENTS (4 Servings)

3 potatoes, boiled and mashed
1 cup cooked crabmeat
¼ cup red onions, chopped
1 tbsp fresh basil, chopped
½ celery stalk, chopped
½ bell red pepper, chopped

1 tbsp Dijon mustard
½ lemon, zested and juiced
¼ cup breadcrumbs
1 tsp ground allspice
½ cup mayonnaise
Salt and black pepper to taste

DIRECTIONS (Prep + Cook Time: 20 minutes + chilling time)

Place the mashed potatoes, red onions, allspice, breadcrumbs, celery, bell pepper, mustard, lemon zest, crabmeat, salt, and black pepper in a large bowl and mix well. Make patties from the mixture and refrigerate for 30 minutes. Mix the mayonnaise, lemon juice, basil, salt, and pepper and set aside.

Preheat the air fryer to 390 F. Remove the patties from the fridge and place them in the greased frying basket. AirFry for 12-14 minutes, flipping once until golden. Serve the patties with the basil-mayo dip.

Fiery Prawns

INGREDIENTS (4 Servings)

8 prawns, cleaned
Salt and black pepper to taste
½ tsp ground cayenne pepper

½ tsp red chili flakes
½ tsp ground cumin
½ tsp garlic powder

DIRECTIONS (Prep + Cook Time: 15 minutes)

In a bowl, season the prawns with salt and black pepper. Sprinkle with cayenne pepper, chili flakes, cumin, and garlic, and stir to coat. Spray the frying basket with oil and lay the prawns in an even layer. AirFry for 8-10 minutes at 340 F, turning once halfway through. Serve with sweet chili sauce if desired.

Crispy Prawns in Bacon Wraps

INGREDIENTS (4 Servings)

8 bacon slices

8 jumbo prawns, peeled and deveined

DIRECTIONS (Prep + Cook Time: 15 minutes)

Preheat the air fryer to 400 F. Wrap each prawn from head to tail in each bacon slice. Make sure to overlap to keep the bacon in place. Secure the ends with toothpicks. Arrange the bacon-wrapped prawns in the greased frying basket and AirFry for 9-12 minutes, turning once. Serve hot.

Chinese Garlic Prawns

INGREDIENTS (4 Servings)

1 lb prawns, peeled and deveined
Juice from 1 lemon
1 tsp sugar
2 tbsp peanut oil
2 tbsp cornstarch

2 scallions, chopped
¼ tsp Chinese powder
1 red chili pepper, minced
Salt and black pepper to taste
4 garlic cloves, minced

DIRECTIONS (Prep + Cook Time: 25 minutes + marinating time)

In a Ziploc bag, mix lemon juice, sugar, black pepper, 1 tbsp of peanut oil, cornstarch, Chinese powder, and salt. Add in the prawns and massage gently to coat well. Let sit for 20 minutes. Heat the remaining peanut oil in a pan over medium heat and sauté garlic, scallions, and red chili pepper for 3 minutes.

Preheat the air fryer to 390 F. Place the marinated prawns in a baking dish and cover with the sautéed vegetables. AirFry for 10-12 minutes, shaking once halfway through, until nice and crispy. Serve warm.

Sesame Prawns with Firecracker Sauce

INGREDIENTS (4 Servings)

1 lb tiger prawns, peeled
Salt and black pepper to taste
2 eggs

Firecracker sauce
⅓ cup sour cream
2 tbsp buffalo sauce

½ cup flour
¼ cup sesame seeds
¾ cup seasoned breadcrumbs

¼ cup spicy ketchup
1 green onion, chopped

DIRECTIONS (Prep + Cook Time: 20 minutes)

Preheat the air fryer to 390 F. In a bowl, beat the eggs with a pinch of salt. In another bowl, mix the breadcrumbs with sesame seeds. In a third bowl, mix flour with salt and pepper. Dip the prawns in the flour, then in the eggs, and finally in the crumbs. Spray with cooking spray.

AirFry for 10-12 minutes, flipping once. Meanwhile, in a bowl mix all sauce ingredients, except for the green onion. Serve the prawns with firecracker sauce and scatter with freshly chopped green onions.

Ale-Battered Scampi with Tartare Sauce

INGREDIENTS (4 Servings)

1 lb prawns, peeled and deveined
1 cup plain flour

Tartare sauce:
½ cup mayonnaise
2 tbsp capers, roughly chopped
2 tbsp fresh dill, chopped

1 cup ale beer
Salt and black pepper to taste

1 pickled cucumber, finely chopped
2 tsp lemon juice
½ tsp Worcestershire sauce

Directions (Prep + Cook Time: 20 minutes)

Preheat the air fryer to 380 F. In a bowl, mix all sauce ingredients and keep in the fridge. Mix flour, ale beer, salt, and pepper in a large bowl. Dip in the prawns and place them in the greased frying basket. AirFry for 10-12 minutes, turning them once halfway through cooking. Serve with the tartare sauce.

Delicious Cayenne Shrimp

INGREDIENTS (2 Servings)

8 large shrimp, peeled and deveined
½ cup breadcrumbs
8 oz coconut milk
½ cup coconut, shredded
Salt to taste

½ cup orange jam
1 tsp mustard
1 tbsp honey
½ tsp cayenne pepper
¼ tsp hot sauce

DIRECTIONS (Prep + Cook Time: 30 minutes)

Combine breadcrumbs, cayenne pepper, shredded coconut, and salt in a bowl. Dip the shrimp in the coconut milk, and then in the coconut crumbs. Arrange them in the greased frying basket and AirFry for 12-14 minutes at 350 F. Whisk jam, honey, hot sauce, and mustard in a bowl. Serve with the shrimp.

Louisiana-Style Shrimp

INGREDIENTS (4 Servings)

1 lb shrimp, peeled and deveined
2 eggs
1 cup flour
1 cup breadcrumbs

2 tbsp Cajun seasoning
Salt and black pepper to taste
1 lemon, cut into wedges

DIRECTIONS (Prep + Cook Time: 20 minutes)

Preheat the air fryer to 390 F. Spray the basket with cooking oil. Beat the eggs in a bowl and season to taste. In a separate bowl, mix the crumbs and Cajun seasoning. In a third bowl, pour the flour. Dip the shrimp in flour, then in the eggs, and finally in the crumbs. AirFry the shrimp in the greased frying basket for 5 minutes. Flip and cook for 3-5 more minutes until crispy. Serve with lemon wedges.

Spicy Shrimp with Coconut-Avocado Dip

INGREDIENTS (4 Servings)

1 ¼ lb tiger shrimp, peeled and deveined
2 garlic cloves, minced
¼ tsp red chili flakes
1 lime, juiced and zested
Salt to taste

1 tbsp fresh cilantro, chopped
1 large avocado, pitted
¼ cup coconut cream
2 tbsp olive oil

DIRECTIONS (Prep + Cook Time: 20 minutes)

Blend avocado, lime juice, coconut cream, cilantro, olive oil, and salt in a food processor until smooth. Transfer to a bowl, cover, and keep in the fridge until ready to use.

Preheat the air fryer to 390 F. In a bowl, place garlic, chili flakes, lime zest, and salt and add in the shrimp; toss to coat. Place them in the greased frying basket and AirFry for 8-10 minutes, turning them once halfway through cooking, until entirely pink. Serve with the chilled avocado dip.

Asian Shrimp Medley

INGREDIENTS (4 Servings)

1 lb shrimp, peeled and deveined
2 whole onions, chopped
3 tbsp butter
1 tbsp sugar

2 tbsp soy sauce
2 cloves garlic, chopped
2 tsp lime juice
1 tsp ginger paste

DIRECTIONS (Prep + Cook Time: 25 minutes + marinating time)

Melt butter in a frying pan over medium heat and stir-fry the onions for 3 minutes until translucent. Mix in the lime juice, soy sauce, ginger paste, garlic, and sugar and stir for 1-2 minutes. Let cool and then pour the mixture over the shrimp. Cover and let marinate for 30 minutes in the fridge.

Preheat the air fryer to 380 F. Transfer the shrimp along with the marinade to a baking dish and place the dish inside the frying basket. AirFry for 12-14 minutes, turning once halfway through. Serve hot.

Mango Shrimp Skewers with Hot Sauce

INGREDIENTS (4 Servings)

20 small-sized shrimp, peeled and deveined
2 tbsp olive oil
½ tsp garlic powder
1 tsp mango powder (or tamarind)
2 tbsp fresh lime juice
Salt and black pepper to taste

2 tbsp fresh cilantro, chopped
1 garlic clove, minced
1 green onion, finely sliced
1 tbsp red chili flakes, crushed
2 tbsp white wine vinegar

DIRECTIONS (Prep + Cook Time: 30 minutes + marinating time)

In a bowl, mix garlic powder, mango powder, lime juice, salt, and pepper. Add the shrimp and toss to coat. Cover and marinate for 20 minutes. Meanwhile, soak wooden skewers in water for 15 minutes. In a small dish, mix cilantro, minced garlic, green onion, chili flakes, olive oil, and vinegar; set aside.

Preheat the air fryer to 390 F. Thread the marinated shrimp onto the skewers and place in the greased frying. AirFry for 10-12 minutes, turn once, until golden. Serve the skewers with the cilantro sauce.

Rosemary Cashew Shrimp

INGREDIENTS (4 Servings)

3 oz cashews, chopped
1 tbsp fresh rosemary, chopped
1 lb shrimp
1 garlic clove, minced

1 tbsp breadcrumbs
1 egg, beaten
1 tbsp olive oil
Salt and black pepper to taste

DIRECTIONS (Prep + Cook Time: 20 minutes)

Preheat the air fryer to 390 F. Whisk oil with garlic, salt, and pepper and brush the shrimp with the mixture. Mix rosemary, cashews, and breadcrumbs in a bowl. Dip the shrimp in the egg and coat in the crumbs. Place in the greased frying basket and AirFry for 4-6 minutes. Turn the shrimp and fry for 4-6 more minutes or until golden and crispy. Cover with a foil and let sit for a few minutes before serving.

Cajun-Rubbed Jumbo Shrimp

INGREDIENTS (2 Servings)

1 lb jumbo shrimp, deveined
Salt to taste
¼ tsp old bay seasoning

⅓ tsp smoked paprika
¼ tsp cayenne pepper
2 tbsp olive oil

DIRECTIONS (Prep + Cook Time: 15 minutes)

Preheat the air fryer to 390 F. In a bowl, add the shrimp, paprika, olive oil, salt, old bay seasoning, and cayenne pepper; mix well. Place the shrimp in the fryer and AirFry for 8-10 minutes, shaking once.

Greek-Style Fried Mussels

INGREDIENTS (4 Servings)

4 lb black mussels
4 tbsp olive oil
1 cup white wine
Salt and black pepper to taste
1 tsp Greek seasoning

2 tbsp white wine vinegar
5 garlic cloves
4 bread slices
½ cup hazelnuts

DIRECTIONS (Prep + Cook Time: 35 minutes)

Add the olive oil, garlic, Greek seasoning, vinegar, salt, black pepper, hazelnuts and bread slices to a food processor and process until you obtain a creamy texture. In a skillet over medium heat, pour the wine and mussels. Bring to a boil, then lower the heat and simmer until the mussels have opened up, about 5 minutes. Then, drain and remove from the shells. Discard any unopened mussels.

Add them to the previously prepared hazelnut mixture and toss to coat. Preheat the fryer to 350 F. Place the mussels in a greased baking dish and Bake in the air fryer for 10-12 minutes, shaking once or twice.

Herbed Garlic Lobster

INGREDIENTS (4 Servings)

4 oz lobster tails, halved
1 garlic clove, minced
2 tbsp butter, melted
Salt and black pepper to taste

½ tbsp lemon juice
1 tbsp fresh parsley, chopped
1 tbsp fresh dill, chopped
1 tbsp fresh thyme, chopped

DIRECTIONS (Prep + Cook Time: 20 minutes)

Whisk the garlic, butter, lemon juice, salt, and pepper in a bowl until well mixed. Clean the skin of the lobster and cover it with the mixture. Preheat the air fryer to 380 F. Place the lobster in the greased frying basket and AirFry for 10 minutes, turning once. Serve sprinkled with parsley, thyme, and dill.

Breaded Scallops

INGREDIENTS (4 Servings)

1 lb fresh scallops
3 tbsp flour
1 egg, lightly beaten

1 cup seasoned breadcrumbs
2 tbsp olive oil
½ tsp fresh parsley, chopped

DIRECTIONS (Prep + Cook Time: 15 minutes)

Preheat the air fryer to 360 F. Coat the scallops in flour. Dip them in the egg, then into the crumbs. Spray with olive oil and AirFry for 6-8 minutes, flipping once until golden. Serve topped with parsley.

Mediterranean Squid Rings with Couscous

INGREDIENTS (4 Servings)

1 cup couscous
1 lb squid rings
2 large eggs
½ cup all-purpose flour

½ cup semolina
1 tsp ground coriander seeds
1 tsp cayenne pepper
Salt and black pepper to taste

DIRECTIONS (Prep + Cook Time: 35 minutes)

Place the couscous in a large bowl and cover with boiling water (about 1 ½ cups). Season with salt and pepper and stir. Cover and set aside for 5-7 minutes until the water is absorbed.

Preheat the air fryer to 390 F.

Beat the eggs in one bowl. In another bowl, combine the flour, semolina, ground coriander, cayenne pepper, salt, and black pepper. Dip the squid rings in the eggs first, then in the flour mixture, and place them in the greased frying basket. AirFry for 13-15 minutes, until golden brown, flipping once. Transfer the couscous to a large platter and serve the squid rings on top.

Calamari Rings with Olives

INGREDIENTS (4 Servings)

1 lb calamari rings
2 tbsp fresh cilantro, chopped
1 chili pepper, finely chopped

2 tbsp olive oil
1 cup pimiento-stuffed green olives
Salt and black pepper to taste

DIRECTIONS (Prep + Cook Time: 30 minutes)

Preheat the air fryer to 400 F. In a bowl, mix the chili pepper, salt, black pepper, olive oil, and fresh cilantro. Add in the calamari rings and toss to coat. Marinate for 10 minutes. Then place the calamari in the air fryer and AirFry for 15 minutes, flipping every 5 minutes. Serve with pimiento-stuffed olives.

Cod Fillets with Ginger-Cilantro Sauce

INGREDIENTS (4 Servings)

1 lb cod fillets
2 tbsp fresh cilantro, chopped
Salt to taste
4 green onions, chopped
1 cup water

1 tbsp ginger paste
5 tbsp light soy sauce
2 tbsp olive oil
1 tsp soy sauce
2 cubes rock sugar

DIRECTIONS (Prep + Cook Time: 20 minutes)

Preheat the air fryer to 360 F. Season the fillets with salt and drizzle with olive oil. Place in the frying basket and AirFry for 14-16 minutes, turning once. Meanwhile, heat the remaining oil in a pan over medium heat. Stir-fry the remaining ingredients for 5 minutes. Pour the sauce over the fish to serve.

American Panko Fish Nuggets

INGREDIENTS (4 Servings)

1 lb white fish fillets
1 lemon, juiced
Salt and black pepper to taste
1 tsp dried dill
4 tbsp mayonnaise

2 eggs, beaten
1 tbsp garlic powder
1 cup breadcrumbs
1 tsp paprika

DIRECTIONS (Prep + Cook Time: 20 minutes)

Preheat the air fryer to 400 F. Season the fish with salt and black pepper. In a bowl, mix the beaten eggs, lemon juice, and mayonnaise. In a separate bowl, mix the crumbs, paprika, dill, and garlic.

Dredge the fillets in the eggs and then in the crumbs. Place them in the greased frying basket and AirFry for 14-16 minutes, flipping once halfway through cooking. Serve with tomato chutney if desired.

Buttered Crab Legs

INGREDIENTS (4 Servings)

2 lb crab legs
2 tbsp butter, melted

1 tbsp fresh parsley

DIRECTIONS (Prep + Cook Time: 15 minutes)

Preheat the air fryer to 380 F. Place the legs in the greased frying basket and AirFry for 10-12 minutes, shaking once or twice. Pour the butter over crab legs, sprinkle with parsley, and serve. Work in batches.

Air-Fried Seafood Mix

INGREDIENTS (4 Servings)

1 lb fresh scallops, mussels, fish fillets, prawns, shrimp
2 eggs

Salt and black pepper to taste
1 cup breadcrumbs mixed with the zest of 1 lemon

DIRECTIONS (Prep + Cook Time: 20 minutes)

Beat the eggs with salt and black pepper in a bowl. Dip in each piece of seafood and then coat in the crumbs. Place them in the greased frying basket and AirFry for 10-12 minutes at 400 F, turning once.

Golden Cod Fish Fillets

INGREDIENTS (4 Servings)

1 cup breadcrumbs
2 tbsp olive oil
2 eggs, beaten

4 cod fillets
A pinch of salt
1 cup flour

DIRECTIONS (Prep + Cook Time: 20 minutes)

Preheat the air fryer to 390 F. Mix the crumbs, olive oil, and salt in a bowl. In another bowl, beat the eggs. Put the flour into a third bowl. Toss the cod fillets in the flour, then in the eggs, and finally in the crumbs mixture. Place them in the greased frying basket and AirFry for 10 minutes. At the 6-minute mark, quickly turn the fillets. Remove to a plate and serve with dill-yogurt sauce if desired.

Cod Finger Pesto Sandwich

INGREDIENTS (4 Servings)

4 cod fillets
4 bread rolls
1 cup breadcrumbs

4 tbsp pesto sauce
4 lettuce leaves
Salt and black pepper to taste

DIRECTIONS (Prep + Cook Time: 20 minutes)

Preheat the air fryer to 370 F. Season the fillets with salt and black pepper and coat them in breadcrumbs. Arrange them on the greased frying basket and Bake for 13-15 minutes, flipping once.

Cut the bread rolls in half. Divide lettuce leaves between the bottom halves and place the fillets over. Spread the pesto sauce on top of the fillets and cover with the remaining halves. Serve warm.

Cod Cornflake Nuggets with Avocado Dip

INGREDIENTS (4 Servings)

1 ¼ lb cod fillets, cut into 4 chunks each
½ cup flour
2 eggs, beaten
1 cup cornflakes

1 tbsp olive oil
Salt and black pepper to taste
1 avocado, chopped
1 lime, juiced

DIRECTIONS (Prep + Cook Time: 25 minutes)

Mash the avocado with a fork in a small bowl. Stir in the lime juice and salt and set aside. Pour the olive oil and cornflakes in a food processor and process until crumbed.

Season the fish with salt and pepper. Preheat the air fryer to 350 F. Place flour, eggs and cornflakes in 3 separate bowls. Coat the fish in flour, dip in the eggs, then coat in the cornflakes. AirFry in the greased frying basket for 14-16 minutes, shaking once or twice, until golden. Serve with the avocado dip.

Soy Sauce-Glazed Cod

INGREDIENTS (2 Servings)

2 cod fillets
1 tbsp olive oil
Salt and black pepper to taste
1 tbsp soy sauce

1 tbsp sesame oil
¼ tsp ginger powder
¼ tsp honey

DIRECTIONS (Prep + Cook Time: 15 minutes)

Preheat the air fryer to 370 F. In a bowl, combine olive oil, salt, and black pepper. Massage the fillets with the mixture. Place them on the greased frying basket and Bake in the fryer for 6 minutes.

Meanwhile, combine the soy sauce, ginger powder, honey, and sesame oil in a small bowl. Flip the fillets and brush them with the glaze. Bake for 3-5 more minutes until golden and crispy. Serve warm.

Gourmet Black Cod with Fennel & Pecans

INGREDIENTS (2 Servings)

2 black cod fillets
Salt and black pepper to taste
1 small fennel bulb, sliced

½ cup pecans
2 tsp white balsamic vinegar
2 tbsp olive oil

DIRECTIONS (Prep + Cook Time: 25 minutes)

Preheat the air fryer to 400 F. Season the fillets with salt and pepper and drizzle with some olive oil. Place in them the frying basket and AirFry for 10-12 minutes, flipping once, or until golden brown.

Meanwhile, warm the remaining olive oil in a skillet over medium heat. Stir-fry the fennel for 5 minutes. Add in the pecans and cook for 3-4 minutes until toasted. Drizzle with the balsamic vinegar and season with salt and pepper. Stir well and remove from heat. Pour the mixture over the black cod and serve.

Pistachio-Crusted Salmon Fillets

INGREDIENTS (2 Servings)

2 salmon fillets
1 tsp yellow mustard
4 tbsp pistachios, chopped
Salt and black pepper to taste

1 tsp garlic powder
2 tsp lemon juice
2 tbsp Parmesan cheese, grated
1 tsp olive oil

DIRECTIONS (Prep + Cook Time: 25 minutes)

Preheat the air fryer to 350 F. Whisk together the mustard, olive oil, lemon juice, salt, black pepper, and garlic powder in a bowl. Rub the mustard mixture evenly onto the salmon fillets.

Lay the fillets on the greased frying basket, skin side down and spread the pistachios and Parmesan cheese all over; press down gently to make a crust. Bake the salmon for 12-15 minutes until golden.

Korean Kimchi-Spiced Salmon

INGREDIENTS (4 Servings)

2 tbsp soy sauce
2 tbsp sesame oil
2 tbsp mirin
1 tbsp ginger puree

1 tsp kimchi spice
1 tsp sriracha sauce
2 lb salmon fillets
1 lime, cut into wedges

DIRECTIONS (Prep + Cook Time: 20 minutes)

Preheat the air fryer to 350 F. Grease the frying basket with cooking spray. In a bowl, mix together soy sauce, mirin, ginger puree, kimchi spice, and sriracha sauce. Add the salmon and toss to coat.

Place the fillets in the frying basket and drizzle with sesame oil. Bake for 10-12 minutes, flipping once halfway through. Garnish with lime wedges and serve.

Tandoori-Style Crispy Salmon

INGREDIENTS (2 Serving)

2 salmon fillets
1 tsp ginger powder
1 garlic clove, minced
½ green bell pepper, sliced
1 tsp sweet paprika, minced

1 tsp honey
1 tsp garam masala
1 tbsp fresh cilantro, chopped
¼ cup yogurt
Juice and zest from 1 lime

DIRECTIONS (Prep + Cook Time: 25 minutes + marinating time)

In a bowl, mix all the ingredients, except for the fish. Coat the fillets in the mixture and let sit for 15 minutes. Preheat the air fryer to 400 F. Place the fillets in the greased frying basket and Bake for 12-15 minutes, flipping once, or until golden and crispy. Serve on a bed of basmati rice if desired.

Easy Salmon with Greek Sauce

INGREDIENTS (4 Servings)

1 lb salmon fillets
Salt and black pepper to taste
2 tsp olive oil

2 tbsp fresh dill, chopped
1 cup sour cream
1 cup Greek yogurt

DIRECTIONS (Prep + Cook Time: 20 minutes)

In a bowl, mix the sour cream, Greek yogurt, dill, and salt. Keep in the fridge until ready to use. Preheat the air fryer to 340 F. Drizzle the fillets with olive oil and sprinkle with salt and pepper. Place the fish in the frying basket and Bake for 10-12 minutes, flipping once. Serve drizzled with the Greek sauce.

Salmon Cakes

INGREDIENTS (4 Servings)

12 oz cooked salmon
2 potatoes, boiled and mashed
½ cup flour
2 tbsp capers, chopped

2 tbsp fresh parsley, chopped
1 tbsp olive oil
Zest of 1 lemon

DIRECTIONS (Prep + Cook Time: 25 minutes + marinating time)

Place the mashed potatoes in a bowl and flake the salmon over. Stir in capers, parsley, and lemon zest. Mix well and shape into 4 cakes. Roll them up in flour, shake off, and refrigerate for 1 hour.

Preheat the air fryer to 350 F. Remove the cakes and brush them with olive oil. Bake in the greased frying basket for 12-14 minutes, flipping once halfway through cooking. Serve warm.

Salmon & Spring Onion Balls

INGREDIENTS (2 Servings)

1 cup tinned salmon
¼ celery stalk, chopped
1 spring onion, sliced
4 tbsp wheat germ

2 tbsp olive oil
1 large egg
1 tbsp fresh dill, chopped
½ tsp garlic powder

DIRECTIONS (Prep + Cook Time: 20 minutes)

Preheat the air fryer to 390 F. In a large bowl, mix tinned salmon, egg, celery, onion, dill, and garlic. Shape the mixture into balls and roll them up in wheat germ. Carefully flatten and place them in the greased frying basket. AirFry for 8-10 minutes, flipping once halfway through, or until golden.

Smoked Salmon & Cheddar Taquitos

INGREDIENTS (4 Servings)

1 lb smoked salmon, chopped
Salt to taste
1 tbsp taco seasoning
1 cup cheddar cheese, shredded

1 lime, juiced
½ cup fresh cilantro, chopped
8 corn tortillas
1 cup hot salsa

DIRECTIONS (Prep + Cook Time: 15 minutes)

Preheat the air fryer to 390 F.

In a bowl, mix the salmon, taco seasoning, lime juice, cheddar cheese, salt, and cilantro. Divide the mixture between the tortillas. Wrap the tortillas around the filling and place them in the greased frying basket. Bake for 10-12 minutes, turning once halfway through cooking. Serve with hot salsa.

Salmon Fillets with Broccoli

INGREDIENTS (2 Servings)

2 salmon fillets
2 tsp olive oil
Juice of 1 lime

1 tsp red chili flakes (optional)
Salt and black pepper to taste
5 oz broccoli florets, steamed

DIRECTIONS (Prep + Cook Time: 25 minutes)

In a bowl, add 1 tbsp of olive oil, lime juice, salt, and pepper and rub the mixture onto the fillets. Transfer to them to the frying basket. Drizzle the florets with the remaining olive oil and arrange them around the salmon. Bake in the preheated at 340 F air fryer for 14 minutes or until the salmon is fork-tender and crispy on top. Sprinkle the fillets with red chili flakes (optional) and serve with broccoli.

Wild Salmon with Creamy Parsley Sauce

INGREDIENTS (4 Servings)

4 Alaskan wild salmon fillets
2 tsp olive oil
Salt and black pepper to taste

½ cup heavy cream
½ cup milk
2 tbsp fresh parsley, chopped

DIRECTIONS (Prep + Cook Time: 20 minutes)

Preheat the air fryer to 380 F. Drizzle the fillets with olive oil and season with salt and black pepper. Place in them in the frying basket and Bake for 14-16 minutes, turning once, until tender and crispy. In a bowl, mix the milk, parsley, salt, and heavy cream. Serve the salmon with the sauce and enjoy!

Sweet Caribbean Salmon Fillets

INGREDIENTS (4 Servings)

4 salmon fillets
½ tsp brown sugar
1 tbsp Cajun seasoning

1 lemon, zested and juiced
1 tbsp fresh parsley, chopped
2 tbsp mango salsa

DIRECTIONS (Prep + Cook Time: 20 minutes)

Preheat the air fryer to 350 F. In a bowl, mix the sugar, Cajun seasoning, lemon juice and zest, and coat the salmon in the mixture. Line the frying basket with parchment paper and grease it with oil. Place in the fish and Bake for 11-13 minutes, turning once. Top with parsley and mango salsa to serve.

Classic Mediterranean Salmon

INGREDIENTS (2 Servings)

2 salmon fillets
Salt and black pepper to taste

1 lemon, cut into wedges
8 asparagus spears, trimmed

DIRECTIONS (Prep + Cook Time: 20 minutes)

Preheat the air fryer to 350 F. Spritz the salmon with cooking spray. Season the fillets and asparagus with salt and pepper. Arrange the asparagus evenly in a single layer in the greased frying basket and top with the fillets. AirFry for 10-12 minutes at 350 F, turning the fish once. Serve with lemon wedges.

French Trout Meunière

INGREDIENTS (4 Servings)

4 trout pieces
½ cup flour
Salt to taste

2 tbsp butter
1 lemon, juiced
2 tbsp chervil (French parsley), chopped

DIRECTIONS (Prep + Cook Time: 20 minutes)

Preheat the air fryer to 380 F. Season the trout with salt and dredge in the flour. Spritz with cooking oil and AirFry for 12-14 minutes, flipping once, until crispy. Remove and tent with foil to keep warm.

Melt the butter in a skillet over medium heat. Stir for 1-2 minutes until the butter becomes golden brown. Turn off the heat and stir in chervil and lemon juice. Pour the sauce over the fish and serve.

Easy Creole Trout

INGREDIENTS (4 Servings)

4 skin-on trout fillets
2 tsp creole seasoning

2 tbsp fresh dill, chopped
1 lemon, sliced

DIRECTIONS (Prep + Cook Time: 20 minutes)

Preheat the air fryer to 350 F. Season the trout with creole seasoning on both sides and spray with cooking spray. Place in the frying basket and Bake for 10-12 minutes, flipping once. Serve sprinkled with dill and garnished with lemon slices.

Smoked Trout Frittata

INGREDIENTS (4 Servings)

2 tbsp olive oil
1 onion, sliced
1 egg, beaten
6 tbsp crème fraiche

½ tbsp horseradish sauce
1 cup smoked trout, diced
2 tbsp fresh dill, chopped

DIRECTIONS (Prep + Cook Time: 25 minutes)

Preheat the fryer to 350 F. Heat olive oil in a pan over medium heat and sauté the onion, 3 minutes. In a bowl, mix the egg with crème fraiche and horseradish sauce. Add the onion, dill, and trout; mix well. Pour the mixture into a greased baking dish and Bake inside the fryer for 14 minutes or until golden.

Baked Trout en Papillote with Herbs

INGREDIENTS (2 Servings)

2 whole trouts, scaled and cleaned
¼ bulb fennel, sliced
½ brown onion, sliced
1 tbsp fresh parsley, chopped

1 tbsp fresh dill, chopped
1 tbsp olive oil
1 lemon, sliced
Garlic salt and black pepper to taste

DIRECTIONS (Prep + Cook Time: 25 minutes)

In a bowl, whisk the olive oil, brown onion, parsley, dill, fennel, garlic salt, and pepper.

Preheat the air fryer to 350 F. Open the cavity of the fish and fill with the spicy mixture. Wrap the fish completely in parchment paper and then in foil. Place the fish in the frying basket and Bake for 15 minutes. Remove the foil and paper. Top with lemon slices and serve warm.

Lovely "Blackened" Catfish

INGREDIENTS (2 Servings)

2 catfish fillets
2 tsp blackening seasoning
Juice of 1 lime

2 tbsp butter, melted
1 garlic clove, minced
2 tbsp fresh cilantro, chopped

DIRECTIONS (Prep + Cook Time: 25 minutes)

Preheat the air fryer to 360 F. In a bowl, mix garlic, lime juice, cilantro, and butter. Divide the sauce into two parts, rub 1 part of the sauce onto the fillets. Sprinkle with the seasoning. Place the fillets in the greased frying basket and Bake for 14-16 minutes, flipping once. Serve with the remaining sauce.

Rosemary Catfish

INGREDIENTS (4 Servings)

4 catfish fillets
¼ cup seasoned fish fry

1 tbsp olive oil
1 tbsp fresh rosemary, chopped

DIRECTIONS (Prep + Cook Time: 20 minutes)

Preheat the air fryer to 400 F. Add the seasoned fish fry and the fillets to a large Ziploc bag; massage to coat. Place the fillets in the greased frying basket and AirFry for 6-8 minutes. Flip the fillets and cook for 2-4 more minutes or until golden and crispy. Top with freshly chopped rosemary and serve.

Golden Batter Fried Catfish Fillets

INGREDIENTS (2 Servings)

4 catfish fillets, cut into strips
½ cup polenta
½ cup flour
¼ tsp cayenne pepper
1 tbsp fresh parsley, chopped

Salt and black pepper to taste
1 tsp onion powder
1 (7-oz) bottle club soda
1 lemon, sliced

DIRECTIONS (Prep + Cook Time: 25 minutes)

Preheat the fryer to 400 F. Sift the flour into a large bowl. Add in the onion powder, salt, black pepper, and cayenne pepper and stir to combine. Pour in the soda and whisk until a smooth batter is formed.

Lightly spray the fish with cooking spray. Dip the fish strips into the batter, then into the polenta. Put the fillets in the lightly greased frying basket and AirFry for 6-7 minutes. Flip or shake and cook further for 4-5 minutes or until brown and crispy. Garnish with parsley and lemon slices and serve.

Jamaican Fish Fillets

INGREDIENTS (4 Servings)

4 hoki fillets
1 tbsp ground Jamaican allspice
1 tsp paprika
Salt and garlic powder to taste

½ red onion, sliced
2 tomatoes, chopped
½ cup canned corn, drained
½ lemon, juiced

DIRECTIONS (Prep + Cook Time: 20 minutes)

In a bowl, mix the red onion, tomatoes, corn, salt, and lemon juice; toss to coat and set aside.

Preheat the air fryer to 390 F. In a bowl, mix paprika, garlic powder, and Jamaican seasoning. Rub the hoki fillets with the spices mixture. Spritz with cooking spray. Transfer to the frying basket and AirFry for 8 minutes, turn the fillets, and cook further for 5 minutes or until crispy. Serve with the corn salsa.

Ale-Battered Fish with Tartar Sauce

INGREDIENTS (4 Servings)

4 lemon wedges
2 eggs
1 cup ale beer
1 cup flour
Salt and black pepper to taste
4 white fish fillets

½ cup light mayonnaise
½ cup Greek yogurt
2 dill pickles, chopped
1 tbsp capers
1 tbsp fresh dill, roughly chopped
Lemon wedges to serve

DIRECTIONS (Prep + Cook Time: 25 minutes)

Preheat the air fryer to 390 F. Beat the eggs in a bowl along with the ale beer, salt, and pepper. Dredge the fillets in the flour and shake off the excess. Dip them into the egg mixture and then in the flour again. Spray with cooking spray and place in the frying basket. AirFry for 10-12 minutes, turning once.

In a bowl, mix the mayonnaise, Greek yogurt, capers, salt, and dill pickles. Sprinkle the fish with a little bit of dill and serve with the sauce and some freshly cut lemon wedges on the side.

Parmesan Tilapia Fillets

INGREDIENTS (4 Servings)

¾ cup Parmesan cheese, grated
2 tbsp olive oil
2 tsp paprika

2 tbsp fresh parsley, chopped
¼ tsp garlic powder
4 tilapia fillets

DIRECTIONS (Prep + Cook Time: 20 minutes)

Preheat the air fryer to 350 F. Mix parsley, Parmesan cheese, garlic powder, and paprika in a shallow bowl. Coat fillets in the mixture and brush with olive oil. Place the filets in the frying basket and AirFry for 10-12 minutes, flipping once, until golden brown. Serve immediately.

Air-Fried Broiled Tilapia

INGREDIENTS (4 Servings)

1 lb tilapia fillets
1 tsp old bay seasoning
2 tbsp canola oil

2 tbsp lemon pepper
Salt to taste
2 butter buds

DIRECTIONS (Prep + Cook Time: 20 minutes)

Preheat the air fryer to 400 F. Drizzle the fillets with canola oil. In a bowl, mix salt, lemon pepper, butter buds, and old bay seasoning; spread onto the fish. Place the fillets in the frying basket and AirFry for 10-12 minutes, turning once, until crispy. Serve with green salad.

Air Fried Tilapia Bites

INGREDIENTS (4 Servings)

1 lb tilapia fillets, cut into chunks
½ cup cornflakes
1 cup flour

2 eggs, beaten
Salt to taste
Lemon wedges for serving

DIRECTIONS (Prep + Cook Time: 25 minutes)

Preheat the fryer to 390 F. Pour the flour, eggs, and cornflakes each into 3 different bowls. Salt the fish and dip first in the flour, then in the eggs, and finally in the cornflakes. Put in the greased frying basket and AirFry for 6 minutes. Shake or flip, and cook for 5 more minutes or until crispy. Serve with lemon.

Peppery & Lemony Haddock

INGREDIENTS (4 Servings)

4 haddock fillets
1 cup breadcrumbs
2 tbsp lemon juice
Salt and black pepper to taste

¼ cup potato flakes
2 eggs, beaten
¼ cup Parmesan cheese, grated
3 tbsp flour

DIRECTIONS (Prep + Cook Time: 20 minutes)

In a bowl, combine flour, salt, and pepper. In another bowl, mix breadcrumbs, Parmesan, and potato flakes. Dip fillets in the flour first, then in the eggs, and coat them in the crumbs mixture. Place them in the greased frying basket and AirFry for 14-16 minutes at 370 F, flipping once. Serve with lemon juice.

Crumbly Haddock Patties

INGREDIENTS (2 Servings)

8 oz haddock, cooked and flaked
2 potatoes, cooked and mashed
2 tbsp green olives, pitted and chopped

1 tbsp fresh cilantro, chopped
1 tsp lemon zest
1 egg, beaten

DIRECTIONS (Prep + Cook Time: 25 minutes + refrigerating time)

Mix haddock, lemon zest, olives, cilantro, egg, and potatoes. Shape into patties and chill for 60 minutes.

Preheat the air fryer to 350 F. Place the patties in the greased frying basket and AirFry for 12-14 minutes, flipping once, halfway through cooking until golden. Serve with green salad or steamed rice.

Barramundi Fillets in Lemon Sauce

INGREDIENTS (4 Servings)

4 barramundi fillets
1 lemon, juiced
Salt and black pepper to taste
2 tbsp butter

½ cup white wine
8 black peppercorns
2 cloves garlic, minced
2 shallots, chopped

DIRECTIONS (Prep + Cook Time: 30 minutes)

Preheat the air fryer to 390 F. Season the fillets with salt and black pepper. Place them in the greased frying basket. AirFry for 15 minutes, flipping once, until the edges are golden brown. Remove to a plate.

Melt the butter in a pan over low heat. Add in garlic and shallots and stir-fry for 3 minutes. Pour in the white wine, lemon juice, and peppercorns. Cook until the liquid is reduced by three quarters, about 3-5 minutes. Adjust the seasoning and strain the sauce. Drizzle the sauce over the fish and serve warm.

Hot Sardine Cakes

INGREDIENTS (4 Servings)

2 (4-oz) tins sardines, chopped
2 eggs, beaten
½ cup breadcrumbs
⅓ cup green onions, finely chopped
2 tbsp fresh parsley, chopped

1 tbsp mayonnaise
1 tsp sweet chili sauce
½ tsp paprika
Salt and black pepper to taste
2 tbsp olive oil

DIRECTIONS (Prep + Cook Time: 20 minutes)

In a bowl, add sardines, eggs, breadcrumbs, green onions, parsley, mayonnaise, sweet chili sauce, paprika, salt, and black pepper. Mix well with hands. Shape into 8 cakes and brush them lightly with olive oil. AirFry them for 8-10 minutes at 390 F, flipping once halfway through cooking. Serve warm.

Effortless Tuna Fritters

INGREDIENTS (2 Servings)

5 oz canned tuna
1 tsp lime juice
½ tsp paprika
¼ cup flour
½ cup milk

1 small onion, diced
2 eggs
1 tsp chili powder, optional
½ tsp salt

DIRECTIONS (Prep + Cook Time: 25 minutes + refrigerating time)

Place all ingredients in a bowl and mix well. Make two large patties out of the mixture. Refrigerate them for 30 minutes. Then, remove and AirFry the patties in the greased frying basket for 13-15 minutes at 350 F, flipping once halfway through cooking. Serve warm.

Air Fried Tuna Sandwich

INGREDIENTS (2 Servings)

4 white bread slices
1 (5-oz) can tuna, drained
½ onion, finely chopped

2 tbsp mayonnaise
1 cup mozzarella cheese, shredded
1 tbsp olive oil

DIRECTIONS (Prep + Cook Time: 20 minutes)

In a small bowl, mix tuna, onion, and mayonnaise. Spoon the mixture over two bread slices, top with mozzarella cheese, and cover with the remaining bread slices. Brush with olive oil and arrange the sandwiches in the frying basket. Bake at 360 F for 7-10 minutes, flipping once halfway through. Serve.

Smoked Fish Quiche

INGREDIENTS (4 Servings)

1 (16-oz) pie crust
4 eggs, lightly beaten
4 tbsp heavy cream
¼ cup green onions, finely chopped
2 tbsp fresh parsley, chopped

1 tsp baking powder
Salt and black pepper to taste
1 lb smoked salmon, chopped
1 cup mozzarella cheese, shredded

DIRECTIONS (Prep + Cook Time: 40 minutes)

In a bowl, whisk eggs, heavy cream, green onions, parsley, baking powder, salt, and pepper. Stir in the salmon and mozzarella cheese. Roll out the pie crust and press it gently into a greased quiche pan that fits in your air fryer. Prick the pie all over with a fork. Pour in the salmon mixture and place the pan inside the fryer. Bake for 22-25 minutes at 360 F. Let cool slightly before slicing. Serve and enjoy!

Delicious Seafood Casserole

INGREDIENTS (4 Servings)

1 cup seafood mix
1 lb russet potatoes, peeled and quartered
1 carrot, grated
½ fennel bulb, sliced
2 tbsp fresh parsley, chopped
10 oz baby spinach
1 small tomato, diced

½ celery stick, grated
2 tbsp butter
4 tbsp milk
½ cup cheddar cheese, grated
1 small red chili, minced
Salt and black pepper to taste

DIRECTIONS (Prep + Cook Time: 60 minutes + cooling time)

Cover the potatoes with salted water in a pot and cook over medium heat for 18-20 minutes or until tender. Drain and mash them along with butter, milk, salt, and pepper. Mix until smooth and set aside.

In a bowl, mix celery, carrot, red chili, fennel, parsley, seafood mix, tomato, spinach, salt, and pepper.

Preheat the air fryer to 330 F. In a casserole baking dish, spread the seafood mixture. Top with the potato mash and level. Sprinkle with cheddar cheese and place the dish in the air fryer. Bake for 20-25 minutes or until golden and bubbling at the edges. Let cool for 10 minutes, slice, and serve.

Sesame Halibut Fillets

INGREDIENTS (4 Servings)

1 lb halibut fillets
4 biscuits, crumbled
3 tbsp flour
1 egg, beaten

Salt and black pepper to taste
¼ tsp dried rosemary
3 tbsp olive oil
2 tbsp sesame seeds

DIRECTIONS (Prep + Cook Time: 25 minutes)

Preheat the air fryer to 390 F.

In a bowl, combine flour, black pepper, and salt. In another bowl, combine sesame seeds, crumbled biscuits, olive oil, and rosemary. Dip the fish fillets into the flour mixture first, then into the beaten egg.

Finally, coat them in the sesame/biscuit mixture. Arrange them on the greased frying basket and AirFry for 8 minutes. Flip the fillets and cook for 4-5 more minutes or until golden. Serve immediately.

Oaty Fishcakes

INGREDIENTS (4 Servings)

4 potatoes, cooked and mashed
2 salmon fillets, cubed
1 haddock fillet, cubed
1 tsp Dijon mustard

½ cup oats
2 tbsp fresh dill, chopped
2 tbsp olive oil
Salt and black pepper to taste

DIRECTIONS (Prep + Cook Time: 30 minutes)

Preheat the air fryer to 400 F. Boil salmon and haddock cubes in a pot filled with salted water over medium heat, for 5-8 minutes. Drain, cool, and pat dry. Flake or shred the fish and transfer to a bowl.

Let cool slightly and mix in the mashed potatoes, mustard, oats, dill, salt, and black pepper. Shape into balls and flatten to make patties. Brush with olive oil and arrange them in the greased frying basket. Bake for 10-13 minutes, flipping once halfway through, until golden. Let cool slightly before serving.

Ponzu Marinated Tuna

INGREDIENTS (4 Servings)

4 tuna steaks
1 cup Japanese ponzu sauce
2 tbsp sesame oil
1 tbsp red pepper flakes

2 tbsp ginger paste
¼ cup scallions, sliced
Salt and black pepper to taste

DIRECTIONS (Prep + Cook Time: 25 minutes + marinating time)

In a bowl, mix the ponzu sauce, sesame oil, red pepper flakes, ginger paste, salt, and black pepper. Add in the tuna and toss to coat. Cover and marinate for 60 minutes in the fridge.

Preheat the air fryer to 380 F. Remove tuna from the marinade and arrange the steaks on the greased frying basket. AirFry for 14-16 minutes, turning once. Top with scallions and serve with fresh salad.

Peach Salsa & Beer Halibut Tacos

INGREDIENTS (4 Servings)

4 corn tortillas
1 lb halibut fillets, sliced into strips
2 tbsp olive oil
1 ½ cups flour
1 (12-oz) can beer

A pinch of salt
4 tbsp peach salsa
4 tsp fresh cilantro, chopped
1 tsp baking powder

DIRECTIONS (Prep + Cook Time: 25 minutes)

Preheat the fryer to 390 F. In a bowl, mix flour, baking powder, and salt. Pour in 1-2 oz of beer, enough to form a batter-like consistency. Save the rest of the beer to gulp with the tacos. Dip the fish strips into the beer batter. Arrange them in the greased frying basket and AirFry them for 8-10 minutes, shaking or flipping once. Spread the peach salsa on the tortillas. Serve topped with the strips and cilantro.

Italian-Style White Fish

INGREDIENTS (4 Servings)

2 tbsp fresh basil, chopped
1 tsp garlic powder
2 tbsp Romano cheese, grated

Salt and black pepper to taste
4 white fish fillets

DIRECTIONS (Prep + Cook Time: 20 minutes)

Preheat the air fryer to 350 F. Season fillets with garlic, salt, and pepper. Place them in the greased frying basket and AirFry for 8-10 minutes, flipping once. Serve topped with Romano cheese and basil.

VEGETABLES & VEGETARIAN

Mushroom Balls with Tomato Sauce

INGREDIENTS (4 Servings)

⅓ cup cooked rice
1 lb mushrooms, chopped
½ onion, chopped
½ green bell pepper, chopped
Celery salt to taste

1 tbsp Worcestershire sauce
1 garlic clove, minced
2 cups tomato juice
1 tsp oregano

DIRECTIONS (Prep + Cook Time: 30 minutes)

Preheat the air fryer to 370 F. In a food processor, blend the mushrooms until they resemble large crumbs. In a bowl, combine the rice, ground mushrooms, onion, celery salt, green pepper, and garlic. Shape into balls, and arrange them in the greased frying basket. AirFry for 18 minutes, turning once.

Meanwhile, place a saucepan over medium heat and pour in tomato juice, oregano, celery salt, and Worcestershire sauce. Cook until reduced by half, 6 minutes. Drizzle the sauce over the balls to serve.

Fried Green Tomato Bites with Remoulade

INGREDIENTS (2 Servings)

2 green tomatoes, sliced
¼ tbsp creole seasoning
¼ cup flour

1 egg, beaten
1 cup breadcrumbs
1 cup remoulade sauce

DIRECTIONS (Prep + Cook Time: 15 minutes)

Add flour to one bowl and the egg to another. Make a mix of creole seasoning and breadcrumbs in a third bowl. Coat the tomato slices in the flour, then dip in the egg, and then in the crumbs. AirFry in the greased frying basket for 5-6 minutes at 400 F, turning once. Serve with remoulade sauce.

Roasted Tomatoes with Cheese Topping

INGREDIENTS (4 Servings)

½ cup cheddar cheese, shredded
¼ cup Parmesan cheese, grated
4 tomatoes, cut into ½ inch slices

2 tbsp fresh parsley, chopped
Salt and black pepper to taste

DIRECTIONS (Prep + Cook Time: 20 minutes)

Preheat the air fryer to 380 F. Lightly salt the tomato slices and put them in the greased frying basket in a single layer. Top with cheddar and Parmesan cheeses and sprinkle with black pepper. AirFry for 5-6 minutes until the cheese is melted and bubbly. Serve topped with fresh parsley and enjoy!

Roasted Brussels Sprouts

INGREDIENTS (4 Servings)

1 lb Brussels sprouts
1 tsp garlic powder

2 tbsp olive oil
Salt and black pepper to taste

DIRECTIONS (Prep + Cook Time: 25 minutes)

Preheat the air fryer to 380 F. Trim off the outer leaves, keeping only the head of each sprout. In a bowl, mix olive oil, garlic powder, salt, and black pepper. Coat in the Brussels sprouts and transfer them to the greased frying basket. AirFry for 15 minutes, shaking once halfway through cooking.

Honey Baby Carrots

INGREDIENTS (4 Servings)

1 lb baby carrots
1 tsp dried dill
2 tbsp olive oil

1 tbsp honey
1 cup feta cheese, crumbled
Salt and black pepper to taste

DIRECTIONS (Prep + Cook Time: 20 minutes)

Preheat the air fryer to 350 F. In a bowl, mix olive oil, carrots, and honey, and stir to coat. Season with dill, black pepper, and salt. Place the coated carrots in the greased frying basket and AirFry for 12-14 minutes, shaking once or twice. Serve warm or chilled topped with feta cheese.

Authentic Spanish Patatas Bravas

INGREDIENTS (4 Servings)

1 lb waxy potatoes, into bite-size chunks
4 tbsp olive oil
1 tsp smoked paprika
1 shallot, chopped
2 tomatoes, chopped
1 tbsp tomato paste

1 tbsp flour
2 tbsp sriracha hot chili sauce
1 tsp sugar
2 tbsp fresh parsley, chopped
Salt to taste

DIRECTIONS (Prep + Cook Time: 40 minutes)

Heat 2 tbsp of olive oil in a skillet over medium heat and sauté the shallot for 3 minutes until fragrant. Stir in the flour for 2 more minutes. Add in the remaining ingredients and 1 cup of water. Bring to a boil, reduce the heat, and simmer for 6-8 minutes until the sauce becomes pulpy. Remove to a food processor and blend until smooth. Let cool completely.

Preheat the air fryer to 400 F. Coat the potatoes in the remaining olive oil and AirFry in the fryer for 20-25 minutes, shaking once halfway through. Sprinkle with salt and spoon over the sauce to serve.

Delicious Potato Patties

INGREDIENTS (4 Servings)

4 potatoes, shredded
1 onion, chopped
1 egg, beaten
¼ cup milk

2 tbsp butter
½ tsp garlic powder
Salt and black pepper to taste
3 tbsp flour

DIRECTIONS (Prep + Cook Time: 25 minutes)

Preheat the air fryer to 390 F. In a bowl, add the egg, potatoes, onion, milk, butter, black pepper, flour, garlic powder, and salt and mix well to form a batter. Mold the mixture into four patties. Place them in the greased frying basket and AirFry for 14-16 minutes, flipping once. Serve warm with garlic mayo.

Sweet & Spicy French Fries

INGREDIENTS (4 Servings)

½ tsp salt
½ tsp garlic powder
½ tsp chili powder

¼ tsp cumin
3 tbsp olive oil
4 sweet potatoes, cut into thick strips

DIRECTIONS (Prep + Cook Time: 30 minutes)

Preheat the air fryer to 380 F. In a bowl, whisk olive oil, salt, garlic, chili powder, and cumin. Coat the strips in the mixture and place them in the frying basket. AirFry for 20 minutes, shaking once, until crispy.

Curly Fries with Gochujang Ketchup

INGREDIENTS (2 Servings)

2 potatoes, spiralized
Salt and black pepper to taste
2 tbsp coconut oil
1 tbsp Gochujang chili paste

½ cup tomato ketchup
2 tsp soy sauce
¼ tsp ginger powder

DIRECTIONS (Prep + Cook Time: 35 minutes)

In a small bowl, whisk together the ketchup, Gochujang paste, soy sauce, and ginger powder; reserve.

Preheat the air fryer to 390 F. In a bowl, coat the potatoes in coconut oil, salt, and pepper. Place in the frying basket and AirFry for 20-25 minutes, shaking once. Serve with Gochujang ketchup and enjoy!

Traditional Jacket Potatoes

INGREDIENTS (4 Servings)

1 lb potatoes
2 garlic cloves, minced
Salt and black pepper to taste

1 tbsp fresh rosemary, chopped
1 tbsp fresh parsley, chopped
2 tsp butter, melted

DIRECTIONS (Prep + Cook Time: 30 minutes)

Preheat the air fryer to 360 F. Prick the potatoes with a fork. Place them in the greased frying basket and Bake for 23-25 minutes, turning once halfway through. Remove and cut a cross on top. Squeeze the sides and drizzle with melted butter. Sprinkle with garlic, rosemary, parsley, salt, and pepper. Serve.

Cheesy Potatoes & Asparagus

INGREDIENTS (4 Servings)

4 potatoes, cut into wedges
1 bunch of asparagus, trimmed
2 tbsp olive oil
¼ cup buttermilk

¼ cup cottage cheese, crumbled
1 tbsp whole-grain mustard
Salt and black pepper to taste

DIRECTIONS (Prep + Cook Time: 30 minutes)

Preheat the fryer to 400 F. Place the potatoes in the greased frying basket and Bake for 14-16 minutes. Drizzle the asparagus with olive oil and season with salt and pepper. Slide the frying basket out and shake the potatoes. Spread the asparagus all over and Bake for 7 minutes, turning the spears once.

In a bowl, mix well the cottage cheese, buttermilk, and whole-grain mustard. Arrange potatoes and asparagus on a serving platter and drizzle with the cheese sauce. Serve and enjoy!

Balsamic Bell Pepper Bites

INGREDIENTS (4 Servings)

1 red bell pepper, cut into small portions
1 yellow pepper, cut into small portions
1 green bell pepper, cut into small portions
3 tbsp balsamic vinegar
2 tbsp olive oil

1 garlic clove, minced
½ tsp dried basil
½ tsp dried parsley
Salt and black pepper to taste
½ cup garlic mayonnaise

DIRECTIONS (Prep + Cook Time: 20 minutes)

Preheat the air fryer to 390 F. In a bowl, mix bell peppers, olive oil, garlic, balsamic vinegar, basil, and parsley and season with salt and black pepper. Transfer to the greased frying basket and Bake in the air fryer for 12-15 minutes, tossing once or twice. Serve with garlic mayonnaise.

Quick Beetroot Chips

INGREDIENTS (2 Servings)

2 golden beetroots, thinly sliced
2 tbsp olive oil

1 tbsp yeast flakes
1 tsp Italian seasoning

DIRECTIONS (Prep + Cook Time: 20 minutes)

Preheat the air fryer to 360 F. In a bowl, add olive oil, beetroot slices, Italian seasoning, and yeast and mix well. Dump the coated chips in the greased frying basket and AirFry for 12 minutes, shaking once.

Brussels Sprouts with Garlic Aioli

INGREDIENTS (4 Servings)

3 garlic cloves, minced
1 lb Brussels sprouts, trimmed and halved
Salt and black pepper to taste

2 tbsp olive oil
2 tsp lemon juice
¾ cup mayonnaise

DIRECTIONS (Prep + Cook Time: 25 minutes)

Place a pot with water over medium heat; bring to a boil. Blanch in the sprouts for 3 minutes; drain.

Preheat the air fryer to 350 F. Drizzle the Brussels sprouts with olive oil and season to taste. Pour them into the frying basket and AirFry for 5 minutes, shaking once. In a bowl, whisk the mayonnaise, garlic, lemon juice, salt and black pepper to taste, to make aioli. Serve the sprouts with aioli.

Easy Cabbage Steaks

INGREDIENTS (3 Servings)

1 cabbage head
1 tbsp garlic paste
2 tbsp olive oil

Salt and black pepper to taste
2 tsp fennel seeds

DIRECTIONS (Prep + Cook Time: 25 minutes)

Preheat the air fryer to 350 F. Cut the cabbage into 1½-inch thin slices. In a small bowl, combine all the other ingredients and brush the cabbage with the mixture. Arrange the steaks in the greased frying basket and Bake for 14-16 minutes, flipping once halfway through cooking. Serve warm or chilled.

Green Cabbage with Blue Cheese Sauce

INGREDIENTS (4 Servings)

1 head green cabbage, cut into wedges
1 cup mozzarella cheese, shredded

4 tbsp butter, melted
½ cup blue cheese sauce

DIRECTIONS (Prep + Cook Time: 25 minutes)

Preheat the air fryer to 380 F. Brush the wedges with butter and sprinkle with mozzarella. Transfer to the greased frying basket and Bake in the air fryer for 18-20 minutes. Serve with blue cheese sauce.

Crispy Bell Peppers with Tartare Sauce

INGREDIENTS (4 Servings)

1 egg, beaten
2 bell peppers, cut into ½-inch-thick slices
⅔ cup panko breadcrumbs
½ tsp paprika
½ tsp garlic powder

Salt to taste
1 tsp lime juice
½ cup mayonnaise
2 tbsp capers, chopped
2 dill pickles, chopped

DIRECTIONS (Prep + Cook Time: 25 minutes)

Preheat the air fryer to 390 F. Mix the breadcrumbs, paprika, garlic powder, and salt in a shallow bowl. In a separate bowl, whisk the egg with 1½ teaspoons of water to make an egg wash. Coat the bell pepper slices in the egg wash, then roll them up in the crumbs mixture until fully covered.

Put the peppers in the greased frying basket in a single layer and spray with olive oil, AirFry for 4-7 minutes until light brown. Meanwhile, in a bowl, mix the mayonnaise, lime juice, capers, pickles, and salt. Remove the peppers from the fryer and serve with the tartare sauce. Enjoy!

Indian Fried Okra

INGREDIENTS (4 Servings)

1 tbsp chili powder	Salt and black pepper to taste
2 tbsp garam masala	½ lb okra, trimmed and halved lengthwise
1 cup cornmeal	1 egg
¼ cup flour	1 cup Cholula hot sauce

DIRECTIONS (Prep + Cook Time: 20 minutes)

Preheat the air fryer to 380 F. In a bowl, mix cornmeal, flour, chili powder, garam masala, salt, and black pepper. In another bowl, whisk the egg and season with salt and pepper.

Dip the okra in the egg and then coat in the cornmeal mixture. Spray with cooking spray and place in the frying basket. AirFry for 6 minutes, shake, and cook for another 5-7 minutes or until golden brown. Serve with hot sauce.

Zucchini Fries with Tabasco Dip

INGREDIENTS (4 Servings)

2 zucchinis, sliced	Salt and black pepper to taste
2 egg whites	1 cup mayonnaise
½ cup seasoned breadcrumbs	¼ cup heavy cream
2 tbsp Parmesan cheese, grated	1 tbsp Tabasco sauce
¼ tsp garlic powder	1 tsp lime juice

DIRECTIONS (Prep + Cook Time: 25 minutes)

Preheat the air fryer to 400 F. In a bowl, beat egg whites with salt and black pepper. In another bowl, mix garlic powder, Parmesan cheese, and breadcrumbs. Dip zucchini strips in the egg whites, then in the crumbs and spray them with cooking oil. AirFry them for 13-15 minutes, turning once.

Meanwhile, in a bowl, mix mayonnaise, heavy cream, Tabasco sauce, and lime juice. Serve as a dip for the strips.

Parmesan Zucchini Boats

INGREDIENTS (4 Servings)

4 small zucchinis, cut lengthwise	¼ cup fresh parsley, chopped
½ cup Parmesan cheese, grated	4 garlic cloves, minced
½ cup breadcrumbs	Salt and black pepper to taste
¼ cup melted butter	

DIRECTIONS (Prep + Cook Time: 25 minutes)

Preheat the air fryer to 370 F. Scoop out the insides of the zucchini halves with a spoon. In a bowl, mix breadcrumbs, garlic, and parsley. Season with salt and pepper and stir in the zucchini flesh. Spoon the mixture into the zucchini "boats" and sprinkle with Parmesan cheese. Drizzle with melted butter. Arrange the boats on the greased frying basket and Bake for 12 minutes or until the cheese is golden.

Bulgarian "Burek" Pepper with Yogurt Sauce

INGREDIENTS (4 Servings)

4 red bell peppers, roasted
1 cup feta cheese, crumbled
4 eggs
1 cup breadcrumbs
4 garlic cloves, chopped
1 tomato, peeled and chopped

1 tsp fresh dill, chopped
1 tbsp fresh parsley, chopped
Salt and black pepper to taste
1 tbsp olive oil
½ cup flour
1 cup Greek yogurt

DIRECTIONS (Prep + Cook Time: 30 minutes)

In a small bowl, mix yogurt, olive oil, half of the garlic, and dill. Keep the sauce in the fridge.

Preheat the air fryer to 350 F. In a bowl, beat 3 eggs with salt and black pepper. Add in feta cheese, the remaining garlic, tomato, and parsley and mix to combine. Fill the peppers with the mixture.

Beat the remaining egg with salt and pepper in a bowl. Coat the peppers first in flour, then dip in the egg, and finally in the crumbs. Arrange them in the greased frying basket and AirFry for 10-12 minutes until golden brown, turning once. Serve the peppers with the yogurt sauce on the side and enjoy!.

Green Pea Arancini with Tomato Sauce

INGREDIENTS (4 Servings)

1 cup rice, rinsed
½ green peas
1 tbsp butter
1 onion, chopped
2 garlic cloves, minced
1 egg

3 tbsp Parmesan cheese, shredded
½ cup breadcrumbs
2 tbsp olive oil
Salt and black pepper to taste
1 lb Roma tomatoes, chopped
2 tbsp fresh basil, chopped

DIRECTIONS (Prep + Cook Time: 60 minutes + chilling time)

Fill a shallow saucepan with water and place over medium heat. Bring to a boil and add in the rice, salt, and pepper. Cook for 20-22 minutes, stirring often. Drain and transfer to a bowl; mix in the green peas.

Mix in the onion, garlic, Parmesan cheese, and egg. Mold the mixture into golf-size balls and roll them in breadcrumbs. Place them in a baking sheet and refrigerate for 1 hour. Preheat the air fryer to 360 F. Remove the arancini from the fridge and arrange them in the greased frying basket. AirFry for 14-16 minutes, shaking from time to time until nicely browned.

Meanwhile, heat the olive oil in the skillet and stir-fry the tomatoes for 6-8 minutes until the sauce thickens. Season with salt and black pepper. Scatter basil on top and serve with the arancini.

Aunt's Roasted Carrots with Cilantro Sauce

INGREDIENTS (4 Servings)

¼ cup olive oil
2 shallots, cut into wedges
4 carrots, halved lengthways
4 garlic cloves, lightly crushed
¼ tsp nutmeg

¼ tsp allspice
¼ cup cilantro, chopped
¼ lime, zested and juiced
1 tbsp Parmesan cheese, grated
1 tbsp pine nuts

DIRECTIONS (Prep + Cook Time: 25 minutes)

Preheat the air fryer to 370 F. Coat the carrots and shallots with allspice, nutmeg, and some olive oil. Put in the frying basket. Sprinkle with garlic and Bake for 15-20 minutes, shaking halfway through.

In a food processor, blitz the remaining olive oil, cilantro, lime zest and juice, Parmesan cheese, and pine nuts until the mixture forms a paste. Remove and serve on the side of the roasted veggies.

Mediterranean Eggplant Burgers

INGREDIENTS (2 Servings)

2 hamburger buns, halved
2 (2-inch) eggplant slices, cut along the round axis
2 mozzarella slices
1 red onion, cut into rings

2 lettuce leaves
1 tbsp tomato sauce
1 pickle, sliced
Salt to taste

DIRECTIONS (Prep + Cook Time: 20 minutes)

Preheat the air fryer to 360 F. Season the eggplant slices with salt and place them in the greased frying basket. Bake for 6 minutes, flipping once. Top with mozzarella slices and cook for 30 more seconds.

Spread the tomato sauce on the bun bottoms. Top with the cheesy eggplant slices followed by the red onion rings, sliced pickle, and lettuce leaves. Finish with the bun tops and serve immediately.

Sesame Balsamic Asparagus

INGREDIENTS (4 Servings)

1 ½ lb asparagus, trimmed
4 tbsp balsamic vinegar
4 tbsp olive oil

2 tbsp fresh rosemary, chopped
Salt and black pepper to taste
2 tbsp sesame seeds

DIRECTIONS (Prep + Cook Time: 30 minutes)

Preheat the air fryer to 360 F. Whisk the olive oil, sesame seeds, balsamic vinegar, salt, and pepper to make a marinade. Place the asparagus on a baking dish and pour the marinade all over. Toss to coat and let them sit for 10 minutes. Transfer the asparagus to the frying basket and AirFry for 10-12 minutes, shaking once, or until tender and lightly charred. Serve the asparagus topped with rosemary.

Cheesy Eggplant Schnitzels

INGREDIENTS (4 Servings)

2 eggplants
½ cup mozzarella cheese, grated
2 tbsp milk

1 egg, beaten
2 cups breadcrumbs
2 tomatoes, sliced

DIRECTIONS (Prep + Cook Time: 15 minutes)

Preheat the air fryer to 400 F. Cut the eggplants lengthways into ½-inch thick slices. In a bowl, mix the egg and milk. In another bowl, combine the breadcrumbs and mozzarella cheese. Dip the eggplant slices in the egg mixture, followed by the crumbs mixture and place them in the greased frying basket. AirFry for 10-12 minutes, turning once halfway through. Top with tomato slices and serve.

Involtini di Melanzane (Eggplant Rollups)

INGREDIENTS (4 Servings)

2 eggplants, thinly sliced
1 tsp Italian seasoning
1 cup wheat flour

1 cup ricotta cheese, crumbled
Salt to taste
2 tbsp Parmesan cheese, grated

DIRECTIONS (Prep + Cook Time: 30 minutes)

Preheat the air fryer to 390 F. Season the eggplant slices with salt and dust them in the flour, shaking off the excess. Place them in the greased frying basket and AirFry for 5-6 minutes, turning once. Remove to a kitchen paper to remove any excess moisture. Then spread them with the ricotta cheese.

Sprinkle with Italian seasoning and roll them up. Coat in the Parmesan cheese and transfer the rolls to the greased frying basket. Bake for 10-12 minutes or until the cheese is lightly browned. Serve warm.

Air Fried Eggplant Bruschetta

INGREDIENTS (2 Servings)

2 large eggplant slices
1 large spring onion, finely sliced
½ cup sweet corn

1 egg white, whisked
1 tbsp black sesame seeds
Salt to taste

DIRECTIONS (Prep + Cook Time: 12 minutes)

Preheat the air fryer to 380 F. Salt the eggplant slices on both sides and place them in the greased frying basket. AirFry for 8-10 minutes, flipping once. In a bowl, place the corn, spring onion, egg white, and sesame seeds and mix well. Spread the mixture over the eggplant slices and place them in the air fryer again. Bake for 4-5 minutes or until the top is golden. Serve immediately.

Easy Eggplant & Zucchini Chips

INGREDIENTS (4 Servings)

1 large eggplant, cut into strips
1 zucchini, cut into strips
½ cup cornstarch

3 tbsp olive oil
Salt to season

DIRECTIONS (Prep + Cook Time: 20 minutes)

Preheat the fryer to 390 F. In a bowl, mix cornstarch, salt, pepper, oil, eggplant and zucchini strips. Place the coated veggies in the greased frying basket and AirFry for 10-12 minutes, shaking once.

Homemade Blooming Onion

INGREDIENTS (4 Servings)

2 eggs
½ cup milk
1 large yellow onions
1 cup flour
1 tsp garlic powder

Salt and black pepper to taste
1 tsp paprika
1 tsp cayenne pepper
1 cup garlic or chili mayonnaise

DIRECTIONS (Prep + Cook Time: 45 minutes)

Cut the top of the onion (not root) about half inch down to make it flat. Peel the onion and trim just the tip of the root. Lay the onion flat side down and make 4 vertical cuts, leaving the root intact. Make 3 more cuts between each of the 4 original cuts, so you have 12-16 cuts in total. Turn around and separate the petals resembling a flower. Place the onion in a deep bowl. Preheat the air fryer to 360 F.

In another bowl, mix flour, garlic powder, salt, pepper, paprika, and cayenne pepper. In a third bowl, whisk the eggs with the milk. Pour the flour mixture over the onion and thoroughly coat it with hands, making sure there is enough flour between the petals. Pick the onion up, turn it and shake it off. Place the onion in a clean bowl and pour the egg mixture over. Coat well and transfer the onion to another clean bowl. Dust the flour over and coat again. Spray generously with cooking oil and AirFry for 22-25 minutes until golden and crispy. Serve with garlic or chili mayonnaise, and enjoy!

Breaded Italian Green Beans

INGREDIENTS (4 Servings)

1 cup panko breadcrumbs
2 eggs, beaten
½ cup Parmesan cheese, grated
½ cup flour

1 tsp cayenne pepper
1 ½ lb green beans
1 cup tomato pasta sauce
Salt and black pepper to taste

DIRECTIONS (Prep + Cook Time: 25 minutes)

Preheat the air fryer to 400 F. In a bowl, mix breadcrumbs, Parmesan cheese, cayenne pepper, salt, and black pepper. Coat the beans in the flour, then dip them in the beaten egg and finally in the crumbs. AirFry in the fryer for 14-16 minutes, turning once halfway through. Serve with tomato sauce.

Russian-Style Eggplant Caviar

INGREDIENTS (4 Servings)

2 eggplants
½ red onion, chopped
2 tbsp balsamic vinegar

½ cup olive oil
Salt to taste
1 baguette, sliced

DIRECTIONS (Prep + Cook Time: 20 minutes + chilling time)

Preheat the air fryer to 380 F. Place the eggplants in the greased frying basket and Bake for 20 minutes, turning every 5 minutes. Remove and let them cool. Then, peel the skin, and transfer the flesh to a food processor. Add in red onion and olive oil; process until pureed. Season with balsamic vinegar and a bit of salt. Serve at room temperature with sliced baguette.

Avocado Fries with Pico de Gallo

INGREDIENTS (6 Servings)

3 eggs, beaten in a bowl
4 avocados, cut in half, pits removed
2 tbsp olive oil
1 ½ cups panko breadcrumbs
1 ½ tsp paprika
Salt and black pepper to taste

2 tbsp fresh cilantro, chopped
2 tomatoes, chopped
1 jalapeño pepper, minced
¼ cup red onions, finely chopped
1 lime, juiced
6 corn tortillas

DIRECTIONS (Prep + Cook Time: 30 minutes)

In a mixing bowl, thoroughly combine the cilantro, tomatoes, jalapeño pepper, red onion, lime juice, and salt. Place in the fridge to allow the flavors to incorporate; until pico de gallo is ready to use.

Preheat the air fryer to 360 F. Remove the skin from the avocado, leaving the flesh intact. Cut the halves into 5-6 lengthwise slices. Mix the breadcrumbs, salt, pepper, and paprika in a bowl. Dip each avocado slice in the eggs, then in the crumbs mixture, pressing gently into the avocado, so it sticks.

Put the avocado slices in a single layer on the greased fryer basket and brush with some olive oil. AirFry for 8-10 minutes, turning once, until light brown and crispy. Serve with pico de gallo on the side.

Cheese & Cauliflower Tater Tots

INGREDIENTS (4 Servings)

1 large egg
¼ cup Pecorino cheese, grated
¼ cup sharp cheddar cheese, shredded
1 lb cauliflower florets
1 garlic clove, minced

½ cup breadcrumbs
1 tbsp olive oil
2 tbsp scallions, chopped
Salt and black pepper to taste

DIRECTIONS (Prep + Cook Time: 35 minutes + chilling time)

Cook the florets in boiling salted water until al dente. Drain well and let dry on absorbent paper for 10 minutes. Then finely chop the florets and place into a bowl. Add in the egg, garlic, Pecorino cheese, cheddar cheese, breadcrumbs, salt, and black pepper; stir to combine. Refrigerate for 10 minutes.

Preheat the air fryer to 380 F. Shape the cauliflower mixture into bite-sized oval 'tater tots.' Lay them into the greased frying basket, giving them plenty of space. Brush the tots with oil and AirFry for 14-16 minutes, turning once, until crispy and browned. Top with scallions and serve with your favorite sauce.

Tasty Balsamic Beets

INGREDIENTS (2 Servings)

2 beets, cubed
⅓ cup balsamic vinegar
2 tbsp olive oil

1 tbsp honey
Salt and black pepper to taste
2 springs rosemary, chopped

DIRECTIONS (Prep + Cook Time: 25 minutes)

Preheat the air fryer to 400 F. In a bowl, mix beets, olive oil, rosemary, black pepper, and salt and toss to coat. AirFry the beets in the frying basket for 13-15 minutes, shaking once halfway through.

Meanwhile, pour the vinegar and honey into a pan over medium heat. Bring to a boil and cook until reduced by half. Drizzle the beets with balsamic sauce and serve.

Teriyaki Cauliflower

INGREDIENTS (4 Servings)

1 big cauliflower head, cut into florets
½ cup soy sauce
1 tbsp brown sugar
1 tsp sesame oil

½ chili powder
2 cloves garlic, chopped
1 tsp cornstarch

DIRECTIONS (Prep + Cook Time: 20 minutes)

In a bowl, whisk soy sauce, brown sugar, sesame oil, ⅓ cup of water, chili powder, garlic, and cornstarch until smooth. In a bowl, add the cauliflower and pour teriyaki sauce over; toss to coat.

Place the cauliflower in the greased frying basket and AirFry for 13-15 minutes at 380 F, turning once halfway through. When ready, check if the cauliflower is cooked but not too soft. Serve warm.

Easy Cauliflower Popcorn

INGREDIENTS (4 Servings)

1 head cauliflower, cut into florets
1 tsp garlic powder
1 tsp turmeric

1 tsp cumin
1 tbsp olive oil
Salt and black pepper to taste

DIRECTIONS (Prep + Cook Time: 35 minutes)

Preheat the air fryer to 390 F. In a mixing bowl, thoroughly combine the turmeric, cumin, garlic powder, salt, and black pepper. Add in the cauliflower florets and toss to coat well.

Add the florets to the greased frying basket and brush with olive oil. AirFry until browned and crispy, about 20 minutes, shaking the basket every 4-6 minutes. Serve hot.

Almond-Crusted Cauliflower Florets

INGREDIENTS (4 Servings)

1 head of cauliflower, cut into florets
2 eggs
1 cup ground almonds

4 tbsp Parmesan cheese, grated
Garlic salt and black pepper to taste
2 tbsp fresh cilantro, chopped

DIRECTIONS (Prep + Cook Time: 20 minutes)

Preheat the air fryer to 380 F. In a bowl, mix the Parmesan cheese, ground almonds, garlic salt, and black pepper. In another bowl, whisk the eggs. Dip the florets into the eggs, then roll them up in the almond crumbs. Lay the florets in the greased frying basket and spritz with cooking spray. AirFry for 8-10 minutes, shaking once, until crispy. Serve sprinkled with fresh cilantro.

Chili Corn on the Cob

INGREDIENTS (4 Servings)

4 ears of sweet corn, shucked
1 clove garlic, minced
1 green chili, minced
1 lemon, zested

2 tbsp olive oil
2 tbsp butter, melted
Fine salt to taste

DIRECTIONS (Prep + Cook Time: 25 minutes)

Preheat the air fryer to 380 F. in a bowl, mix olive oil, garlic, lemon zest, and green chili. Rub the mixture on all sides of the corn ears. Place the ears in the greased frying basket (work in batches). AirFry for 14-16 minutes, turning once, until lightly browned. Remove to a platter and drizzle with melted butter. Scatter with salt and serve.

Cholula Seasoned Broccoli

INGREDIENTS (4 Servings)

1 lb broccoli florets
½ tsp lemon zest
1 garlic clove, minced
1 tsp olive oil

1 ½ tbsp soy sauce
1 tsp lemon juice
1 tsp Cholula hot sauce
Salt and black pepper to taste

DIRECTIONS (Prep + Cook Time: 30 minutes)

Preheat the air fryer to 390 F. Put the broccoli florets, olive oil, and garlic in a bowl and season with salt. Toss well, then transfer the florets to the greased frying basket. AirFry for 15-20 minutes or until light brown and crispy. Shake the basket every 5 minutes.

Meanwhile, whisk the soy sauce, hot sauce, and lemon juice in a bowl. Toss the broccoli and sauce mixture into a large bowl and mix well. Sprinkle with lemon zest, salt, and pepper, and serve.

Parmesan Broccoli Bites

INGREDIENTS (4 Servings)

1 small head broccoli
3 eggs
1 carrot, shredded

½ cup roasted red pepper, chopped
Salt and black pepper to taste
2 tbsp Parmesan cheese, grated

DIRECTIONS (Prep + Cook Time: 25 minutes)

Blanch the broccoli in salted boiling water for 4-5 minutes until just tender. Drain and let cool slightly.

Preheat the air fryer to 340 F. In a bowl, mix all the remaining ingredients. Cut the cooled broccoli into florets and mix in the egg mixture. Spoon the mixture into greased muffin cups and place in the air fryer. Bake for 12-14 minutes or until set and just turning golden. Let cool completely before serving.

Catalan-Style "Escalivada" Veggie Spread

INGREDIENTS (6 Servings)

1 lb green peppers
1 lb tomatoes
1 medium onion

3 tbsp olive oil
½ tbsp salt
4 garlic cloves, peeled

DIRECTIONS (Prep + Cook Time: 25 minutes)

Preheat the air fryer to 360 F. Place green peppers, tomatoes, and onion in the greased frying basket and Bake for 5 minutes, flip, and cook for 8-10 more minutes. Remove and peel the skin. Place the vegetables in a blender and add garlic, olive oil, and salt and pulse until smooth. Serve warm or cooled.

Zucchini & Turnip Bake

INGREDIENTS (4 Servings)

1 lb turnips, sliced
1 large red onion, cut into rings
1 large zucchini, sliced

Salt and black pepper to taste
2 cloves garlic, crushed
2 tbsp olive oil

DIRECTIONS (Prep + Cook Time: 30 minutes)

Preheat the air fryer to 360 F. Place turnips, red onion, garlic, and zucchini in the greased frying basket. Drizzle with olive oil and season with salt and pepper. Bake in the fryer for 18-20 minutes, turning once.

Black Beans & Veggie Burgers

INGREDIENTS (4 Servings)

1 parsnip, chopped
1 carrot, chopped
½ lb mushrooms, chopped
1 (15-oz) can black beans, drained and rinsed
2 tbsp olive oil
1 egg, beaten

2 tbsp tomato paste
2 garlic cloves, minced
½ tsp onion powder
½ cup breadcrumbs
Salt and black pepper to taste
4 hamburger buns

DIRECTIONS (Prep + Cook Time: 45 minutes)

Preheat the air fryer to 360 F. Put the parsnip and carrot in the greased frying basket, drizzle with some olive oil, and season with salt and pepper. AirFry for 8 minutes. Toss the mushrooms in the frying basket, spray with oil, and season with salt and black pepper. AirFry for 5 more minutes.

Mash the black beans in a bowl. Mix in the egg, tomato paste, garlic, onion powder, salt, cooked veggies and mash the veggies with a fork. Add the breadcrumbs and stir to combine. Make 4 patties out of the mixture. Put the patties in the greased frying basket, giving each patty plenty of room. AirFry for 5 minutes, flip, spray with oil, and fry for 5-7 more minutes. Serve on buns.

Roasted Pumpkin with Goat Cheese

INGREDIENTS (2 Servings)

1 lb pumpkin, cut into wedges
2 tbsp olive oil
½ tsp red pepper flakes

1 tbsp fresh sage, chopped
1 cup goat cheese, crumbled
Salt and garlic powder to taste

DIRECTIONS (Prep + Cook Time: 35 minutes)

Preheat the air fryer to 390 F. Brush the pumpkin wedges with olive oil and arrange them on the frying basket. Sprinkle with salt, red pepper flakes, and garlic powder. Roast for 18-20 minutes, tossing once halfway through, or until browned and crisp. Top with goat cheese and sage and serve warm.

Sweet Butternut Squash with Walnuts

INGREDIENTS (4 Servings)

1 lb butternut squash, halved and seeded
2 tbsp sugar
⅓ cup walnuts, chopped

2 tsp olive oil
1 tsp ground cinnamon

DIRECTIONS (Prep + Cook Time: 30 minutes)

Preheat the air fryer to 390 F. Cut the squash into large pieces similar in size, leaving the skin on, and arrange them on the greased frying basket. Drizzle with olive oil and Roast for 8-10 minutes. Slide the basket out, and sprinkle with sugar. Cook until the sugar is caramelized, and the squash is lightly charred, 6-8 minutes. Top with walnuts and dust with cinnamon and serve.

Spicy Vegetable Skewers

INGREDIENTS (2 Servings)

2 large sweet potatoes
1 beetroot
1 green bell pepper
1 tsp chili flakes
Salt and black pepper to taste

½ tsp turmeric
¼ tsp garlic powder
¼ tsp paprika
1 tbsp olive oil
½ cup tomato chili sauce

DIRECTIONS (Prep + Cook Time: 35 minutes)

Preheat the air fryer to 350 F. Peel the veggies and cut them into bite-sized chunks. Place the chunks in a bowl along with the remaining ingredients and mix until completely coated. Thread the vegetables, alternately, onto skewers in this order: potato, pepper, and beetroot. Place in the greased frying basket and AirFry for 18-20 minutes, turning once. Serve with tomato chili sauce on the side.

Tempura Veggies with Sesame Soy Sauce

INGREDIENTS (4 Servings)

2 lb chopped veggies: carrot, parsnip, green beans, zucchini, onion rings, asparagus, cauliflower

1 ½ cups plain flour
Salt and black pepper to taste

1 ½ tbsp cornstarch
¾ cup cold water

Dipping sauce:
4 tbsp soy sauce
Juice of 1 lemon
½ tsp sesame oil

½ tsp sugar
½ garlic clove, chopped
½ tsp sweet chili sauce

DIRECTIONS (Prep + Cook Time: 30 minutes)

Line the frying basket with baking paper. In a bowl, mix flour, salt, pepper, and cornstarch; whisk to combine. Keep whisking as you add in cold water, so a smooth batter is formed. Dip each veggie piece into the batter and place it into the greased frying basket. AirFry for 10-12 minutes at 360 F, turning once; cook until crispy. Mix all dipping ingredients in a bowl. Serve with the crispy veggies.

Crispy Fried Tofu

INGREDIENTS (4 Servings)

14 oz firm tofu, cut into ½-inch thick strips
2 tbsp olive oil
½ cup flour

½ cup crushed cornflakes
Salt and black pepper to taste

DIRECTIONS (Prep + Cook Time: 20 minutes)

On a plate, mix flour, cornflakes, salt, and black pepper. Dip each tofu strip to coat, spray with olive oil, and arrange them on the frying basket. AirFry for 13-15 minutes at 360 F, turning once, until golden.

Classic French Ratatouille

INGREDIENTS (2 Servings)

2 tbsp olive oil
2 Roma tomatoes, thinly sliced
2 garlic cloves, minced
1 zucchini, thinly sliced

2 yellow bell peppers, sliced
1 tbsp vinegar
2 tbsp herbs de Provence
Salt and black pepper to taste

DIRECTIONS (Prep + Cook Time: 30 minutes)

Preheat the fryer to 390 F. Place all ingredients in a bowl and stir to coat. Transfer them to the greased frying basket and Bake in the fryer for 15-20 minutes, shaking every 5 minutes, until slightly charred.

Indian Aloo Tikki

INGREDIENTS (2 Servings)

4 boiled potatoes, shredded
3 tbsp lemon juice
1 roasted bell pepper, chopped
Salt to taste
2 onions, chopped

¼ cup fennel, chopped
5 tbsp flour
2 tbsp ginger-garlic paste
1 tbsp mint leaves, chopped
1 tbsp fresh cilantro, chopped

DIRECTIONS (Prep + Cook Time: 25 minutes)

Preheat the air fryer to 360 F. In a bowl, mix cilantro, mint, fennel, ginger-garlic paste, flour, salt, and lemon juice. Add in the potatoes, bell pepper, and onions, and mix to combine. Make balls from the mixture and flatten them to form patties. Place them into the greased frying basket and AirFry them for 14-16 minutes, flipping once. Serve with mint chutney if desired.

Roasted Balsamic Veggies

INGREDIENTS (4 Servings)

2 lb chopped veggies: potatoes, parsnips, zucchini, pumpkin, carrot, leeks
3 tbsp olive oil
1 tbsp balsamic vinegar

1 tbsp agave syrup
Salt and black pepper to taste

DIRECTIONS (Prep + Cook Time: 30 minutes)

In a bowl, add olive oil, balsamic vinegar, agave syrup, salt, and black pepper; mix well. Arrange the veggies on a baking tray and place them in the frying basket. Drizzle with the dressing and massage with hands until well-coated. AirFry for 18-22 minutes at 360 F, tossing once halfway through. Serve.

Party Crispy Nachos

INGREDIENTS (2 Servings)

1 cup sweet corn
1 cup all-purpose flour + some more
1 tbsp butter

½ tsp chili powder
Salt to taste
½ cup guacamole

DIRECTIONS (Prep + Cook Time: 20 minutes)

Add a small amount of water to the sweet corn and grind until you obtain a very fine paste. In a bowl, mix flour, salt, chili powder, and butter; stir into the corn. Knead with your palm until you obtain a stiff dough.

Preheat the air fryer to 350 F. On a working surface, dust a little bit of flour and spread the dough with a rolling pin. Make it around ¼-inch thickness. Cut into triangle shapes, as many as you can. AirFry the nachos in the greased frying basket for 9-12 minutes, shaking once, until crispy. Serve with guacamole.

Charred Broccolini with Lemon-Caper Sauce

INGREDIENTS (4 Servings)

1 lb broccolini
2 tbsp olive oil
2 garlic cloves, sliced
½ tsp red chili flakes

2 tsp lemon juice
2 tbsp capers
Salt and black pepper to taste
1 tbsp fresh parsley, chopped

DIRECTIONS (Prep + Cook Time: 25 minutes)

Preheat the air fryer to 380 F. Season the broccolini with salt and black pepper. Place them in the frying basket and drizzle with some olive oil. AirFry until tender and charred, 8-10 minutes.

Meanwhile, warm the remaining oil in a pan and sauté the garlic for 35 seconds; remove from heat. Stir in lemon juice, capers, and chili flakes. Pour the sauce over the broccolini and top with parsley.

Winter Vegetable Traybake

INGREDIENTS (2 Servings)

1 potato, cut into ½-inch half-moons
6 oz sliced butternut squash
1 small red onion, cut into wedges

1 carrot, sliced into rounds
1 tsp Italian seasoning
2 tsp olive oil

DIRECTIONS (Prep + Cook Time: 20 minutes)

Preheat the air fryer to 380 F. Coat the vegetables with olive oil and Italian seasoning in a bowl. Transfer them to the frying basket and AirFry for 14-16 minutes, tossing once, or until golden brown.

Winter Root Vegetable Medley

INGREDIENTS (4 Servings)

8 shallots, halved
2 carrots, sliced
1 turnip, cut into chunks
1 rutabaga, cut into chunks
2 potatoes, cut into chunks

1 beet, cut into chunks
Salt and black pepper to taste
2 tbsp fresh thyme, chopped
2 tbsp olive oil
2 tbsp pesto sauce

DIRECTIONS (Prep + Cook Time: 30 minutes)

Preheat the air fryer to 400 F.

In a bowl, combine all the root vegetables, salt, pepper, and olive oil. Toss to coat and transfer to the frying basket. AirFry for 10 minutes, shake, and cook for 8-10 more minutes or until crispy. Meanwhile, mix the pesto with 2 tbsp water and drizzle over the vegetables, and serve sprinkled with thyme.

Turmeric Crispy Chickpeas

INGREDIENTS (4 Servings)

1 (15-oz) can chickpeas, rinsed
1 tbsp salted butter, melted

½ tsp dried rosemary
¼ tsp turmeric

DIRECTIONS (Prep + Cook Time: 20 minutes)

Preheat the air fryer to 380 F. In a bowl, combine together chickpeas, salted butter, rosemary, and turmeric; toss to coat. Place them in the greased frying basket and AirFry for 6 minutes. Shake, and cook for 4-6 more minutes or until golden and crispy.

Middle Eastern Veggie Kofta

INGREDIENTS (4 Servings)

2 tbsp cornflour
1 cup canned white beans
⅓ cup carrots, grated
2 potatoes, boiled and mashed
¼ cup fresh mint leaves, chopped
½ tsp ras el hanout powder

2 tbsp pine nuts
½ cup fresh mozzarella, chopped
3 garlic cloves, chopped
A bunch of skewers, soaked in water
Salt to taste

DIRECTIONS (Prep + Cook Time: 30 minutes)

Preheat the air fryer to 390 F. Place the beans, carrots, pine nuts, garlic, mozzarella cheese, and mint in a food processor. Blend until smooth, then transfer to a bowl. Add in the mashed potatoes, cornflour, salt, and ras el hanout and mix until fully incorporated. Divide the mixture into equal shaped-patties, about 3 inches long by 1 inch thick. Thread shapes on skewers and Bake in the greased frying basket for 10-12 minutes, turning once halfway through. Serve warm.

Air Fried Cheesy Ravioli

INGREDIENTS (4 Servings)

1 package cheese ravioli
2 cup Italian breadcrumbs
¼ cup Pecorino cheese, grated

1 cup buttermilk
2 tsp olive oil
¼ tsp garlic powder

DIRECTIONS (Prep + Cook Time: 20 minutes)

Preheat the air fryer to 390 F. In a small bowl, combine breadcrumbs, Pecorino cheese, garlic powder, and olive oil. Dip the ravioli in the buttermilk and then coat them in the breadcrumb mixture.

Line the frying basket with parchment paper and arrange the ravioli inside. Bake for 7-9 minutes, turning once halfway through cooking, until nice and golden. Serve with marinara or carbonara sauce.

Cashew & Chickpea Balls

INGREDIENTS (4 Servings)

¼ cup rolled oats
½ cup cashews
15 oz canned chickpeas, drained
2 eggs

½ cup sweet onions, chopped
1 tsp cumin
1 tsp garlic powder
1 cup horseradish sauce

DIRECTIONS (Prep + Cook Time: 30 minutes)

Preheat the air fryer to 380 F. Ground the oats and cashews in a food processor. Add in the chickpeas and process until mostly smooth. Transfer to a bowl and mix in the eggs, onions, garlic powder, and cumin. Make falafel-sized balls out of the mixture. Place the balls in the greased frying basket and AirFry for 14-16 minutes, shaking once, until golden and crispy. Serve warm with horseradish sauce.

Chili Falafel with Cheesy Sauce

INGREDIENTS (4 Servings)

1 (14-oz) can chickpeas, drained
2 tbsp fresh parsley, chopped
6 spring onions, sliced
1 tsp garlic powder
Salt to taste
¼ tsp chili powder
1 cup cream cheese, softened

1 clove garlic, finely chopped
½ tsp dried dill
1 tsp hot paprika
2 tbsp olive oil
2 tbsp plain yogurt
1 tsp apple cider vinegar

DIRECTIONS (Prep + Cook Time: 35 minutes + chilling time)

Place the cream cheese, chopped garlic, dill, hot paprika, olive oil, yogurt, and vinegar in a bowl and whisk until you obtain a smooth and homogeneous sauce consistency. Keep covered in the fridge.

In a blender, place chickpeas, parsley, spring onions, garlic powder, chili powder, and salt and process until crumbly. Transfer the mixture to a bowl and refrigerate covered for 20 minutes. For each falafel, take 2 tablespoons to form a round ball, flattened around the edges.

Preheat the air fryer to 370 F and arrange falafels on the greased frying basket. AirFry for 14-16 minutes, flipping once, until lightly browned and cooked through. Serve with the cream cheese sauce.

Quinoa & Veggie Stuffed Peppers

INGREDIENTS (2 Servings)

1 cup cooked quinoa
2 red bell peppers, cored and cleaned

½ onion, diced
½ cup tomatoes, diced

¼ tsp smoked paprika
Salt and black pepper to taste

1 tsp olive oil
¼ tsp dried basil

DIRECTIONS (Prep + Cook Time: 25 minutes)

Preheat the air fryer to 350 F. In a bowl, mix quinoa, onion, basil, tomatoes, smoked paprika, salt, and pepper and stir. Stuff the peppers with the filling and brush them with olive oil. Place the peppers in the greased frying basket and Bake for 12-15 minutes until cooked through and slightly charred. Serve.

Fava Bean Falafel with Tzatziki

INGREDIENTS (4 Servings)

2 cups cooked fava beans
½ cup flour
2 tbsp fresh parsley, chopped
Juice of 1 lemon
2 garlic cloves, chopped

1 onion, chopped
½ tsp ground cumin
1 cup tzatziki sauce
4 pita wraps, warm
Salt and black pepper to taste

DIRECTIONS (Prep + Cook Time: 30 minutes)

In a blender, add fava beans, flour, parsley, lemon juice, garlic, onion, cumin, salt, and pepper; blend until well-combined but not too battery; there should be some lumps. Shape the mixture into balls.

Press them with hands, making sure they are still around. Spray with olive oil and arrange in the paper-lined frying basket. AirFry for 13-15 minutes at 360 F, turning once halfway through, until crunchy and golden. Serve in the pita wraps drizzled with tzatziki sauce.

Greek Halloumi Cheese with Veggies

INGREDIENTS (2 Servings)

6 oz halloumi cheese, grated
2 zucchinis, cut into even chunks
1 carrot, cut into chunks
1 eggplant, peeled, cut into chunks

2 tsp olive oil
1 tsp dried Greek seasoning
Salt and black pepper to taste

DIRECTIONS (Prep + Cook Time: 25 minutes)

Preheat the air fryer to 350 F. In a bowl, add zucchinis, carrot, eggplant, olive oil, Greek seasoning, salt, and pepper. Transfer to the greased frying basket and AirFry for 12-14 minutes, shaking once. Sprinkle with halloumi cheese and Bake for 3-4 more minutes until the cheese is melted. Serve.

Green Vegetable Rotini Pasta Bake

INGREDIENTS (4 Servings)

1 cup green peas
1 lb broccoli florets, steamed
1 cup kale, chopped
1 garlic clove, minced
2 tbsp flour
2 cups milk

¼ cup mozzarella cheese, grated
16 oz rotini pasta
3 tbsp butter
1 tbsp fresh basil, chopped
Salt and black pepper to taste

DIRECTIONS (Prep + Cook Time: 40 minutes)

Bring a large saucepan of salted water to a boil. Add in the rotini pasta and cook following the package instructions. Drain and set aside. Melt butter in a skillet over medium heat and sauté garlic for 1 minute. Stir in the flour for 1 minute. Gradually add in the milk and simmer until slightly thickened, 3 minutes.

Preheat the air fryer to 350 F. Transfer the milk mixture to a baking dish and add in the pasta, broccoli, kale, green peas, salt, and pepper; stir to combine. Top with the mozzarella cheese and sprinkle with basil. Place in the air fryer and Bake for 10-12 minutes or until the cheese is golden. Serve warm.

Easy Vegetable Croquettes

INGREDIENTS (4 Servings)

1 lb red potatoes
1 ¼ cups milk
Salt to taste
3 tbsp butter
2 tsp olive oil
1 red bell pepper, chopped
½ cup baby spinach, chopped
½ lb mushrooms, chopped

½ lb broccoli florets, chopped
1 green onion, sliced
1 red onion, chopped
2 garlic cloves, minced
1 cup flour
2 eggs, beaten
1 ½ cups breadcrumbs

DIRECTIONS (Prep + Cook Time: 60 minutes + chilling time)

Cover the potatoes with salted water in a pot over medium heat and cook for 18-20 minutes until fork-tender. Drain and place them in a bowl. Add in 2 tbsp of butter, 1 cup of milk, and salt. Mash with a potato masher. In a food processor, place red onion, garlic, bell pepper, broccoli, mushrooms, green onion, baby spinach, olive oil, salt, and the remaining milk and pulse until a crumbs texture is formed.

Mix in the mashed potatoes' bowl. Using your hands, create oblong balls out of the mixture and place them on a baking sheet in a single layer. Refrigerate for 30 minutes.

Preheat the air fryer to 390 F. Take 3 separate bowls, pour the breadcrumbs in one, flour in another, and eggs in a third bowl. Remove the croquettes from the fridge and dredge them first in flour, then in the eggs, and finally in the crumbs. Arrange them in the greased frying basket without overlapping. AirFry for 12-15 minutes, flipping once. Remove to a wire rack to let cool a bit and serve.

Asian-Style Spring Rolls

INGREDIENTS (4 Servings)

½ lb shiitake mushrooms, chopped
2 tbsp canola oil
1 clove garlic, minced
1-inch piece ginger, grated
2 cups green cabbage, shredded

1 carrot, shredded
1 green onion, thinly sliced
1 tbsp soy sauce
1 tbsp hoisin sauce
12 wonton wrappers

DIRECTIONS (Prep + Cook Time: 30 minutes)

Warm 1 tbsp of the canola oil in a pan over medium heat and sauté green onion, garlic, and ginger for 30 seconds. Add in shiitake mushrooms, carrot, and cabbage and stir-fry until tender, about 4 minutes. Stir in soy sauce and hoisin sauce. Preheat the air fryer to 390 F.

Distribute the mixture across the wrappers and roll them up. Place the rolls in the greased frying basket and AirFry for 14-16 minutes, turning once, until golden and crispy. Serve warm with sweet chili sauce.

Egg & Cauliflower Rice Casserole

INGREDIENTS (4 Servings)

1 head cauliflower, cut into florets
2 tbsp olive oil
1 yellow bell pepper, chopped
1 cup okra, chopped

½ onion, chopped
Salt and black pepper to taste
1 tbsp soy sauce
2 eggs, beaten

DIRECTIONS (Prep + Cook Time: 20 minutes)

Preheat the air fryer to 380 F. Grease a baking dish with cooking spray.

Pulse cauliflower in a food processor until it resembles rice. Add the cauli rice to the baking dish and mix in bell pepper, okra, onion, soy sauce, salt, and black pepper. Pour the beaten eggs over and drizzle with olive oil. Place the dish in the air fryer and Bake for 12-14 minutes until golden. Serve.

Greek-Style Stuffed Bell Peppers

INGREDIENTS (4 Servings)

4 red bell peppers, tops sliced off
2 cups cooked rice
1 onion, chopped
1 tbsp Greek seasoning
¼ cup Kalamata olives, pitted and sliced

¾ cup tomato sauce
Salt and black pepper to taste
1 cup feta cheese, crumbled
2 tbsp fresh dill, chopped

DIRECTIONS (Prep + Cook Time: 30 minutes)

Preheat the air fryer to 360 F. Microwave the bell peppers for 1-2 minutes to soften.

In a bowl, combine rice, onion, Greek seasoning, feta cheese, olives, tomato sauce, salt, and pepper. Divide the mixture between the bell peppers and arrange them on the greased frying basket. Bake for 14-16 minutes. When ready, remove to a serving plate, scatter with dill and serve with yogurt if desired.

Poblano & Tomato Stuffed Squash

INGREDIENTS (4 Servings)

1 butternut squash
6 grape tomatoes, halved
1 poblano pepper, cut into strips

¼ cup mozzarella cheese, grated
2 tsp olive oil
Salt and black pepper to taste

DIRECTIONS (Prep + Cook Time: 45 minutes)

Preheat the air fryer to 350 F. Trim the ends and cut the squash lengthwise. You'll only need half of the squash for this recipe. Scoop the flesh out to make room for the filling. Brush the squash with olive oil.

Place in the air fryer and Bake for 15 minutes. Combine the remaining olive oil with tomatoes and poblano pepper, season with salt and pepper. Fill the squash half with the mixture and Bake for 12 more minutes. Top with mozzarella cheese and cook further for 3-5 minutes or until the cheese melts.

Cheesy English Muffins

INGREDIENTS (2 Servings)

2 English muffins, halved and toasted
½ cup cheddar cheese, shredded
1 ripe avocado, mashed
2 tbsp ranch-style salad dressing

½ cup alfalfa sprouts
1 tomato, chopped
½ sweet onion, chopped
1 tbsp sesame seeds, toasted

DIRECTIONS (Prep + Cook Time: 20 minutes)

Preheat the air fryer to 350 F. Arrange the muffins open-faced on the greased frying basket. Spread the mashed avocado on each half of the cupcakes. Top with sprouts, tomato, onion, ranch dressing, and cheddar cheese. Bake in the air fryer for 7-10 minutes. Serve sprinkled with sesame seeds.

Cheesy Vegetable Quesadilla

INGREDIENTS (1 Serving)

2 flour tortillas
¼ cup gouda cheese, shredded
¼ yellow bell pepper, sliced
¼ zucchini, sliced

½ green onion, sliced
1 tbsp fresh cilantro, chopped
1 tsp olive oil

DIRECTIONS (Prep + Cook Time: 20 minutes)

Preheat the air fryer to 390 F. Place a flour tortilla in the greased frying basket and top with gouda cheese, bell pepper, zucchini, cilantro, and green onion. Cover with the other tortilla and brush with olive oil. Bake for 10 minutes or until lightly browned. Cut into 4 wedges and serve.

Italian-Style Stuffed Mushrooms

INGREDIENTS (4 Servings)

4 oz mascarpone cheese, softened
1 egg
1 cup fresh baby spinach
12 large mushrooms, stems removed

¾ cup shredded Italian blend cheese
¼ cup breadcrumbs
1 tbsp olive oil
Salt and black pepper to taste

DIRECTIONS (Prep + Cook Time: 30 minutes)

Preheat the air fryer to 375 F. Whisk the mascarpone cheese, Italian blend cheese, breadcrumbs, egg, salt, and pepper with an electric mixer. Stir in the spinach with a spoon until everything is well combined. Divide the mixture between the mushrooms, leaving some of it popping out of the top.

Put the mushrooms in the greased frying basket and drizzle them with olive oil. Bake for 7-10 minutes, until the mushrooms have begun to brown and the cheese on top is a light brown color. Serve warm.

Chili Roasted Pumpkin with Orzo

INGREDIENTS (4 Servings)

1 lb pumpkin, peeled and cubed
2 red bell peppers, diced
2 shallots, quartered
1 red chili pepper, minced

1 tsp ground caraway seeds
1 cup orzo
Salt and black pepper to taste

DIRECTIONS (Prep + Cook Time: 35 minutes)

Preheat the air fryer to 380 F. In a bowl, place the pumpkin, bell peppers, shallots, chili pepper, ground caraway seeds, salt, and pepper; toss to coat. Transfer to the greased frying basket. Bake for 20-25 minutes, shaking once, until golden.

Place a pot filled with salted water over medium heat and bring to a boil. Add in the orzo and cook for 4 minutes. Drain and place on a serving platter. Spread the baked veggies all over and serve.

Portuguese-Style Veggies with Cheese

INGREDIENTS (4 Servings)

2 tbsp olive oil
1 tsp paprika
2 tsp ground cumin
1 tbsp tomato purée
1 lemon, juiced
2 yellow bell peppers, cut into chunks

1 zucchini, sliced
1 eggplant, cut into chunks
1 red onion, cut into wedges
2 garlic cloves, minced
6 oz fontina cheese, grated
10 green olives

DIRECTIONS (Prep + Cook Time: 35 minutes)

Preheat the air fryer to 370 F. In a small bowl, combine paprika, garlic, cumin, tomato purée, lemon juice, and olive oil. Add in the bell peppers, zucchini, eggplant, and red onion and mix well.

Transfer to the greased frying basket. Bake for 18-20 minutes, shaking once, until golden. Sprinkle with fontina cheese and olives and Bake for another 5 minutes or until the cheese is melted.

Southern-Style Corn Cakes

INGREDIENTS (6 Servings)

2 cups corn kernels, canned, drained
2 eggs, lightly beaten
⅓ cup green onions, finely chopped
¼ cup parsley, chopped

1 cup flour
½ tsp baking powder
Salt and black pepper to taste
⅓ cup sour cream

DIRECTIONS (Prep + Cook Time: 25 minutes)

Preheat the air fryer to 380 F. In a bowl, add corn kernels, eggs, parsley, and green onions and season with salt and pepper; mix well. Sift flour and baking powder into the bowl and stir. Line the frying basket with parchment paper and spoon batter dollops, making sure they are separated by at least one inch. Bake in the fryer for 10-12 minutes, turning once halfway through, until golden. Serve with sour cream.

Eggplant Gratin with Mozzarella Crust

INGREDIENTS (2 Servings)

1 cup eggplants, cubed
¼ cup red peppers, chopped
¼ cup green peppers, chopped
¼ cup onion, chopped
⅓ cup tomatoes, chopped
1 garlic clove, minced
1 tbsp sliced pimiento-stuffed olives

1 tsp capers
¼ tsp dried basil
¼ tsp dried marjoram
Salt and black pepper to taste
¼ cup mozzarella cheese, grated
1 tbsp breadcrumbs

DIRECTIONS (Prep + Cook Time: 30 minutes)

Preheat the air fryer to 300 F. In a bowl, add eggplants, green peppers, red peppers, onion, tomatoes, olives, garlic, basil, marjoram, capers, salt, and pepper; mix well. Spoon the eggplant mixture into a greased baking dish and level it using the vessel. Sprinkle mozzarella cheese on top and cover with breadcrumbs. Place the dish in the air fryer and Bake for 17-23 minutes until golden. Serve warm.

Vegetable & Goat Cheese Tian

INGREDIENTS (4 Servings)

2 tbsp butter
1 garlic clove, minced
2 tomatoes, sliced
1 cup canned chickpeas, drained
¼ cup black olives, pitted and chopped

1 fennel bulb, sliced
1 zucchini, sliced into rounds
4 oz goat cheese, sliced into rounds
1 tsp dried thyme
Salt and black pepper to taste

DIRECTIONS (Prep + Cook Time: 45 minutes)

Preheat the air fryer to 360 F. Melt the butter in a skillet over medium heat and sauté the fennel, garlic, and chickpeas for 5-6 minutes, stirring often until soft. Season with thyme, salt, and black pepper.

Transfer to a baking dish and arrange tomato, zucchini, and cheese slices on top. Scatter with black olives. Place the dish in the air fryer and Bake for 20-25 minutes until the cheese is melted and golden in color. Remove and let sit for a few minutes before serving.

Chickpea & Spinach Casserole

INGREDIENTS (4 Servings)

2 tbsp olive oil
1 onion, chopped
Salt and black pepper to taste
2 garlic cloves, minced
1 can coconut milk

1 tbsp ginger, minced
1 lb spinach
½ cup dried tomatoes, chopped
1 (14-oz) can chickpeas, drained
1 chili pepper, minced

DIRECTIONS (Prep + Cook Time: 20 minutes)

Heat olive oil in a saucepan over medium heat and sauté onion, garlic, chili pepper, ginger, salt, and black pepper for 3 minutes. Add in spinach and stir for 4 minutes or until wilted.

Transfer to a baking dish and mix in the remaining ingredients. Preheat the air fryer to 370 F. Place the baking dish in the air fryer and Bake for 14-16 minutes or until golden on top. Serve warm.

Dilled Zucchini Egg Cakes

INGREDIENTS (4 Servings)

12 oz thawed puff pastry
4 large eggs
1 medium zucchini, chopped

4 oz feta cheese, drained and crumbled
2 tbsp fresh dill, chopped
Salt and black pepper to taste

DIRECTIONS (Prep + Cook Time: 30 minutes)

Preheat the air fryer to 360 F. In a bowl, whisk the eggs with salt and black pepper. Stir in zucchini, dill, and feta cheese. Grease a muffin tin tray with cooking spray. Roll the pastry out and arrange them to cover the sides of the muffin holes. Divide the egg mixture evenly between the holes. Place the muffin tray in the frying basket and Bake for 13-15 minutes, until golden. Let cool a bit and serve warm.

Roasted Veggies with Penne Pasta

INGREDIENTS (4 Servings)

1 lb penne pasta
1 zucchini, sliced
1 bell pepper, sliced
½ lb acorn squash, sliced
½ cup mushrooms, sliced
½ cup Kalamata olives, pitted and halved

¼ cup olive oil
1 tsp Italian seasoning
1 cup grape tomatoes, halved
3 tbsp balsamic vinegar
2 tbsp fresh basil, chopped
Salt and black pepper to taste

DIRECTIONS (Prep + Cook Time: 40 minutes)

Fill a pot with salted water and bring to a boil over medium heat. Add in the penne pasta and cook until al dente, about 8-10 minutes. Drain and place in a bowl; set aside. Preheat the air fryer to 380 F.

In the frying basket, combine bell pepper, zucchini, acorn squash, mushrooms, and olive oil. Season with salt and pepper. Bake in the air fryer for 15 minutes, shaking once. Remove the veggies to the pasta bowl. Mix in tomatoes, olives, Italian seasoning, and balsamic vinegar. Sprinkle with basil to serve.

Tomato Sandwiches with Feta & Pesto

INGREDIENTS (2 Servings)

1 heirloom tomato
1 (4-oz) block feta cheese
1 small red onion, thinly sliced
1 garlic clove
Salt to taste

2 tsp + ¼ cup olive oil
1 ½ tbsp pine nuts, toasted
2 tbsp fresh parsley, chopped
¼ cup Parmesan cheese, grated
¼ cup fresh basil, chopped

DIRECTIONS (Prep + Cook Time: 25 minutes)

Add basil, pine nuts, garlic, Parmesan cheese, and salt to a food processor. Pulse while slowly adding ¼ cup of olive oil. Preheat the air fryer to 390 F. Slice feta cheese and the tomato into ½-inch slices.

Spread the obtained pesto sauce on the tomato slices. Top with feta cheese and onion and drizzle with olive oil. Place the tomato in the greased frying basket and Bake for 6-8 minutes. Remove to a serving platter, sprinkle lightly with salt, and top with fresh parsley. Serve chilled.

Cheesy Green Beans & Egg Cups

INGREDIENTS (4 Servings)

1 lb green beans, steamed and chopped
4 eggs, beaten
1 cup sharp cheese, shredded
1 cup heavy cream

½ tsp nutmeg
½ tsp ginger powder
Salt and black pepper to taste

DIRECTIONS (Prep + Cook Time: 25 minutes)

Place the green beans in a bowl and mix in the eggs, heavy cream, nutmeg, ginger powder, salt, and black pepper. Divide the mixture between 4 greased ramekins. Top with the cheese and Bake in the air fryer for 12-14 minutes at 330 F. Remove and let cool for a few minutes before serving.

Jalapeño & Bean Tacos

INGREDIENTS (4 Servings)

4 soft taco shells, warm
½ cup kidney beans, drained
½ cup black beans, drained
1 tbsp tomato puree
1 fresh jalapeño pepper, chopped
2 tbsp fresh cilantro, chopped

1 cup corn kernels
½ tsp cumin
½ tsp cayenne pepper
Salt and black pepper to taste
1 cup mozzarella cheese, grated
Guacamole to serve

DIRECTIONS (Prep + Cook Time: 25 minutes)

In a bowl, add the beans, tomato puree, jalapeño, cilantro, corn, cumin, cayenne, salt, and black pepper and stir. Fill the taco shells with the bean mixture and sprinkle with mozzarella. Lay the tacos in the greased frying basket and Bake for 12-14 minutes at 360 F, turning once. Serve with guacamole.

Air Fried Veggie Sushi

INGREDIENTS (4 Servings)

2 cups cooked sushi rice
4 nori sheets
1 carrot, sliced lengthways
1 red bell pepper, sliced
1 avocado, sliced

1 tbsp sesame oil
1 tbsp rice wine vinegar
1 cup panko crumbs
2 tbsp sesame seeds
Soy sauce, wasabi, and pickled ginger to serve

DIRECTIONS (Prep + Cook Time: 30 minutes)

Prepare a clean working board, a small bowl of lukewarm water, and a sushi mat. Wet your hands, and lay a nori sheet onto the sushi mat, and spread half cup of sushi rice, leaving a half-inch of nori clear, so you can seal the roll. Place carrot, bell pepper, and avocado sideways of the rice. Roll the sushi tightly and rub warm water along the clean nori strip to seal. In a bowl, mix sesame oil and vinegar.

In another bowl, mix the crumbs and sesame seeds. Roll each sushi log in the vinegar mixture and then into the sesame bowl to coat. Arrange the sushi in the greased frying basket and Bake for 11-13 minutes at 360 F, turning once. Slice and serve with soy sauce, pickled ginger, and wasabi.

Potato Filled Bread Rolls

INGREDIENTS (4 Servings)

8 slices sandwich bread
4 large potatoes, boiled and mashed
½ tsp turmeric
2 green chilies, seeded and chopped

1 onion, finely chopped
½ tsp mustard seeds
1 tbsp olive oil
Salt to taste

DIRECTIONS (Prep + Cook Time: 30 minutes)

Preheat the air fryer to 350 F. In a skillet over medium heat, warm the olive oil and stir-fry onion and mustard seeds, 3 minutes. Remove to a bowl and add in potatoes, chilies, turmeric, and salt; mix well.

Trim the crust sides of the bread, and roll out with a rolling pin. Spread a spoonful of the potato mixture on each bread sheet, and roll the bread over the filling, sealing the edges. Place the rolls in the greased frying basket and Bake for 11-14 minutes until golden and crispy. Serve warm.

Mexican Chile Relleno

INGREDIENTS (4 Servings)

2 (8-oz) cans whole green chiles, drained
2 cups Mexican cheese, shredded
1 cup all-purpose flour

2 whole eggs
½ cup milk

DIRECTIONS (Prep + Cook Time: 20 minutes)

Preheat the air fryer to 380 F. Lay the green chilies on a plate, cut them open at the top and fill them with cheese. In a bowl, whisk the eggs, milk, and half of the flour. Pour the remaining flour on a flat plate. Dip the chilies in the flour first, then in the egg mixture, and arrange them in the greased frying basket. AirFry for 8-10 minutes, flipping once halfway through. Serve with slices of avocado if desired.

Crispy Mozzarella Sliders

INGREDIENTS (4 Servings)

8 mozzarella cheese slices
8 Pepperidge farm rolls, halved
1 tbsp butter, softened

1 tsp mustard seeds
1 tsp poppy seeds
1 small onion, chopped

DIRECTIONS (Prep + Cook Time: 25 minutes)

Preheat the air fryer to 350 F. In a bowl, mix butter, mustard seeds, onion, and poppy seeds. Spread the mixture on-farm roll bottoms, top with a slice of mozzarella cheese, and cover with the farm roll tops. Arrange the sliders in the greased frying basket and Bake 13-16 minutes until golden. Serve.

Vegetable Tortilla Pizza

INGREDIENTS (1 Serving)

¼ tbsp tomato paste
1 tbsp cheddar cheese, grated
1 tbsp mozzarella cheese, grated
1 tbsp canned sweet corn
4 zucchini slices

4 eggplant slices
4 red onion rings
½ green bell pepper, chopped
1 large tortilla
A few fresh basil leaves, chopped

DIRECTIONS (Prep + Cook Time: 25 minutes)

Preheat the air fryer to 350 F. Spread the tomato paste on the tortilla. Arrange zucchini and eggplant slices first, then green bell peppers and onion rings. Sprinkle the corn all over. Top with cheddar and mozzarella cheeses. Place the pizza in the frying basket and Bake in the fryer for 10-12 minutes until nice and lightly browned on top. Sprinkle with freshly chopped basil leaves and serve.

Spanish-Style Huevos Rotos (Broken Eggs)

INGREDIENTS (2 Servings)

½ tsp salt
½ tsp garlic powder
3 tbsp olive oil

1 tsp sweet paprika
2 russet potatoes, cut into wedges
2 eggs

DIRECTIONS (Prep + Cook Time: 36 minutes)

Preheat the air fryer to 390 F. In a bowl, mix salt, garlic powder, and 1 tbsp of olive oil. Add in the potatoes and toss to coat. Arrange them in the greased frying basket without overcrowding.

AirFry for 20-25 minutes, shaking regularly to get crispy on all sides. Heat the remaining olive oil in a pan over medium heat and fry the eggs until the whites are firm and the yolks are still runny, about 5 minutes. Place the potatoes on a serving bowl and top with the fried eggs and paprika. Break the eggs with a fork, and stir a bit. Serve with cold beer.

Homemade Pie with Root Vegetables

INGREDIENTS (4 Servings)

1 lb potatoes, cubed
1 parsnip, chopped
½ cup Parmesan cheese, grated
1 cup crème fraiche
1 bread slice, diced

½ tsp dried sage
2 tbsp butter
1 tsp yellow mustard
Salt and black pepper to taste

DIRECTIONS (Prep + Cook Time: 40 minutes)

Boil the potatoes and parsnip in a pot filled with salted water over medium heat for 15 minutes. Drain and transfer to a bowl. Add in mustard, crème fraiche, sage, butter, salt, and pepper and mash them with a masher. Mix in the bread and Parmesan cheese. Preheat the air fryer to 360 F. Add the resulting batter to the greased frying basket and place it in the fryer. Bake for 14-16 minutes until golden. Serve.

Plantain Fritters

INGREDIENTS (4 Servings)

3 ripe plantains, sliced diagonally
2 tbsp cornflour
1 egg white

¼ cup breadcrumbs
Salt and black pepper to taste

DIRECTIONS (Prep + Cook Time: 25 minutes)

Preheat the air fryer to 340 F. Pour the breadcrumbs into a plate; season with salt and pepper. Coat the plantain slices in the cornflour, brush with the egg white, and roll in the crumbs. Arrange on the greased frying basket and lightly spray with oil. Bake for 8-10 minutes, flipping once, until golden.

Baked Mediterranean Shakshuka

INGREDIENTS (4 Servings)

1 onion, sliced
2 garlic cloves, minced
2 tbsp olive oil
1 tsp ground cumin
2 tsp paprika
¼ tsp chili powder

1 red bell pepper, seeded and diced
2 (14.5-oz) cans tomatoes, diced
4 eggs
2 tbsp fresh parsley, chopped
4 tbsp feta cheese, crumbled
Salt and black pepper to taste

DIRECTIONS (Prep + Cook Time: 25 minutes)

Preheat the air fryer to 390 F. Heat olive oil in a skillet over medium heat and sauté bell pepper, onion, and garlic for 5 minutes until tender. Stir in paprika, parsley, chili, cumin, salt, and pepper and pour in the tomatoes. Simmer for 10 minutes; transfer to a baking dish. Crack in the eggs. Bake in the air fryer for 12-15 minutes or until the egg whites are set but the yolks are still runny. Top with feta to serve.

Brussels Sprouts with Raisins & Pine Nuts

INGREDIENTS (4 Servings)

1 lb Brussels sprouts, stems cut off and halved
2 tbsp olive oil
1 ¾ oz raisins, soaked and drained

Juice of 1 orange
Salt to taste
2 tbsp pine nuts, toasted

DIRECTIONS (Prep + Cook Time: 20 minutes)

Preheat the air fryer to 390 F. In a bowl, toss the Brussels sprouts with olive oil and salt and stir to combine. Place them in the frying and AirFry for 14-16 minutes, shaking once halfway through, until slightly charred. Top with toasted pine nuts and raisins. Drizzle with orange juice and serve.

SWEETS & DESSERTS

Spanish Churros con Chocolate

INGREDIENTS (4 Servings)

1 tsp vanilla extract
¼ cup butter
½ cup water
1 pinch of salt
½ cup all-purpose flour

2 eggs
¼ cup + 1 tbsp white sugar
½ tsp ground cinnamon
4 oz dark chocolate chips
¼ cup milk

DIRECTIONS (Prep + Cook Time: 30 minutes + cooling time)

In a skillet over medium heat, pour water, ¼ cup of sugar, butter, and salt; bring to a boil. Stir in the flour until the mixture thickens, about 3 minutes. Remove to a bowl, mix in vanilla, and let cool slightly.

Preheat the air fryer to 360 F. Gently stir the eggs in the cooled bowl, one at a time, until glossy and smooth. Place the dough in a piping bag and generously grease the frying basket with cooking spray. Pipe in the batter into long and thick strips. AirFry them for 8-10 minutes or until golden, flipping once.

Mix the chocolate with cinnamon in a heatproof bowl and microwave for 60-90 seconds or until the chocolate is melted. Stir in milk until smooth. Sprinkle the churros with sugar and serve with the hot chocolate as a dip and enjoy!

Chocolate & Peanut Butter Fondants

INGREDIENTS (4 Servings)

¾ cup dark chocolate
½ cup peanut butter, crunchy
2 tbsp butter
½ cup sugar, divided

4 eggs, room temperature
⅛ cup flour, sieved
1 tsp salt
¼ cup water

DIRECTIONS (Prep + Cook Time: 45 minutes)

Make the praline by adding ¼ cup of sugar, 1 tsp of salt, and ¼ cup of water in a saucepan over low heat. Stir and bring to a boil. Simmer until the mixture reduces by half, about 5 minutes.

Spread on a baking tray to freeze up to harden. Then break into pieces and set the pralines aside.

Preheat the air fryer to 300 F. Place a pot of water over medium heat and place a heatproof bowl on top. Add in chocolate, butter, and peanut butter. Stir continuously until fully melted, combined, and smooth. Remove the bowl and let cool slightly. Whisk in the eggs, add flour and the remaining sugar; mix well.

Grease 4 small loaf pans with cooking spray and divide the chocolate mixture between them. Place them in the air fryer and Bake for 7-8 minutes until browned. Remove and serve with a piece of praline.

Mock Blueberry Pie

INGREDIENTS (6 Servings)

2 store-bought pie crusts
21 oz blueberry pie filling

1 egg yolk, beaten
Powdered sugar, to dust

DIRECTIONS (Prep + Cook Time: 35 minutes)

Preheat air fryer to 340 F. Place one pie crust into a greased pie pan. Poke holes into the crust and Bake for 5 minutes in the air fryer. Remove the pan and spread the blueberry pie filling on top. Cut the other crust into strips and make a lattice over the filling. Brush the lattice with the yolk and Bake the pie in the fryer for 15-20 minutes until golden. Dust with sugar and serve chilled.

French Sour Cherry Clafoutis

INGREDIENTS (4 Servings)

½ lb sour cherries, pitted
½ cup all-purpose flour
¼ tsp salt
2 tbsp sugar
2 eggs + 2 yolks

1 tsp vanilla extract
1 tbsp lemon zest
2 tbsp butter, melted
1 ¼ cups milk
Icing sugar to dust

DIRECTIONS (Prep + Cook Time: 40 minutes + cooling time)

Preheat air fryer to 380 F. In a bowl, mix the flour, sugar, and salt. Whisk in the eggs, egg yolks, vanilla extract, lemon zest, and melted butter until creamy. Gradually, add in the milk and stir until bubbly.

Spread the sour cherries on a greased baking dish and pour the batter over. Bake in the air fryer for 25-30 minutes or until a lovely golden crust is formed. Dust the top with icing sugar and serve warm.

Chocolate Fudge Squares

INGREDIENTS (6 Servings)

1 cup sugar
½ cup plain flour
1 tbsp honey
1 tsp baking powder
1 tsp vanilla extract
Chocolate Topping:
2 tbsp chocolate chips

1 tbsp cocoa powder
3 eggs
½ cup butter, softened
1 orange, zested
½ cup dark chocolate, melted

2 tbsp heavy cream

DIRECTIONS (Prep + Cook Time: 45 minutes + cooling time)

Preheat air fryer to 350 F. In a bowl, whisk the eggs with sugar and honey until pale and creamy. Sift the flour into another bowl and mix in the baking powder and cocoa powder. Gently stir in the egg mixture to combine. Stir in orange zest, melted chocolate, and vanilla extract, be careful not to overmix.

Transfer the batter to a greased cake pan and Bake in the air fryer for 23-26 minutes, until set in the center and the top is slightly crusty. Remove and let cool completely. Microwave the chocolate chips and heavy cream in a heatproof bowl for 60-90 seconds. Remove and stir until smooth. Drizzle over the chilled cake. Cut into squares and enjoy!

Classic Crème Brûlée

INGREDIENTS (4 Servings)

1 cup whipped cream
¾ cup milk
1 vanilla pod

5 egg yolks
⅓ cup + 1 tbsp sugar

DIRECTIONS (Prep + Cook Time: 60 minutes + cooling time)

Place a saucepan over low heat and add the milk and whipped cream. Cut the vanilla pods open and scrape the seeds into the saucepan along with the pods. Cook until almost boiled, stirring regularly, about 6-8 minutes. Turn off the heat and remove the vanilla pods. Preheat air fryer to 300 F.

Beat egg yolks in a bowl and whisk in ⅓ cup of sugar, but not too bubbly. Slowly pour in the egg yolk mixture and beat until combined. Fill 4 ramekins with the custard mix. Place the ramekins in a baking pan and pour in boiling water to reach halfway up ramekins. Bake in the fryer for 25-30 minutes.

Remove the ramekins and let them cool at room temperature, then refrigerate for 1 hour. Sprinkle the remaining sugar over the crème brûlée and use a torch to caramelize the top. Serve and enjoy!

Vanilla & Chocolate Brownies

INGREDIENTS (6 Servings)

6 oz dark chocolate
6 oz butter
¾ cup white sugar
3 eggs
2 tsp vanilla extract

¾ cup flour
¼ cup cocoa powder
1 cup walnuts, chopped
1 cup white chocolate chips

DIRECTIONS (Prep + Cook Time: 45 minutes)

Preheat air fryer to 340 F. Line a baking dish with waxed paper. Melt the dark chocolate and butter in a saucepan over low heat, stirring constantly until a smooth mixture is obtained; let cool slightly.

In a bowl, whisk eggs, sugar, and vanilla. Fold in the flour and cocoa powder and mix to combine. Stir in the white chocolate chips and melted dark chocolate. Sprinkle the walnuts over. Spread the batter onto the baking dish and Bake in the fryer for 20-25 minutes. Transfer to a wire rack to cool before slicing.

Easy Lemony Cheesecake

INGREDIENTS (6 Servings)

8 oz graham crackers, crushed
4 oz butter, melted
16 oz cream cheese, at room temperature
3 eggs

3 tbsp sugar
1 tbsp vanilla extract
Zest of 2 lemons

DIRECTIONS (Prep + Cook Time: 40 minutes + chilling time)

Line a cake tin that fits in your air fryer with baking paper. Mix together the crackers and butter and press them at the bottom of the tin. In a bowl, add cream cheese, eggs, sugar, vanilla, and lemon zest and beat with a hand mixer until well combined and smooth. Pour the mixture on top of the crackers.

Bake in the air fryer for 20-25 minutes at 350 F. Regularly check to ensure it's set but still a bit wobbly. Let cool, then refrigerate overnight. Serve at room temperature or chilled.

Apple Caramel Relish

INGREDIENTS (4 Servings)

1 vanilla box cake mix
2 apples, peeled, sliced
3 oz butter, melted
½ cup brown sugar

1 tsp cinnamon
½ cup flour
1 cup caramel sauce

DIRECTIONS (Prep + Cook Time: 40 minutes)

Line a cake tin with baking paper. In a bowl, mix butter, brown sugar, cinnamon, and flour until you obtain a crumbly texture. Prepare the cake mix according to the instructions (no baking).

Pour the obtained batter into the tin and arrange the apple slices on top. Spoon the caramel over the apples and pour the crumbly flour mixture over the sauce. Bake in the preheated air fryer for 18-20 minutes at 360 F. Check regularly to avoid overcooking. Serve chilled.

Oat & Walnut Granola

INGREDIENTS (4 Servings)

¼ cup walnuts, chopped
½ cup oats
3 tbsp canola oil

½ cup maple syrup
2 tbsp muscovado sugar
1 cup fresh blueberries

DIRECTIONS (Prep + Cook Time: 35 minutes + cooling time)

Preheat air fryer to 380 F. In a bowl, place oil, maple syrup, and muscovado sugar; mix well. Fold in the oats and walnuts. Spread out the mixture on a greased baking dish. Bake in the air fryer for 20-25 minutes. Sprinkle with blueberries and bake for 3 minutes. Let cool. Break it up and store it in a jar.

White Chocolate Pudding

INGREDIENTS (2 Servings)

3 oz white chocolate	1 tbsp melted butter
4 egg whites	1 tbsp cold butter
2 egg yolks, at room temperature	¼ tsp vanilla extract
¼ cup sugar	1 ½ tbsp flour

DIRECTIONS (Prep + Cook Time: 30 minutes)

Brush two ramekins with melted butter. Swirl in 2 tbsp of sugar to coat the butter. Melt the cold butter with the chocolate in a heatproof bowl, inside the microwave, then set aside. In another bowl, beat the egg yolks vigorously. Add the vanilla and the remaining sugar; beat to incorporate fully. Mix in the melted chocolate. Add the flour and mix until there are no lumps.

Preheat air fryer to 330 F. Whisk the egg whites in another bowl until the mixture holds stiff peaks. Fold in the chocolate mixture and divide the mixture between the ramekins. Place them in the frying basket, and Bake for 14-16 minutes or until cooked through and golden.

Soft Buttermilk Biscuits

INGREDIENTS (10 Biscuits)

1 cup all-purpose flour	4 tbsp butter, cubed
¾ tsp salt	1 tsp sugar
½ tsp baking powder	¾ cup buttermilk

DIRECTIONS (Prep + Cook Time: 30 minutes)

Preheat air fryer to 360 F. In a bowl, stir the flour, baking powder, sugar, and salt until well combined. Add in butter and rub it into the flour mixture until crumbed. Stir in the buttermilk until a dough is formed.

Flour a flat and dry surface and roll the dough out until half-inch thick. Cut out 10 rounds with a small cookie cutter. Arrange the biscuits on a greased baking tray. Working in batches, Bake in the air fryer for 16-18 minutes. Let cool for a few minutes before serving.

Orange Sponge Cake

INGREDIENTS (4 Servings)

1 cup white sugar	Zest and juice from 1 orange
1 cup self-rising flour	2 egg whites
3 eggs	4 tbsp superfine sugar
1 tsp vanilla extract	½ cup ground walnuts

DIRECTIONS (Prep + Cook Time: 45 minutes)

Preheat air fryer to 360 F. In a bowl, beat white sugar, flour, eggs, vanilla, and orange zest with an electric mixer until creamy and fluffy, about 8 minutes. Transfer half of the batter into a greased and floured cake pan and Bake in the air fryer for 15 minutes. Repeat the process for the remaining batter.

Meanwhile, prepare the frosting by beating egg whites, orange juice, and superfine sugar together. Spread half of the frosting mixture on top of one cooled cake. Top with the other cake and spread the remaining frosting all over. Top with walnuts, slice, and serve.

Almond & Berry Crumble

INGREDIENTS (4 Servings)

2 tbsp flaked almonds
1 ⅓ cups frozen mixed berries
1 tsp lemon zest

⅔ cup all-purpose flour
4 tbsp caster sugar
2 tbsp unsalted butter, softened

DIRECTIONS (Prep + Cook Time: 30 minutes)

Preheat air fryer to 380 F. Spread the mixed berries on a 6-by-2-inch baking dish and sprinkle them with some sugar, lemon zest, and almonds. In a bowl, mix the remaining sugar and flour. Rub the butter into the mixture with your fingertips until it becomes crumbly. Pour the crumble topping on top of the almonds and bake in your air fryer for 11-16 minutes until golden and bubbling. Serve warm.

Madrid-Style Almond Meringues

INGREDIENTS (4 Servings)

8 egg whites
½ tsp almond extract
1 ⅓ cups sugar

2 tsp lemon juice
1 ½ tsp vanilla extract
Melted dark chocolate, to drizzle

DIRECTIONS (Prep + Cook Time: 60 minutes + cooling time)

In a bowl, beat egg whites and lemon juice with an electric mixer until foamy. Slowly beat in the sugar until thoroughly combined. Add almond and vanilla extracts. Beat until glossy and stiff peaks form.

Line a baking dish that fits in the fryer with parchment paper. Fill a piping bag with the mixture and pipe as many mounds in the baking dish as you can, leaving 1½-inch spaces between each mound.

Place the baking dish inside the frying basket and Bake at 250 F for 5 minutes. Reduce the temperature to 220 F and bake for 15 more minutes. Then, reduce the temperature to 190 F and cook for 13-15 more minutes. Let the meringues cool. Drizzle with dark chocolate and serve.

White Chocolate Cookies

INGREDIENTS (4 Servings)

1 cup self-rising flour
4 tbsp brown sugar
1 egg
2 oz white chocolate chips

1 tbsp honey
1 ½ tbsp milk
1 tsp baking soda
½ cup butter, softened

DIRECTIONS (Prep + Cook Time: 40 minutes)

Preheat air fryer to 350 F. In a bowl, beat butter and sugar until fluffy. Mix in honey, egg, and milk. In a separate bowl, mix flour and baking soda and gradually add the butter/egg mixture, stirring constantly.

Gently fold in the chocolate chips. Drop spoonfuls of the mixture onto a greased cookie sheet and press down slightly to flatten. Bake in the air fryer for 18-20 minutes. Remove to a wire rack to cool completely before serving.

Chocolate & Raspberry Cake

INGREDIENTS (6 Servings)

1 cup flour
⅓ cup cocoa powder
1 tsp baking powder
½ cup white sugar
¼ cup brown sugar
½ cup butter, melted

1 tsp vanilla extract
⅔ cup milk
2 eggs, beaten
1 cup raspberries
1 cup chocolate chips

DIRECTIONS (Prep + Cook Time: 40 minutes)

Line a cake tin with baking paper. In a bowl, sift flour, cocoa powder, and baking powder. In another bowl, whisk butter, white and brown sugar, vanilla, and milk until creamy. Mix in the eggs.

Pour the wet ingredients into the dry ones, and whisk to combine. Add in the raspberries and chocolate chips. Pour the batter into the cake tin and Bake in the fryer for 18-22 minutes at 350 F. Serve cooled.

Effortless Pecan Pie

INGREDIENTS (4 Servings)

¾ cup maple syrup
2 eggs
¼ tsp ground nutmeg
½ tsp cinnamon
2 tbsp almond butter

2 tbsp brown sugar
½ cup pecans, chopped
1 tbsp butter, melted
1 (8-inch) pie dough
¾ tsp vanilla extract

DIRECTIONS (Prep + Cook Time: 50 minutes + cooling time)

Preheat air fryer to 360 F.

Coat the pecans with melted butter. Place them in the frying basket and AirFry for 8-10 minutes, shaking once. Lay the pie crust into a 7-inch round pie pan and pour the pecans over.

Whisk together all the remaining ingredients in a bowl. Spread the mixture over the pecans. Set the air fryer to 320 F and Bake the pie for 22-25 minutes. Serve chilled.

Pineapple Cake

INGREDIENTS (4 Servings)

2 oz dark chocolate, grated
8 oz self-rising flour
4 oz butter, melted
7 oz pineapple chunks

½ cup pineapple juice
1 egg
2 tbsp milk
½ cup sugar

DIRECTIONS (Prep + Cook Time: 40 minutes + cooling time)

Preheat air fryer to 350 F. In a large bowl, combine the flour, sugar, and chocolate. In another bowl, beat the egg, butter, pineapple juice, and milk, without overmixing. Mix the wet ingredients with the dry ingredients, then fold in the pineapple chunks. Spread the batter on a greased cake pan. Bake in the air fryer for 20-25 minutes or until a toothpick comes out dry and clean. Let cool before serving.

Lemon-Glazed Cupcakes

INGREDIENTS (6 Servings)

1 cup flour
½ cup sugar
1 egg
1 tsp lemon zest
¾ tsp baking powder

2 tbsp vegetable oil
½ cup milk
½ tsp vanilla extract
½ cup powdered sugar
2 tsp lemon juice

DIRECTIONS (Prep + Cook Time: 30 minutes + cooling time)

Preheat air fryer to 360 F. In a bowl, combine flour, sugar, lemon zest, and baking powder. In another bowl, whisk together egg, vegetable oil, milk, and vanilla extract. Gently combine the two mixtures to obtain a smooth batter. Divide the batter between greased muffin tins or a 6-hole muffin tray.

Place the muffin tins or tray in the air fryer and Bake for 12-14 minutes. Remove the muffins and let cool. Whisk the sugar with lemon juice until smooth. Pour the glaze on top of the muffins and serve.

Cinnamon Grilled Pineapples

INGREDIENTS (2 Servings)

1 tsp cinnamon
5 pineapple slices
½ cup brown sugar

1 tbsp mint, chopped
1 tbsp honey

DIRECTIONS (Prep + Cook Time: 20 minutes)

Preheat air fryer to 340 F. In a small bowl, mix the sugar and cinnamon. Drizzle the sugar mixture over the pineapple slices. Place them in the greased frying basket and Bake for 5 minutes. Flip the pineapples and cook for 4 to6 more minutes. Remove, drizzle with honey and sprinkle with fresh mint.

Simple Coffee Cake

INGREDIENTS (2 Servings)

¼ cup butter
½ tsp instant coffee
1 tbsp black coffee, brewed
1 egg

¼ cup sugar
¼ cup flour
1 tsp cocoa powder
Powdered sugar, for icing

DIRECTIONS (Prep + Cook Time: 30 minutes + cooling time)

Preheat air fryer to 320 F. In a bowl, beat sugar and egg until creamy. Mix in cocoa, instant and black coffees; and stir in the flour. Transfer the batter to a greased baking dish. Bake in the air fryer for 15 minutes. Let cool for at least 1 hour at room temperature. Dust with powdered sugar, slice and serve.

Peach Almond Flour Cake

INGREDIENTS (4 Servings)

3 tbsp butter, melted
1 cup peaches, chopped
3 tbsp sugar
1 cup almond flour

1 cup heavy cream
1 tsp vanilla extract
2 eggs, whisked
1 tsp baking soda

DIRECTIONS (Prep + Cook Time: 35 minutes + cooling time)

Preheat air fryer to 360 F. In a bowl, mix all the ingredients and stir well. Pour the mixture into a greased baking dish and insert in the frying basket. Bake for 20-25 minutes. Let cool, slice, and serve.

Dark Rum Pear Pie

INGREDIENTS (4 Servings)

1 cup flour
5 tbsp sugar
3 tbsp butter, softened

1 tbsp dark spiced rum
2 pears, sliced

DIRECTIONS (Prep + Cook Time: 35 minutes + cooling time)

Preheat air fryer to 370 F. In a bowl, place 3 tbsp of the sugar, butter, and flour and mix to form a batter. Roll the butter out onto a floured surface and transfer to a greased baking dish. Arrange the pears slices on top and sprinkle with sugar and dark rum. Bake in the air fryer for 20 minutes. Serve cooled.

Yummy Moon Pie

INGREDIENTS (4 Servings)

4 graham cracker sheets, snapped in half
8 large marshmallows

8 squares each of dark, milk, and white chocolate

IDIRECTIONS (Prep + Cook Time: 15 minutes)

Arrange the crackers on a cutting board. Put 2 marshmallows onto half of the graham cracker halves. Place 2 squares of chocolate on top of the marshmallows. Place the remaining crackers on top to create 4 sandwiches. Wrap each one in baking paper, so it resembles a parcel. Bake in the preheated air fryer for 5 minutes at 340 F. Serve at room temperature or chilled.

Air Fried Donuts

INGREDIENTS (4 Servings)

2 ¼ cups self-rising flour, mixed with ¼ tsp salt
2 ¼ dry active yeast
1/3 cup lukewarm milk

¼ cup unsalted butter, softened
2 eggs, beaten
3 tbsp brown sugar

DIRECTIONS (Prep + Cook Time: 35 minutes)

In a bowl, stir eggs, butter, and milk until well mixed. Mix the flour, brown sugar, and yeast with a mixer on low speed. Slowly add the egg mixture, increase the speed and mix until a elastic, glossy dough forms. Transfer to a oiled bowl, cover, and let it rise for 1 hour. Preheat air fryer to 350 F. Remove and knead for 3-4 minutes. Form donut shapes and cut off the center using cookie cutters. Arrange on a lined baking sheet and Bake in the fryer for 10-12 minutes, flipping once. Serve with your favorite glaze.

Tropical Pineapple Fritters

INGREDIENTS (5 Servings)

1 ½ cups flour
1 pineapple, sliced into rings
3 tbsp sesame seeds

2 eggs, beaten
1 tsp baking powder
½ tbsp sugar

DIRECTIONS (Prep + Cook Time: 25 minutes)

Preheat air fryer to 350 F. In a bowl, mix sesame seeds, flour, baking powder, eggs, sugar, and 1 cup of water. Dip pineapple slices into the flour mixture and arrange them in the greased frying basket. AirFry for 14-16 minutes, turning once, until golden. Serve and enjoy!

Honey & Plum Homemade Rice

INGREDIENTS (4 Servings)

1 cup long-grain rice
2 cups milk
½ cup plums, chopped

3 tbsp honey
1 tsp vanilla extract
1/3 cup heavy cream

DIRECTIONS (Prep + Cook Time: 30 minutes + cooling time)

Preheat the air fryer to 360 F. In a baking dish, combine all the ingredients, except for the ch. Place the dish in the air fryer and Bake for 20 minutes. Spoon into glass cups, top with plums and serve warm.

Chocolate Soufflé

INGREDIENTS (2 Servings)

2 eggs, whites and yolks separated
¼ cup butter, melted
2 tbsp flour

3 tbsp sugar
3 oz chocolate, melted
½ tsp vanilla extract

DIRECTIONS (Prep + Cook Time: 35 minutes)

Preheat air fryer to 320 F. In a bowl, beat yolks, sugar, and vanilla until creamy. Stir in butter, chocolate, and flour. In another bowl, whisk the egg whites until stiff peak forms. Gently combine the egg whites with the chocolate mixture. Divide the batter between 2 greased ramekins and Bake in the air fryer for 14 minutes.

No Flour Lime Cupcakes

INGREDIENTS (4 Servings)

2 eggs + 1 egg yolk
Juice and zest of 1 lime
1 cup yogurt

¼ cup superfine sugar
8 oz cream cheese
1 tsp vanilla extract

DIRECTIONS (Prep + Cook Time: 30 minutes)

Preheat the fryer to 300 F. In a bowl, mix yogurt and cream cheese until uniform. In another bowl, beat the eggs, yolk, sugar, vanilla, lime juice, and zest. Gently fold the in the cheese mixture. Divide the batter between greased muffin tins and Bake in the fryer for 15 minutes or until golden. Serve chilled.

Cheat Apple Pie

INGREDIENTS (4 Servings)

2 apples, diced
2 tbsp butter, melted
2 tbsp white sugar
1 tbsp brown sugar

1 tsp cinnamon
1 egg, beaten
2 large puff pastry sheets
¼ tsp salt

DIRECTIONS (Prep + Cook Time: 30 minutes)

In a bowl, whisk white sugar, brown sugar, cinnamon, salt, and butter. Place the apples in a greased baking dish and coat them with the mixture. Place the dish in the fryer and Bake for 10 minutes at 350 F. Roll out the pastry on a floured flat surface and cut each sheet into 6 equal pieces.

Divide the apple filling between the pieces. Brush the edges of the pastry squares with the egg. Fold the squares and seal the edges with a fork. Place on a lined baking dish and Bake in the fryer at 350 F for 8 minutes. Flip over, and cook for 2-4 more minutes until golden. Serve chilled.

Apricot & Lemon Flapjacks

INGREDIENTS (4 Servings)

¼ cup butter
2 tbsp maple syrup
2 tbsp pure cane sugar

1 ¼ cups rolled oats
2 tsp lemon zest
3 apricots, stoned and sliced

DIRECTIONS (Prep + Cook Time: 35 minutes + cooling time)

Preheat the air fryer to 350 F. Line a baking dish with parchment paper.

Melt the butter in a skillet over medium heat and stir in cane sugar and maple syrup until the sugar dissolves, about 2 minutes. Mix in the remaining ingredients and transfer to the baking dish. Bake for 18-20 minutes or until golden. Let cool for a few minutes before cutting into flapjacks.

Fruit Skewers

INGREDIENTS (2 Servings)

1 cup blueberries
1 banana, sliced
1 mango, peeled and cut into cubes

1 peach, cut into wedges
2 kiwi fruit, peeled and quartered
2 tbsp caramel sauce (optional)

DIRECTIONS (Prep + Cook Time: 25 minutes)

Preheat the air fryer to 340 F. Thread the fruit pieces alternately onto 4-6 previously soaked in water bamboo skewers. Place them in the greased frying basket and AirFry for 6-8 minutes, turning once or until the fruit caramelize slightly. Drizzle with the caramel sauce (optional), let cool slightly and serve.

Mom's Lemon Curd

INGREDIENTS (2 Servings)

3 tbsp butter
3 tbsp sugar
1 whole egg

1 egg yolk
¾ lemon, juiced

DIRECTIONS (Prep + Cook Time: 35 minutes)

Add sugar and butter to a medium-size ramekin and beat evenly. Slowly whisk in the whole egg and egg yolk until fresh yellow color is obtained. Mix in the lemon juice. Place the ramekin in the preheated air fryer and Bake at 220 F for 6 minutes. Increase the temperature to 320 F and cook for 13-15 minutes until golden. Remove the ramekin and use a spoon to check for any lumps. Serve chilled.

Molten Lava Mini Cakes

INGREDIENTS (4 Servings)

2 tbsp butter, melted
3 ½ tbsp sugar
1 ½ tbsp self-rising flour

3 ½ oz dark chocolate, melted
2 eggs
½ tsp ground cinnamon

DIRECTIONS (Prep + Cook Time: 35 minutes)

Preheat the fryer to 360 F. In a bowl, beat the eggs and sugar until frothy. Stir in butter, cinnamon, and chocolate and gently fold in the flour. Divide the mixture between 4 greased ramekins and Bake in the air fryer for 10-12 minutes. Let cool for a few minutes before inverting the cakes onto serving plates.

Snickerdoodle Poppers

INGREDIENTS (5 Servings)

1 box instant vanilla Jell-O mix
1 can (5 pieces) Pillsbury Grands Flaky Layers Biscuits

1 ½ cups cinnamon sugar
2 tbsp butter, melted

DIRECTIONS (Prep + Cook Time: 30 minutes)

Preheat the fryer to 340 F. Unroll the biscuits and cut them into fourths. Shape each ¼-th into a ball. Arrange the balls on a paper-lined baking dish and Bake in the air fryer for 7 minutes or until golden.

Prepare the Jell-O following the package's instructions. Using an injector, insert some of the vanilla pudding into each ball. Brush the balls with melted butter and then coat in cinnamon sugar. Serve cool.

Blueberry Muffins

INGREDIENTS (6 Servings)

1 ½ cups flour
½ tsp salt
½ cup sugar
¼ cup vegetable oil
2 tsp vanilla extract

1 cup fresh blueberries
2 eggs
1 tsp baking powder
1 lemon, zested
¼ cup sour cream

DIRECTIONS (Prep + Cook Time: 30 minutes)

Preheat the air fryer to 340 F. In a bowl, combine flour, sugar, salt, lemon zest, and baking powder. In another bowl, add the vegetable oil, sour cream, vanilla extract, and eggs and whisk until fully incorporated. Combine the wet and dry ingredients, and gently fold in the blueberries.

Divide the mixture between a greased 6-hole muffin tray or 4 muffin cups and Bake in the air fryer for 10-12 minutes or until set and golden. Serve cooled.

MEASUREMENT CONVERSIONS

WEIGHT EQUIVALENTS

US STANDARD	METRIC (APPROXIMATE)
½ OUNCE	15 GRAMS
1 OUNCE	30 GRAMS
2 OUNCES	60 GRAMS
4 OUNCES	115 GRAMS
8 OUNCES	225 GRAMS
12 OUNCES	340 GRAMS
16 OUNCES OR 1POUND	455 GRAMS

VOLUME EQUIVALENTS (DRY)

US STANDARD	METRIC (APPROXIMATE)
¼ TEASPOON	1 ML
½ TEASPOON	2 ML
1 TEASPOON	4 ML
1 TABLESPOON	15 ML
¼ CUP	59 ML
½ CUP	118 ML
¾ CUP	177 ML
1 CUP	235 ML

VOLUME EQUIVALENTS (LIQUID)

US STANDARD	METRIC (APPROXIMATE)
2 TABLESPOONS	30 ML
¼ CUP	60 ML
½ CUP	240 ML
2 CUPS	475 ML

AIR FRYER TEMPERATURES

FAHRENHEIT (F)	CELSIUS (APPROXIMATE)
250°F	120°C
300°F	150°C
325°F	165°C
350°F	180°C
375°F	190°C
400°F	200°C
425°F	220°C

AIR FRYER COOKING CHART

CHICKEN					
ITEM	TEMP (°F)	TIME (MINS)	ITEM	TEMP (°F)	TIME (MINS)
BREASTS, BONELESS (4 OZ)	380	12-14	LEGS, BONE-IN (1.5 LB)	380	30-35
DRUMSTICKS (2.5 LB)	370	20-22	WINGS (2 LB)	400	12-14
THIGHS, BONE-IN (2 LB)	380	20-22	WHOLE CHICKEN (12 OZ)	360	70-75

BEEF					
ITEM	TEMP (°F)	TIME (MINS)	ITEM	TEMP (°F)	TIME (MINS)
BEEF EYE ROUND ROAST (4 LB)	400	45-55	MEATBALLS (1-INCH)	370	7
BURGER PATTY (4 OZ)	370	16-20	MEATBALLS (3-INCH)	380	10
FLANK STEAK (1.5 LB)	400	12	SIRLOIN STEAKS (12 OZ)	400	9-14

PORK AND LAMB					
ITEM	TEMP (°F)	TIME (MINS)	ITEM	TEMP (°F)	TIME (MINS)
PORK LOIN (2 LB)	360	50-55	LAMB CHOPS (1.5 LB)	400	12-14
PORK CHOPS, BONE-IN (6.5 OZ)	400	12-14	WINGS (2 LB)	400	12-14
PORK TENDERLOIN (2 LB)	380	25-30	RACK OF LAMB (2 LB)	380	20-22

FISH AND SEAFOOD					
ITEM	TEMP (°F)	TIME (MINS)	ITEM	TEMP (°F)	TIME (MINS)
FISH FILLET (8 OZ)	400	10-12	CALAMARI (8 OZ)	400	4-10
SALMON FILLET (8 OZ)	300	12-14	SCALLOPS (1 LB)	400	5-8
TUNA STEAK (6 OZ)	400	7-10	SHRIMP (1 LB)	3900	5-8

VEGETABLES					
ITEM	TEMP (°F)	TIME (MINS)	ITEM	TEMP (°F)	TIME (MINS)
FRENCH FRIES (2-4 CUPS)	400	15-20	EGGPLANTS (1 LB)	350	15-20
MUSHROOMS (2-4 CUPS)	380	6-10	GREEN BEANS (1 LB)	350	5-7
VEGETABLES, ROOTS (2-4 CUPS)	400	15-25	ZUCCHINI (1 LB)	400	15-20
ASPARAGUS (2 BUNCHES)	400	12-15	CAULIFLOWER (HEAD)	400	15-20
BELL PEPPERS (1 LB)	400	15-20	ONION (1 LB)	350	4-7

INDEX

Made in the USA
Monee, IL
26 January 2022

89863524R00101